SCIENTIFICALLY Sweet Occasions

THE ULTIMATE RECIPE GUIDE FOR
EVERY HOME BAKER

Written & Photographed by

Christina Marsigliese

RELIABLE RECIPES FOR EVERY OCCASION

Text Copyright 2020 © Christina Marsigliese
Design & Layout Copyright 2020 © Christina Marsigliese

All rights reserved. No reproduction, copy or transmission of any part of this publication may be made without written permission by the publisher. No paragraph or photograph of this publication may be reproduced or copied in accordance with the provision of the Copyright Act 1985.

SCIENTIFICALLY SWEET OCCASIONS
Photography & Food Styling by Christina Marsigliese
www.scientificallysweet.com

Also check out Christina's other cookbooks:

SCIENTIFICALLY SWEET CHOCOLATE (2018)
Irresistible Chocolate Recipes & Helpful Hints

SCIENTIFICALLY SWEET (2012)
A Scientific & Delicious Approach to Artisanal Baking

Thank you
to every single sweet tooth, chocoholic and bakeaholic who can understand and appreciate this obsession with creating delicious things and DEVOURING delicious things.

CONTENTS

Introduction — 6
Measuring Technique & Conversion Charts — 8
Baking FAQ — 10
Flour & Function — 12
What's With The Wheat? — 14
The Creaming Step — 16
About That Oven… — 19

Harvest — 21

Happy Holidays — 43

Happy Birthdays — 83

Sunday Brunch — 119

Light Summer Lunch — 139

Tea Time — 159

Date Night — 183

Index — 206

introduction

The more I bake, the more I realize my desire for simplicity. Onto my third cookbook, I'm learning that even as a skilled baker sometimes I really don't want to dirty 18 bowls and spatulas to make a cake, or that committing to a 13-step recipe feels like work when all I want it to be is pleasure. There is certainly a time and a place (an *occasion*, if you will) for fussy recipes, but more often than not I crave things that are simple and just plain satisfying!

The recipes in this book "Scientifically Sweet Occasions" are approachable and accessible. That means they are unfussy and easy to make with ingredients that are readily available. You'll find all the classics like apple pie, pecan pie, lemon tart, chocolate chip cookies, cheesecake, fudgy brownies and birthday cake, but there are also unique twists on classics like Maple Sesame Snickerdoodles, Irish Cream Coffee Brownies and Sea Salt S'mores Cookies. There's a whole chapter dedicated to holiday favourites including Classic Gingerbread, Vanilla Sugar Cookies and Snowflake Crinkle Cookies. You'll learn how easy it is to make your own ladyfinger biscuits to assemble a traditional tiramisu, and how quickly you can whip up a decadent moist chocolate cake! Impress your guests with a stunning yule log at Christmas time, or layer up a bakery-worthy Cheat's Opera Cake for the next anniversary or graduation party.

Brunch becomes a no-brainer with homemade New York Style Bagels, the fluffiest No Knead Cinnamon Rolls, hearty flavourful granola and a plethora of banana bread variations to satisfy your addiction from a healthy whole wheat version to a decadent double chocolate loaf. One can never have enough banana bread recipes! Don't miss the last chapter for decadent chocolate treats to satisfy your sweetheart!

Look for "gluten free", "egg free" and "vegan" stamps on recipe pages for when you are baking with dietary restrictions in mind. Read the many notes in pink and teal-coloured text boxes for baking tips, fun recipe "switch ups" and convenient ingredient substitutions! This book has something for everyone and any time, so what are you waiting for? Let's start baking!

Hi, it's Me!

I'm Christina and I am IN LOVE with food – especially the sweet stuff! I am a full time Food Product Developer and in between I run the Scientifically Sweet baking blog and develop irresistible recipes for the Scientifically Sweet cookbook series. With a Master's Degree in Food Science and pastry chef training, I know what it takes to make recipes that work! The more I bake the more I come to appreciate uncomplicated food that requires few steps, simple ingredients and the fewest dirty dishes possible (no one likes cleaning up!). Why not whip up a batch of brownies on a Tuesday night? And who said cake was only for holidays and birthday parties? Delicious homemade baked goods can be effortless. So, in between all the real life moments, sprinkle in some sweetness because it's easy and YOU CAN! Now it's time to stock up on butter...

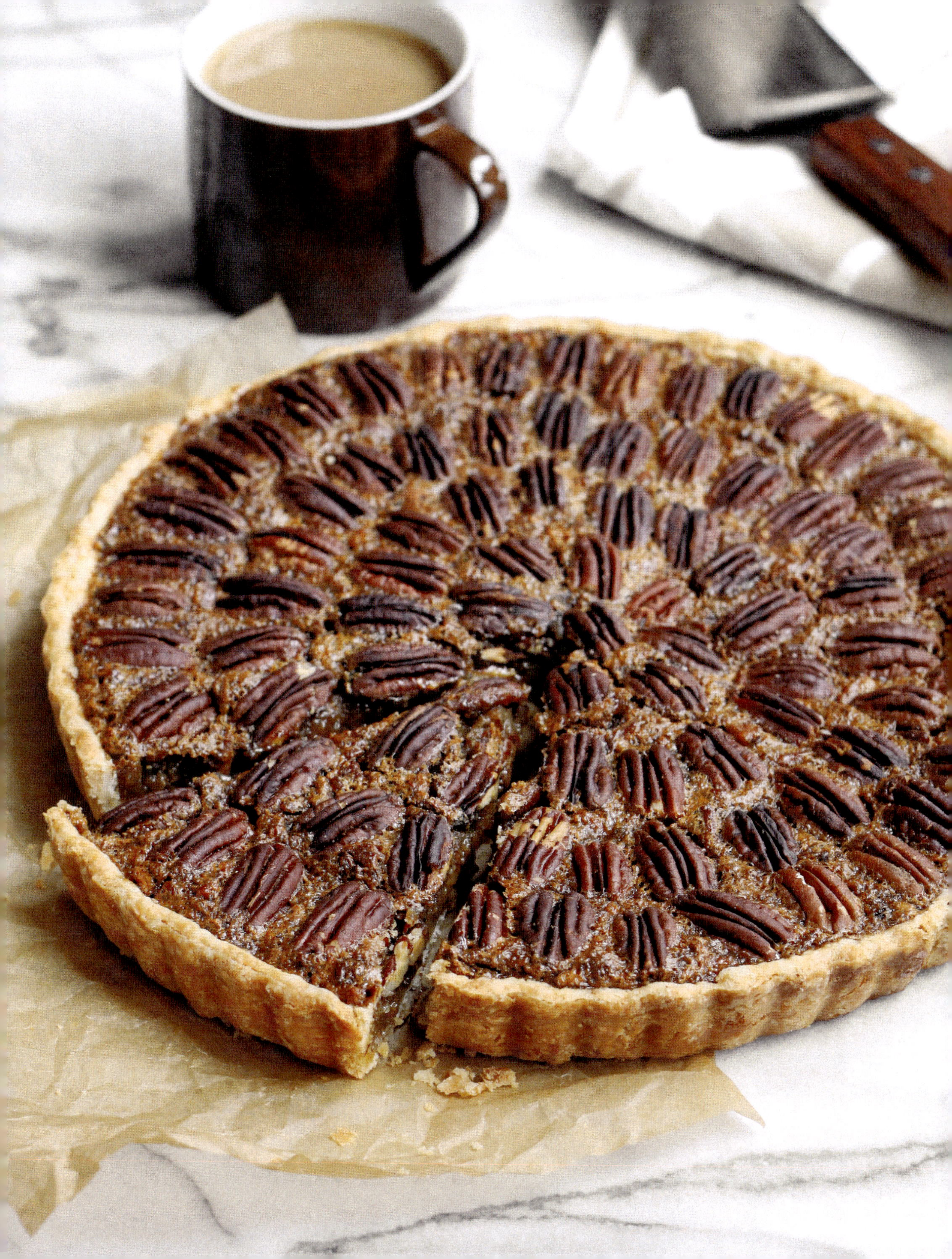

measuring technique

Measuring is one of the most important techniques to learn as a baker. For best results, weigh your ingredients using a small kitchen scale. It is accurate, quick, convenient and requires less measuring tools so you end up with fewer dishes.

WITH A SCALE

Become familiar with the "tare" function on your scale. This button "zeroes" the scale which means that it returns the measurement reading to "0" on the display so that you can continue weighing multiple different ingredients or different amounts into the same vessel. For example, you can measure flour, sugar and cocoa powder directly into a mixing bowl by setting the scale to zero (tare) after each addition. So, instead of dirtying 3 items in measuring scoops, you could simply weigh each amount into the same bowl. Also, recipes can be easily and accurately halved, doubled or multiplied by any amount when converted using weights.

WITHOUT A SCALE

Without a scale, measure your ingredients using the the "Spoon & Sweep" technique. Spoon the ingredient into your measuring cup so that it piles over the rim. Sweep a straight edge like the back side of a knife across the top to scrape off the excess mound so that the amount in the cup is flush with the rim. If measuring very light and powdery ingredients such as flour or cocoa powder, first stir it up in its storage container to lighten it a bit. A cup of flour measured properly should equal 5 ounces (142 grams). Note that different ingredients have different densities, so a cup of sugar and a cup of all-purpose flour do not weigh the same.

All recipes in this cookbook use UNBLEACHED all-purpose flour.

conversions

LIQUIDS		
U.S. standard cups to volume (mL)*		
1 tsp	1/6 oz	5 ml
1 tbsp	½ fl oz	15 ml
¼ cup	2 fl oz	60 ml
⅓ cup	2.7 fl oz	80 ml
½ cup	4 fl oz	120 ml
⅔ cup	5.4 fl oz	160 ml
¾ cup	6 fl oz	180 ml
1 cup	8 fl oz	240 ml

EQUIVALENTS FOR BUTTER		
U.S. standard cups to mass (g)**		
1 tsp	1/6 oz	5 g
1 tbsp	½ oz	14 g
¼ cup	2 oz	56 g
⅓ cup	2 ¾ oz	75 g
½ cup	4 oz	113 g
⅔ cup	5 ⅓ oz	150 g
¾ cup	6 oz	170 g
1 cup	8 oz	227 g

*The Metric System assumes 1 cup = 250 ml, but the "1 cup" marker on your glass measuring jug at home is likely based on the US Customary fluid ounce which assumes 1 cup = 8 fluid ounces = 8 x 29.57ml = 237 ml. The numbers in the top left chart are rounded to the nearest 10.

1 CUP EQUIVALENTS FOR COMMON DRY INGREDIENTS		
1 cup all-purpose flour	5 oz	142 g
1 cup whole wheat flour	4.5 oz	128 g
1 cup icing sugar (sifted/unsifted)	3.5 oz/4.4 oz	100 g/125 g
1 cup granulated sugar	7 oz	200 g
1 cup packed brown sugar	7.7 oz	220 g
1 cup cocoa powder	3 oz	85 g
1 cup corn starch	4.5 oz	130 g

** 1 US ounce (mass) = 28.4g

1 large egg = 57g

FAHRENHEIT to CELSIUS	
250 °F	120 °C
275 °F	135 °C
300 °F	150 °C
325 °F	165 °C
350 °F	175 °C
375 °F	190 °C
400 °F	205 °C
425 °F	220 °C
450 °F	230 °C

baking FAQ

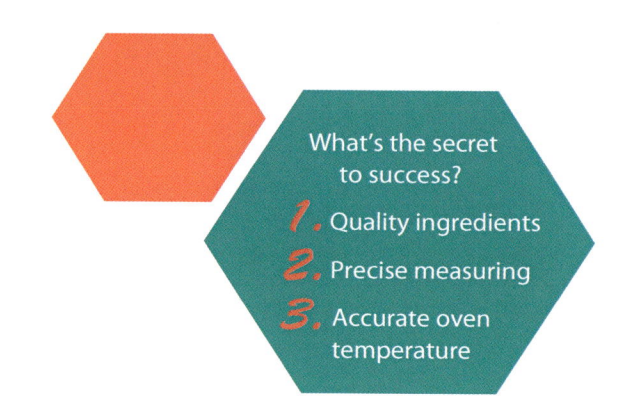

What's the secret to success?
1. Quality ingredients
2. Precise measuring
3. Accurate oven temperature

1. WHAT SIZE EGGS SHOULD I USE WHEN BAKING?

All recipes in this book (and most baking recipes) use large size eggs. They have a rather consistent, standard measure of about 57g each with the shell on. Without the shell, the egg is about 50g or 60ml – the yolk weighs about 20g and the egg white is 30g.

2. CAN I USE SALTED BUTTER FOR BAKING?

You absolutely can! In fact, for some recipes I prefer salted butter. It is rich and delicious and in some cases it can really enhance the flavour of your dessert. However, using unsalted butter allows you to control how much salt goes into the baked good since different recipes require different amounts of salt. Salted butter typically contains about 2% salt, and when used in large quantities it can contribute a significant amount of sodium to the recipe. You can use salted butter in place of unsalted butter in most recipes, but then reduce the amount of added salt by half. I would only *not* recommend salted butter when making buttercream.

3. WHY DO MOST RECIPES CALL FOR UNSALTED BUTTER?

Using unsalted butter puts you in control of flavour and allows you to manage how salty your sweets taste since salt requirements vary depending on the recipe (i.e. chocolate brownies can take more salt than vanilla sponge cakes, fillings or frostings). In some cases where there is little butter in the recipe (such as sponge cakes or chocolate glazes/ganache) it doesn't matter which type you use as the effect would be negligible. But for butter cakes, brownies, cookies, pastries and buttercream that use upwards of ½ cup of butter, I would recommend using the type of butter stated in the recipe.

4. IS THERE A SUBSTITUTE FOR BUTTERMILK?

Buttermilk makes delicious baked goods, especially rich chocolate cakes and flavourful muffins. It is a cultured low fat dairy product that contributes acidity to batters to react with chemical leaveners (baking soda) and it has a thick creamy consistency which helps to add moisture and body to a batter without thinning it out too much. Although there are a lot of sources that recommend substituting a combination of milk and vinegar, it will never produce the same results because it doesn't replicate the same viscosity as buttermilk. A good substitution for 1 cup of buttermilk would be ½ cup of low fat plain stirred yogurt mixed together with ½ cup of skim milk.

5. WHAT'S THE DIFFERENCE BETWEEN DUTCH PROCESS AND NATURAL COCOA POWDER?

Dutch process cocoa is treated with an alkalizing agent (such as potassium carbonate) that neutralizes the natural acidity of cacao and enhances colour, turning it to a deeper dark brown or red (or even black) colour depending on the intensity of the process. The reason for recipes to specify one type over the other is because of how the cocoa interacts with the leavening agents. Recipes that call for baking soda with no other acidic ingredient typically require natural cocoa to provide the acidic component, while Dutch process cocoa is often paired with baking powder unless there are other acid ingredients that are sufficient to react with baking soda.

6. MY OVEN HAS A CONVECTION SETTING – SHOULD I BAKE WITH THE FAN ON?

Most conventional ovens (no fan) heat from the bottom element only and rely on the natural rising of hot air to maintain an even temperature throughout the space. The function of a convection fan is to move the hot air around to promote even cooking and browning. This is great for roasting chicken and potatoes or root vegetables as the constant movement of air will dry out the food for faster caramelization. Although this can produce nicely golden crisp chocolate chip cookies and flaky pastries, the heat can be quite intense and it will dry out delicate cakes or custards. I generally recommend baking in a conventional oven with the fan off and all of the recipes in this book were tested this way.

7. WHAT OVEN RACK SHOULD I USE?

Most recipes, such as cakes, cookies and brownies, are designed for baking on the centre rack of the oven for uniform heat distribution around the product. However some recipes, such as pies and tarts with wet fillings, may benefit from baking part of the time (usually the first 10-20 minutes) on the bottom rack for conventional conduction (no fan) ovens that have a top and bottom heat element. This directs heat to the bottom crust to cook and crisp it up quickly before the filling has a chance to soak in. It also helps cook the base quickly before the top of the pie or tart starts browning.

8. WHAT'S THE DIFFERENCE BETWEEN "DARK" AND "BITTERSWEET" CHOCOLATE?

Dark chocolate is a general term given to chocolate with more than 50% cocoa solids. It encompasses a wide ranch of chocolate products, but to be truly "dark" it should contain >55% cocoa solids. Semi-sweet chocolate is a type of dark chocolate that contains half sugar and half cocoa solids (50% cocoa). Bittersweet chocolate contains at least 70% cocoa.

9. A RECIPE CALLS FOR BITTERSWEET CHOCOLATE. CAN I USE SEMI-SWEET CHOCOLATE?

Generally you can substitute semi-sweet or dark chocolate for bittersweet chocolate, but anticipate that the product will taste sweeter since semi-sweet chocolate contains up to twice as much sugar as bittersweet chocolate. You cannot, however, do the reverse and substitute bittersweet chocolate for semi-sweet with the same results. This is because there is a higher cocoa solids content in bittersweet chocolate that binds up more moisture in a batter and can dry it out. The recipe may rely on the sugar that semi-sweet chocolate contributes for the desired texture and you may need to increase the amount of added sugar to achieve the same results. Bittersweet chocolate also contains more cocoa butter which hardens at room temperature and will result in a stiffer batter or dough.

10. WHY DO MY COOKIES AND CAKES SOMETIMES TURN OUT DRY?

There are so many variables that can affect the texture of baked goods, but one of the most common reasons for dry cakes and cookies is inaccurate measurements for flour. I always use a scale when I bake to ensure that I don't over-measure flour. Using too much flour can yield tough and dry desserts, and it also dilutes the flavour. When measuring ingredients using standard cups, use the "Spoon and Sweep" technique where you gently spoon it into the cup and level it off with a knife. Do not pack it down. Always be cautious of over-baking and check the dessert for doneness after the minimum recommended time stated in the recipe.

11. DO I REALLY NEED TO REFRIGERATE COOKIE DOUGH BEFORE BAKING?

Not all cookie recipes require a refrigeration or "chilling" step before baking. For example, cookie dough that contains melted chocolate cannot rest for too long or the chocolate will harden and make the dough crumbly. Most "drop" cookies, such as classic chocolate chip cookies and sugar cookie dough certainly benefit from time in the fridge. This allows the flour and chemical leaveners (baking soda/powder) to hydrate and the dough equilibrates so it is more uniform. It means that the resulting cookies will brown more quickly and evenly, and it also improves the overall flavour of the cookies!

flour & function

The type of flour used in any recipe will affect the outcome of the finished product. All recipes in this book use unbleached all-purpose flour, unless otherwise specified.

Flour is a quintessential baking ingredient. Considering how it is unquestionably the most abundant ingredient in the majority of recipes, it doesn't receive as much attention as it deserves. Since it is used in such high quantities in recipes, the type you use will have a major effect on the final outcome when you are baking. Wheat flour comes in all different varieties, and choosing the right flour that is best suited to your recipe is very important. It is available under many different labels, including bread flour, all-purpose flour, pastry flour and cake flour. Then there are unbleached, bleached, chlorinated and heat-treated flours. How are we supposed to keep up with all this, right? It's easy to just use all-purpose flour for everything because, well, it's for all purposes! This works just fine in most cases, but knowing a few facts will help you tailor recipes for optimum results.

	Bread/Baker's Flour	All Purpose/Plain Flour	Pie & Pastry Flour	Cake Flour
Protein level	12-14%	10-12%	8-9%	6-8%
Applications	Artisan bread, sourdough, chewy cookies	Cookies, scones, biscuits, muffins, moist chocolate cakes, pastries	Pastry, pie dough	Butter cakes, sponge cakes
Unique qualities	High-quality protein, high strength and elasticity. Never bleached.	Produces acceptable results in most applications (from bread to cupcakes). Can be bleached or unbleached.	Makes tender pastries and delicate shortbread. Usually unbleached.	Makes a uniform, fine, soft crumb in cakes. Is often bleached or heat treated for optimum starch hydration and crumb structure.

Flour ultimately contributes structure, texture and flavour to baked goods and helps to support batters as they expand in the oven. In addition to this, it can be used to thicken gravies and sauces (ex. béchamel), as well as pastry cream, custards and fillings. It is useful to help suspend particulates in a batter when coated over ingredients such as dried fruits, berries, chocolate chips and nuts.

The type of flour used in a recipe will affect the outcome of the finished product since different flours have different compositions and properties. In general, cake flour is used to make delicate white cakes and sponges, while bread flour is used to make rustic, artisan, chewy and resilient loaves of bread. All-purpose flour can make everything in between, including a decent buttercake to a reasonable loaf of bread. In particular, all-purpose flour is ideal for making almost any type of cookie.

For cakes, sometimes a blend of chlorinated cake flour and unbleached all-purpose flour works really well. The former provides a soft, sturdy, uniform crumb and greater volume, while the latter creates moistness and promotes even rising with little contour (perfect for layering!). For pastry, you want extensible but not elastic gluten – resting pastry allows dough to become less elastic (elasticity relaxes with time) as the bonds between aligned proteins weaken to allow the dough to be shaped.

CAKE FLOUR

Cake flour is specially manufactured to produce cakes with optimum crumb quality characteristics. It is made from soft wheat (low gluten) at a low extraction rate, meaning that it is taken from only the finest sieved particles of milled flour. The final product is flour with an overall reduced particle size so it has a larger surface area to allow starch to react more efficiently with other compounds in cake batter. Increasing the surface area of available starch helps support the batter during baking. Ultimately it is capable of absorbing more water and sets the batter more quickly as it bakes to create a very stable structure. Cake flour has a low protein content ranging from 6 to 8%, which limits gluten development in the batter to create a fine, tight and soft crumb texture. Low gluten translates to very little (if any) elasticity in cake batter so that starch solidifies around many small bubbles. This also means that less water is bound by wheat proteins so that more water is available to starch for swelling and better gelatinization or setting (more on gelatinization on page 15).

Almost all cake flour in North America is bleached using any one of many bleaching agents (such as chlorine), and it is this process that weakens proteins further. Bleached flour creates more delicate products like chiffon and angel food cakes. Cakes that have a high ratio of sugar and liquid to flour are best made with bleached flour, whose oxidized starch molecules are able to carry more than their weight in water.

PASTRY FLOUR

Pastry flour is made from soft wheat flour and has a protein content of 8%-10%, putting it somewhere between cake flour and all-purpose flour. What distinguishes it most from cake flour is that it is not chlorinated. It is soft and ivory in color and absorbs less liquid during mixing compared to all-purpose flour, making it ideal for delicate pastries, pie crusts and cookies with a crumbly texture. It also makes soft and tender biscuits and muffins.

ALL-PURPOSE FLOUR

All-purpose or plain flour is usually made from a blend of hard and soft wheat flours with a protein content lower than bread flour, ranging between 9% and 12%. It can be bleached or unbleached, which makes a difference (see page 12) and it is acceptable for most household baking needs. All-purpose flour varies in protein content and quality depending on brand and place of origin. Just like a Cabernet Sauvignon from France tastes different from a Cabernet Sauvignon from Chile, wheat protein quality varies across the globe. Unbleached all-purpose flour creates a moist texture in brownies, cookies and most cakes. It makes excellent pastry too.

BREAD FLOUR

Bread flour contains 12-14% protein and is made from hard wheat. The high gluten content makes for easy dough molding and shaping, it allows bread dough to extend and rise, and then lets the dough hold that shape as it bakes.

HIGH RATIO FLOUR

High Ratio flour refers to soft wheat, low protein flour that has been treated with heat or chlorine to modify its functional properties in favour of recipes that use a high quantity of water and sugar compared to flour for guaranteed moistness. It is commonly subject to post-milling to further reduce flour particle size. Chlorination affects all flour components including starches, proteins and fats by changing their characteristics and how they react with other ingredients in a batter. It alters the properties of wheat starch molecules in a way that allows them to absorb water more readily and lowers their gelatinization temperature so that the cake batter sets faster as it bakes. This helps to retain moisture and air bubbles so that the final cake has better volume and texture. The result is a tender, moist, fine-textured crumb – it's what you'd expect from a box mix or commercial cakes.

> "All-purpose flour varies in protein content and quality depending on brand and place of origin"

what's with the wheat?

> Flour contributes to majority of the structure in most recipes and helps support batters as they expand in the oven via effective proteins and starch.

GLUTEN

Gluten can be thought of as a very strong and elastic network of proteins that allows the expansion and entrapment of large air bubbles. Gliadins and glutenins are two types of proteins in wheat that have special functional properties and provide cohesiveness to breads and cakes. They are insoluble by nature but become mobile in the presence of water and cross-link to transform into this complex network called gluten. When subjected to stress like stirring or kneading, a mixture of flour and water adopts unique properties: elasticity and extensibility. Glutenin proteins are responsible for dough elasticity. Upon agitation they stretch out and link up end-to-end as well as at other sites along their lengths. Think of these proteins as coils that can be stretched and straightened out, but then spring back when released and the kinks re-form. Gliadin proteins provide extensibility and allow the dough to be molded and shaped. These are important characteristics in bread-making where dough needs to stretch to accommodate expanding air bubbles, but resist expansion to the point where the bubble walls break, thus helping to retain bubbles. It is because of this elasticity that gluten contributes a chewy texture to cookies and the crust on artisan breads.

Cake recipes can be classified as having low gluten potential due to minimal mixing required after flour is added. Also, added fat and sugar interfere with gluten development. For this reason the structure is not as strong and elastic so it will let gas bubbles diffuse throughout the batter evenly before they grow too large. Over-mixing can encourage a strong gluten network that has the capacity to stretch and accommodate growing bubbles (like a balloon). These bubbles can expand uncontrollably to form large holes that will collapse during cooling and create a very open, non-uniform structure in the finished cake.

Both the quantity and quality of protein is important when assessing the characteristics of different wheat flours. Quantity of protein is proportional to water absorption which means that flour with a high protein content (bread flour) absorbs more water in a cold batter or dough compared to flour with a low protein content (cake flour). The inherent quality or type of protein is also important as it affects the way flour behaves when mixed in a batter or dough (i.e. elasticity, extensibility, resistance to deformation and stickiness).

STARCH GELATINIZATION

Where wheat protein is the main structure-building ingredient of concern in bread-making, wheat starch is the fundamental functional ingredient in cake batter and cookie dough. Since the starch component of flour takes up about 70%, it is not surprising that it plays a significant role in forming cake structure. It controls batter thickness/viscosity as it heats up during baking and helps trap expanding gases from air introduced during mixing, carbon dioxide from baking powder or baking soda and steam from water in the batter.

When batters and doughs bake in the oven their starch components take up water, swell and transform into a rigid structure that gives cakes, cookies, breads and muffins their shape and texture. This action is called gelatinization and it mainly involves three processes:

1. Swelling: diffusion of water into "starch granules" which are sacs that contain organized starch molecules.
2. Melting: disruption or dissolving of the starch granules so that the starch molecules held inside lose their organized crystalline structure and rearrange to become more random or disordered (amorphous).
3. Leaching: diffusion of the starch molecules out into the surrounding environment.

Cake is best described as a foam where many small air bubbles are suspended in a starch gel. The lack of or diminished functionality of gluten in cake batters allows these air bubbles to diffuse through the batter evenly and maintain a small size (i.e. there is not enough elasticity to sustain and hold large air bubbles). The strength and rigidity of gelatinized starch further stops gases from expanding into large bubbles so instead the small bubbles turn into a series of connected holes.

> "Cake is best described as a foam where many small air bubbles are suspended in a starch gel"

CHLORINATION

Effect on starch

Since the most critical factor in cake quality is starch gelatinization, it is no wonder that chlorination has such an impact on the final product. Chlorine treatment modifies how starch granules perform during baking by making them absorb *more* water and also making them absorb water *faster* so that they swell more and make a stronger starch gel. It also increases the solubility of starch granules which makes them more mobile and allows them to gelatinize more readily. Basically, it helps cake batter set faster, strengthens the crumb and produces a closed structure to prevent collapse during cooling. This is useful in high-sugar recipes since sugar typically competes with starch for moisture (sugar is hygroscopic or *water-loving* and likes to hog the moisture) and would otherwise make a very moist yet fragile and dense cake.

Chlorinated starch, with its improved setting or gelatinization properties, increases the viscosity of cake batter at a faster rate than unbleached starch and this helps hold in air bubbles from baking powder for better volume. It's worth noting that by absorbing more water in the batter it means that there is less available water in the finished cake crumb. This explains why cakes made entirely with chlorinated flour often have a drier mouthfeel compared to those made with unbleached all-purpose flour. If unbleached flour is used in a high-sugar-high-moisture recipe, then the cake can collapse since it lacks the water absorption capacity and will have an open-textured weak crumb structure. It will also feel pasty in the mouth.

Effect on fat

In addition to its effect on starch, chlorine modifies the functionality of wheat protein and fat fractions. It is known to reduce the pH of flour (making it more acidic) and thus changing the structure and properties of wheat proteins to weaken gluten strength or reduce gluten network formation. Chlorination also enhances the emulsification properties of fats in flour by causing them to adhere more readily to starch granule surfaces. This helps disperse the fat phase in cake batter for better aeration and foam stability (retention or suspension of air bubbles), and it ultimately improves cake volume.

the creaming step

Understanding the roles of ingredients and techniques in the theater of baking will help you create consistent and quality products in your home kitchen. The most delicious desserts combine the most basic ingredients like butter, sugar, eggs, milk and flour, and then transform them into a treat with a delightful taste and texture. The goal of many cake and cookie recipes is to promote tenderness through thoughtful selection and proportions of fat, sugar, eggs and flour, or to create a fine soft texture through minimal gluten formation. In the case of cakes we aim to create a smooth homogeneous batter for even rising and to incorporate as much air as possible for optimum volume and lightness.

The Creaming Method

"Creaming" is probably the most referenced baking method for making cakes and cookies. A recipe that uses this technique goes something like this:

1. Beat together solid fat (i.e. butter) and sugar
2. Gradually beat in eggs
3. Combine or sift together dry ingredients (flour, salt, baking powder, baking soda, etc.)
4. Add dry ingredients; alternate with wet ingredients (milk, sour cream, etc.) for cake batters

Creaming is a vigorous method of beating solid fat and sugar until it appears fluffy. It is a great job for an electric stand mixer but can be done by hand using a wide rubber spatula. The change in colour of the mixture from creamy yellow to pale offwhite is a good sign that it is well aerated. Sharp sugar crystals rip through the fat and introduce thousands of tiny air pockets that will expand as they heat in the oven to lift the batter. The smaller the sugar crystals, the more air pockets that will get torn into the fat; the more air pockets, the lighter and fluffier the mixture; the lighter the mixture, the finer the crumb and higher the rise.

Eggs are then beaten into the creamed mixture until smooth thanks to the emulsifying power of egg yolks. Sometimes if the fat and sugar are not creamed well enough, the egg does not incorporate as smoothly and can leave the mixture looking curdled. This isn't such a big deal with cookies, but can really affect the final texture of cakes that benefit from a homogeneous, well emulsified batter for even rising. It's worthwhile noting that more air incorporation, although great for crumb structure, can also create a drier mouthfeel (because, well... air is dry). For this reason, many pastry chefs brush butter cakes with sugar syrup before layering.

For cakes, dry ingredients are usually mixed in alternately with wet ingredients. This action of agitating flour in the presence of water (usually from milk) stimulates gluten formation and can lead to an uneven, open crumb structure. For this reason, most recipes instruct the baker to "fold gently" until "just combined" and "do not over-mix". Some gluten can help provide structure and sturdiness, but is typically not encouraged in cakes. Alternating the dry and liquid ingredients also ensures that they become evenly incorporated with minimal mixing.

HOW IT WORKS

Extent of creaming

When making chewy gooey drop cookies, like traditional chocolate chip cookies, excessive creaming is not desired. We are not looking for "light and fluffy" here, rather a thoroughly blended mixture that looks like a smooth paste and still a bit grainy – it will resemble wet sand. Sometimes I prefer to complete the creaming step by hand for these types of cookies to have better control. Intense creaming is ideal for very crisp and tender cookies that snap when you break them, such as cut-out sugar cookies, but it is not preferred when moist chewiness is desired. When making layer cakes, it is important to beat on high speed for a longer period of time (3-5 minutes) until the butter and sugar is very pale to incorporate a lot of air and build the foundation for a fine-textured, uniform and sturdy crumb.

Ingredient temperature

Ingredients blend together more easily when they are at the same temperature and introduced to each other gradually. Most recipes call for room temperature ingredients, so try to be prepared before baking – I like to pull butter and eggs from the fridge the night before. Temperature can affect the functional properties of ingredients. The ideal temperature for creaming butter is 21°C (70°F). At this point the fat is soft and malleable but still opaque and not weeping, greasy or translucent. It is firm enough to support trapped air bubbles but soft enough to whip. High quality butter with a good fat crystallization profile will hold more air than a lesser quality butter. In addition, smaller sugar crystals, such as caster or superfine sugar, create more air bubbles than standard granulated sugar.

Eggs impart structure, flavour and tenderness (from yolks) to cakes, and they also help aerate. The step of adding eggs to creamed fat and sugar is crucial as you are adding water (mainly from egg whites) to fat. Since water and fat don't mix, it is the powerful action of an emulsifier called lecithin naturally present in egg yolks that binds them together. Making sure the eggs are at room temperature is important to help the two phases come together as a smooth, thick and homogenous mixture. Using cold eggs can cause your batter to seize up and look curdled as the cold liquid hardens the soft butter. This is especially true when a recipe calls for a lot of eggs. If the batter does appear curdled, it will likely come together again once the flour is added (since flour will absorb and bind the free water), but it will ultimately reduce the volume of the finished cake. Curdling can be prevented by lightly beating the eggs separately and slowly drizzling them into the batter as the mixer is running.

Adding extracts and other flavourings to the creamed butter and sugar mixture helps to get the most out of them since many flavour compounds are fat-soluble.

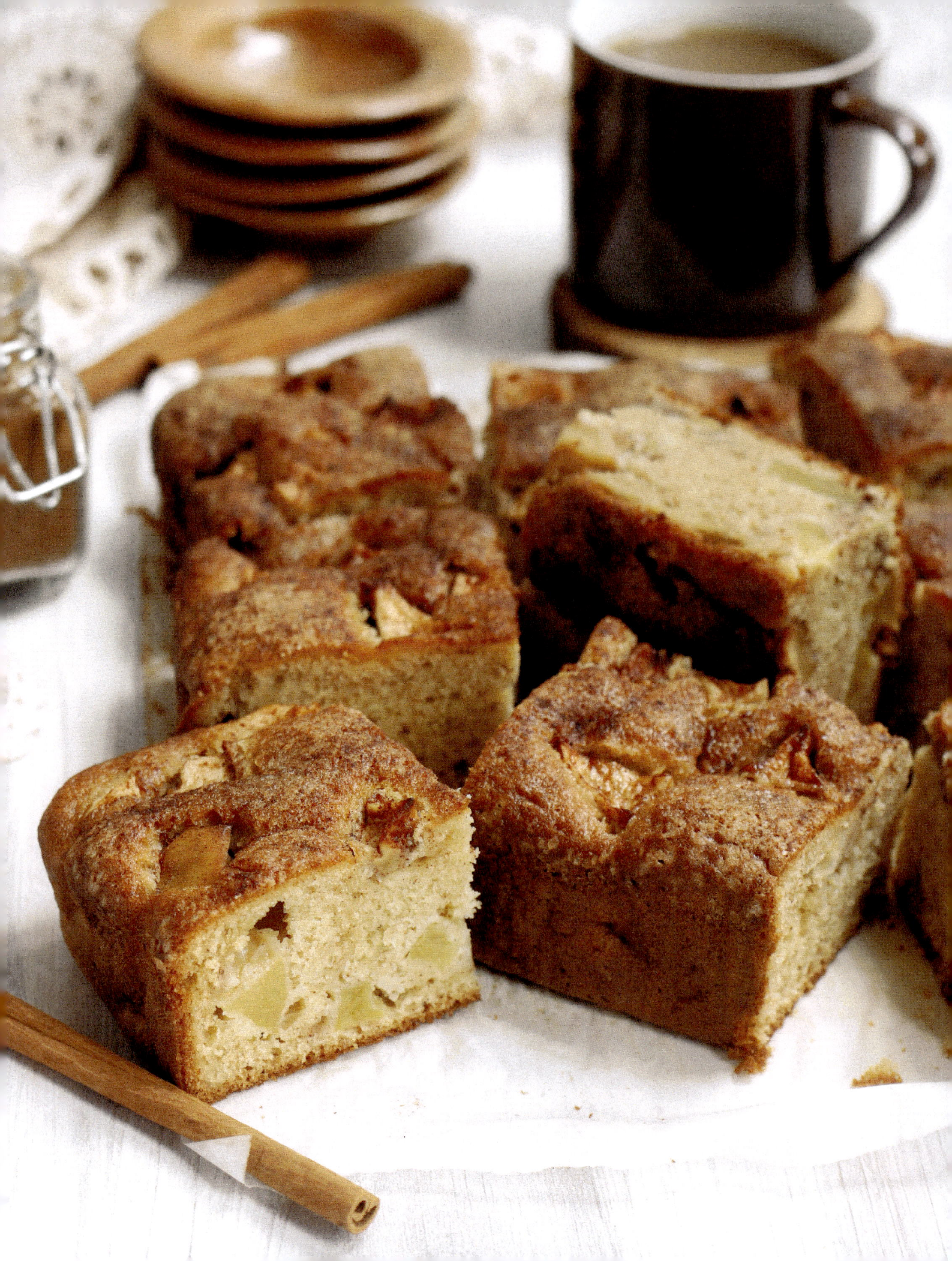

about that oven...

When to use the fan: cookies, fruit pies, tarts, filled pastries.

GET TO KNOW YOUR OVEN

I've baked in every type of oven. What have I learned? They're all different! Hot spots, strong top heat, strong bottom heat, fan-forced, no fan... It doesn't matter if it is the fanciest oven on the market or the cheapest ol' thing. What matters is that you know its nuances. The more you bake, the more familiar you will become with your particular oven settings and will be able to gauge when a cake is well cooked, or when it makes more sense to use the bottom rack or top rack.

When NOT to use the fan: cheesecake, sponge cake, butter cake, cupcakes, crème brulée, crème caramel, brownies, yeasted doughs (cinnamon buns), loaf cakes.

PRE-HEAT FOR PERFECTION

Always Pre-heat your oven for at least 25 minutes (or 10 minutes passed the signal)

CONVECTION vs. CONDUCTION

The difference between the two is a fan.

Convection ovens have a fan and exhaust system that helps circulate hot air over and around food so that it cooks evenly and more rapidly. This provides better browning since its venting system creates a dry environment that caramelizes sugars faster. It creates flaky pies and pastries as well as extra crispy-edged cookies, perfect for classic chocolate chip cookies that are crunchy on the outside and chewy in the middle. Convection setting is not ideal for delicate cakes as the forced air creates a very dry environment and causes rapid rise which means cakes can develop domed or cracked surfaces and hard crusty edges. The fan can also "push" wet cake batters and cause them to rise slanted.

Conduction or conventional ovens heat via top and bottom elements and do not have a fan so the hot air is still. This is why some ovens can have hot spots since the air is not blown around or circulated. It is best suited for cakes and baked custards, puddings or cheesecake since the lack of forced air across the surface of the batter means that the product won't dry out or develop a hard crust which can impact rising. All of the recipes in this book are tested in a conduction oven. However, if you choose to use convection setting I would recommend lowering the oven temperature by 25°F.

mocha berry cheesecake, page 22

HARVEST

This chapter is full of recipes that make the most of all the gorgeous fruits & veg that come with every season – Springtime rhubarb, Summer berries and late Summer stone fruits; Fall apples and pumpkin too! There are Winter bakes using lovely dried fruits and nuts paired with warm spices, as well as a bright citrus tart that leads into late Winter's maple syrup season!

mocha berry cheesecake

makes 8-10 servings

Base:
- ⅔ cup (95g) all-purpose flour
- ¼ cup (21g) cocoa powder
- ⅓ cup (70g) packed light brown sugar
- ¼ tsp espresso powder
- ¼ tsp salt
- ¼ cup (56g) unsalted butter, melted

Filling:
- 2 tbsp (12g) cocoa powder
- 1½ tsp espresso powder
- 2 tbsp (30ml) boiling water
- 2 blocks (500g) cream cheese, softened
- ⅔ cup (145g) packed light brown sugar
- 1 tsp (5ml) pure vanilla extract
- 2 large eggs, at room temperature
- ⅓ cup (80ml) sour cream

Topping:
- 3 tbsp (40g) granulated sugar
- 1 tbsp (8g) corn starch
- 1 cup (120g) fresh or frozen blueberries
- 2 tbsp (30ml) water
- ⅔ cup (80g) fresh or frozen raspberries

1. Preheat oven to 350°F. Line the base of an 8-inch round springform pan with parchment paper.

2. For the crust, blend together flour, cocoa powder, brown sugar, espresso powder and salt in a medium bowl so there are no lumps of brown sugar. Stir in melted butter and use your fingertips to combine all ingredients so it forms damp crumbs. Turn the crumbly mixture out into prepared pan and press it down in an even layer, pushing it about ¾-inch up the sides to form an edge. Run the back of a spoon across the surface to smooth it out. Bake for 8-10 minutes until slightly puffed and feels dry to the touch. Transfer to a wire rack. Reduce oven to 300°F.

3. For the filling, whisk together cocoa, espresso powder and hot water in a small bowl until it forms a smooth paste; set aside. Beat cream cheese using a hand mixer in a large bowl until smooth. Add brown sugar and beat until silky and glossy (you can also use a food processor). Beat in the cocoa mixture and vanilla. Beat in eggs one at a time, then mix in sour cream until evenly blended. Pour the filling over the crust and smooth it out. Bake for 35-45 minutes until set around the edges with a slight wobble in the centre. Turn off the oven and leave the cheesecake in for another 5-10 minutes. This gentle cooking makes the silkiest texture. Transfer to a wire rack to cool completely, then refrigerate for at least 2 hours.

4. For the topping, combine sugar and cornstarch in a small saucepan. Add blueberries and toss to combine. Place over medium heat and cook while stirring gently until the juices start to release from the blueberries. Add water and cook until it comes to a simmer. It will thicken as it changes from opaque to translucent and glossy. Remove the pan from over the heat and gently stir in raspberries so that they don't break down excessively. Let cool completely before spooning it over the cheesecake.

> **Switch Up!** For an extra creamy texture and to prevent cracking, cook in a water bath. Wrap the base of the round springform pan with a double layer of aluminum foil. Place it onto a rimmed baking tray. Pour boiling water into the baking tray so that it comes about ½-inch up the sides of the foil-wrapped pan and bake as directed.

egg free

cherry almond crisp
makes 6-9 servings

Topping:
- ½ cup (71g) all-purpose flour
- ½ cup (50g) large flake rolled oats
- ½ cup (50g) sliced almonds
- ¼ cup (55g) packed light brown sugar
- 1 tsp ground cinnamon
- ¼ tsp coarsely ground black pepper
- ⅛ tsp salt
- 6 tbsp (84g) cold unsalted butter

Cherry filling:
- 4 cups (520g) whole fresh or frozen pitted cherries
- ¼ cup (55g) packed light brown sugar
- 1 ½ tbsp (12g) corn starch
- 1 tsp (5ml) aged balsamic vinegar

1. Preheat oven to 350°F.

2. For the topping, combine flour, oats, almonds, brown sugar, cinnamon, black pepper and salt in the bowl of a food processor. Pulse two or three times to blend and break down the oats and almonds. Cut the cold butter into small pieces, add it to the food processor bowl and pulse until it forms large crumbs. Tip the mixture out into a bowl and rub in the butter further with your fingertips, squeezing it in your hands to form large clumps. Set aside.

3. For the filling, slice about 2 cups of the cherries in half and leave the rest whole. Combine cherries, brown sugar, corn starch and balsamic vinegar in a large bowl until evenly blended. Spread the mixture into an 8x8-inch baking dish and crumble the topping over the fruit in clumps.

4. Bake for 40-50 minutes until the fruit is bubbling and the crumble is golden. If the crumble mixture browns too quickly before the fruit is cooked, cover loosely with foil halfway through baking. Transfer dish to a wire rack to cool for at least 30 minutes before serving (with ice cream!).

egg free

caramel apple crumble bars

makes about 12 bars

Filling:

1 tbsp (14g) unsalted butter

3 tart apples (Granny Smith, Idared or Pink Lady), peeled, cored and very thinly sliced

1 tbsp (15g) packed dark brown sugar

1 tsp (5ml) fresh lemon juice

1 tsp ground cinnamon

1 x Rich Salted Caramel Sauce recipe (page 196)

Crumble:

1 cup (142g) all-purpose flour

1 cup (100g) large flake rolled oats

½ cup (110g) packed dark brown sugar

¼ tsp baking soda

heaped ¼ tsp salt

½ cup (113g) unsalted butter, soft but cool and cut into small pieces

1. For the filling, melt butter in a large skillet over medium-high heat until foamy and it smells nutty. Add sliced apples, sugar, lemon juice and cinnamon and cook for 6-8 minutes while tossing frequently until the apples are soft. Set aside to cool.

2. Preheat oven to 350°F. Line a 9x9-inch baking pan with parchment paper, leaving a 2-inch over hang along each side.

3. Place flour, oats, brown sugar, baking soda and salt in the bowl of a stand mixer fitted with the paddle attachment and blend on low speed for 1 minute until evenly combined. Add butter pieces and blend on medium-low for 3-4 minutes until evenly incorporated. The mixture should be crumbly, like streusel. It will look a bit dry, so use your hands to squeeze the crumble into clumps and press out any lumps of butter.

4. Press about two-thirds of the crumble (about 2 ½ cups) into the prepared pan and pat it down to form an even layer. Spread cooled apples evenly over top and then drizzle over about ½ cup (120ml) of caramel sauce. Squeeze handfuls of the remaining crumbs to form large clumps, break them up and scatter them over top to cover the apples (I like to dampen my hands first to help the crumbs stay in clumps).

5. Bake for 30-35 minutes until evenly golden and the caramel is bubbling. Transfer to a wire rack and let cool completely in the pan. Refrigerate for at least one hour before slicing into bars. Drizzle more caramel over top before serving if desired.

date apricot & pecan seed loaf

makes 8-10 servings

1 ¼ cups (150g) chopped dried dates

½ cup (75g) chopped dried apricots

1 cup (240ml) water

1 ½ cups (215g) all-purpose flour

1 tsp baking powder

½ tsp baking soda

½ tsp salt

½ tsp ground cinnamon

¼ tsp <u>each</u> ground allspice and cardamom

½ cup (60g) chopped pecans

¼ cup (25g) large flake rolled oats

2 tbsp (20g) pumpkin seeds

2 tbsp (18g) sunflower seeds

¼ cup (56g) unsalted butter

¼ cup (60ml) sunflower oil

2 large eggs

¾ cup (165g) packed light brown sugar

1 tbsp sesame seeds for sprinkling

1. Preheat oven to 350°C. Line a 9 x 5-inch loaf pan with parchment paper and grease any exposed sides.

2. Place chopped dates and apricots in a small saucepan with the water. Bring to a boil over medium heat then reduce heat, cover and simmer for 10 minutes. Transfer the mixture (including all the liquid) to a large mixing bowl and mash with the back of a fork until it becomes thick and jammy (like a chunky purée) and it absorbs all of the liquid. Let cool for 10 minutes.

3. Combine flour, baking powder, baking soda, salt, spices, pecans, oats, pumpkin seeds and sunflower seeds in a medium bowl and whisk to blend evenly.

4. Add butter to the warm date mixture, let it melt and then stir it in along with the oil. Stir in eggs and brown sugar until combined. Make a well in the centre of the dry ingredients in the large bowl and add the date mixture. Fold together gently until evenly combined, being sure to reach down to the bottom of the bowl to lift up all of the dry ingredients. Do not over-mix.

5. Spread batter into prepared pan. To help it bake evenly, run a spatula through the centre of the batter along the length of the pan to create a "trench". Sprinkle generously with sesame seeds and extra pumpkin seeds. Bake for 50-55 minutes until a skewer inserted into the centre comes out clean. Transfer pan to a wire rack and cool for 10 minutes. Remove loaf from pan and cool completely on the rack before slicing.

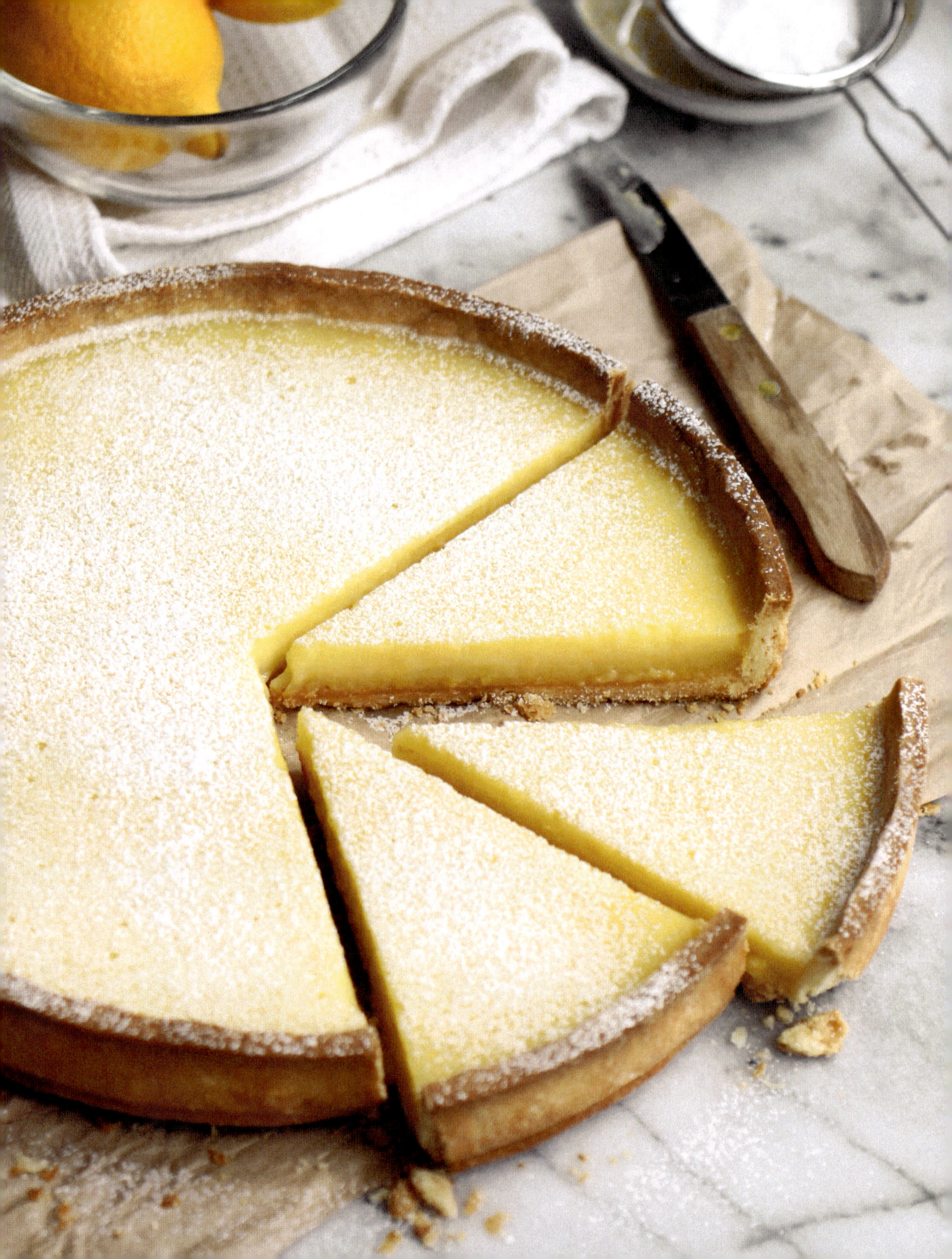

classic creamy lemon tart
makes 8-10 servings

Crust:
½ cup (113g) unsalted butter, softened

½ cup (60g) icing sugar

2 large egg yolks

½ tsp pure vanilla extract

¼ tsp salt

1 ⅓ cups (190g) all-purpose flour

> *This lemon filling can be made with up to 1 ¼ cups (250g) of sugar. I find that 1 cup is just enough to create the right balance of tangy-sweet flavour, but 250g will provide a bit more insurance against over cooking to ensure you get a smooth and silky texture.

Filling:
1 cup (200g) granulated sugar*

2 tsp lemon zest

pinch of salt

4 large eggs, at room temperature

½ cup (120ml) fresh lemon juice (from 3 to 4 lemons)

⅓ cup (80ml) mascarpone (or use 35% whipping cream)

2 tsp (6g) all-purpose flour

1. For the crust, beat butter with icing sugar in a medium bowl using a spatula or wooden spoon until pale, smooth and creamy. Stir in egg yolks, vanilla and salt until well combined. Sift flour over the bowl and fold it in evenly. Wrap dough well and refrigerate for 2 hours.

2. Preheat oven to 350°F. Lightly dust a work surface with flour and roll the dough out to ⅛-inch thickness. Fit it into a 9-inch round tart pan with removable bottom, pressing the dough into the corners and up the sides of the pan. Trim away excess dough. You can also use a springform pan and gently run a knife along the sides (about 1-inch up from the base) to trim away excess dough and make an even edge crust. Cover and refrigerate for 20 minutes. Prick the pastry a few times with a fork to help prevent it from puffing up and bake for about 25 minutes until evenly golden. Reduce oven temperature to 300°F.

3. While the pastry bakes, make the filling. Combine sugar with lemon zest and salt in a large bowl and rub it together with the back of a spoon until fragrant. Whisk in eggs until smooth. Whisk in lemon juice, then mix in mascarpone or cream until evenly blended (if using mascarpone, premix it with about ¼ cup of the lemon mixture until smooth and then mix it in with the rest of the lemon mixture). Avoid beating vigorously at this stage since it's best not to incorporate too much air. Whisk in flour. Let the filling settle for a bit while the pastry finishes baking off, then once the crust is ready, stir up the filling again to re-blend it and immediately pour it into the hot crust. Place the tart onto a rimmed baking sheet to catch any leakage and to help transfer it to the oven more easily with the runny filling.

4. Bake for 22-28 minutes until the filling is set around the edges with a slight wobble in the centre when you gently shake the pan. Do not over-bake or the filling can become rubbery instead of smooth and creamy. Transfer pan to a wire rack to cool completely, then cover and refrigerate for 2 hours until thoroughly chilled. Dust with powdered sugar just before serving and slice using a hot dry knife.

milk chocolate swirl pumpkin spice muffins

makes 12 muffins

1 ⅔ cups (235g) all-purpose flour
⅓ cup (65g) granulated sugar
1 ¼ tsp baking powder
½ tsp baking soda
½ tsp salt
1 tsp ground cinnamon
½ tsp ground ginger
¼ tsp ground nutmeg
⅛ tsp ground clove
1 cup (240ml) pure pumpkin purée
½ cup (110g) packed dark brown sugar
2 large eggs, at room temperature
⅔ cup (160ml) whole milk
1 tsp (5ml) pure vanilla extract
⅓ cup (75g) unsalted butter, melted
3 ½ oz (100g) milk chocolate, melted

Switch Up! Top with chopped roasted hazelnuts before baking!

1. Preheat oven to 350°F. Line the cups of a standard 12-cup muffin pan with paper liners.

2. Whisk together flour, sugar, baking powder, baking soda, salt and spices in a medium bowl until evenly blended.

3. Combine pumpkin purée with brown sugar in a large bowl and whisk it together until sugar is dissolved. Whisk in eggs one at a time, then mix in milk, vanilla and melted butter. Add the flour mixture and stir together gently until just combined. Do not over-mix. A few small lumps are just fine.

4. Divide the batter evenly among prepared muffin cups, filling them to the rim. Drizzle or dollop a teaspoon of melted chocolate over each cup of batter and swirl it through with a knife or a skewer. Bake for 20-25 minutes until golden brown and muffins spring back when pressed gently. Transfer pan to a wire rack to cool for 5 minutes before transferring muffins individually to the rack to finish cooling.

whole wheat maple pecan banana bread

makes 8-10 servings

1 cup (240ml) mashed ripe banana (from about 2 large bananas)
¼ cup (55g) packed light brown sugar
½ cup (120ml) pure maple syrup
¼ cup (56g) unsalted butter, melted
1 large egg, at room temperature
1 tsp (5ml) pure vanilla extract
1 ½ cups (192g) whole wheat flour
1 tsp baking powder
½ tsp baking soda
½ tsp ground cinnamon
¼ tsp salt
½ cup (60g) chopped roasted pecans
½ cup (85g) milk or dark chocolate chips

1. Preheat oven to 350°F. Line an 8x4-inch or 9x5-inch loaf pan with parchment paper, letting it hang about an inch above the sides. Butter any exposed sides.

2. Mash together banana with brown sugar in a large bowl until sugar dissolves. Whisk in maple syrup. Whisk in melted butter, then whisk in egg and vanilla until smooth.

3. Combine flour, baking powder, baking soda, cinnamon and salt in a medium bowl and whisk to blend evenly. Add the dry ingredients to the banana mixture with the pecans and chocolate chips and fold them in gently until just combined. Do not over-mix. Spread batter into prepared pan and bake for 45-55 minutes until the top is evenly browned and a skewer inserted in the centre comes out clean (an 8x4-inch loaf will take longer – closer to 55 minutes).

4. Transfer pan to a wire rack and let cool for 15 minutes. Lift the loaf from the pan using the parchment overhang and let cool completely on the rack before slicing.

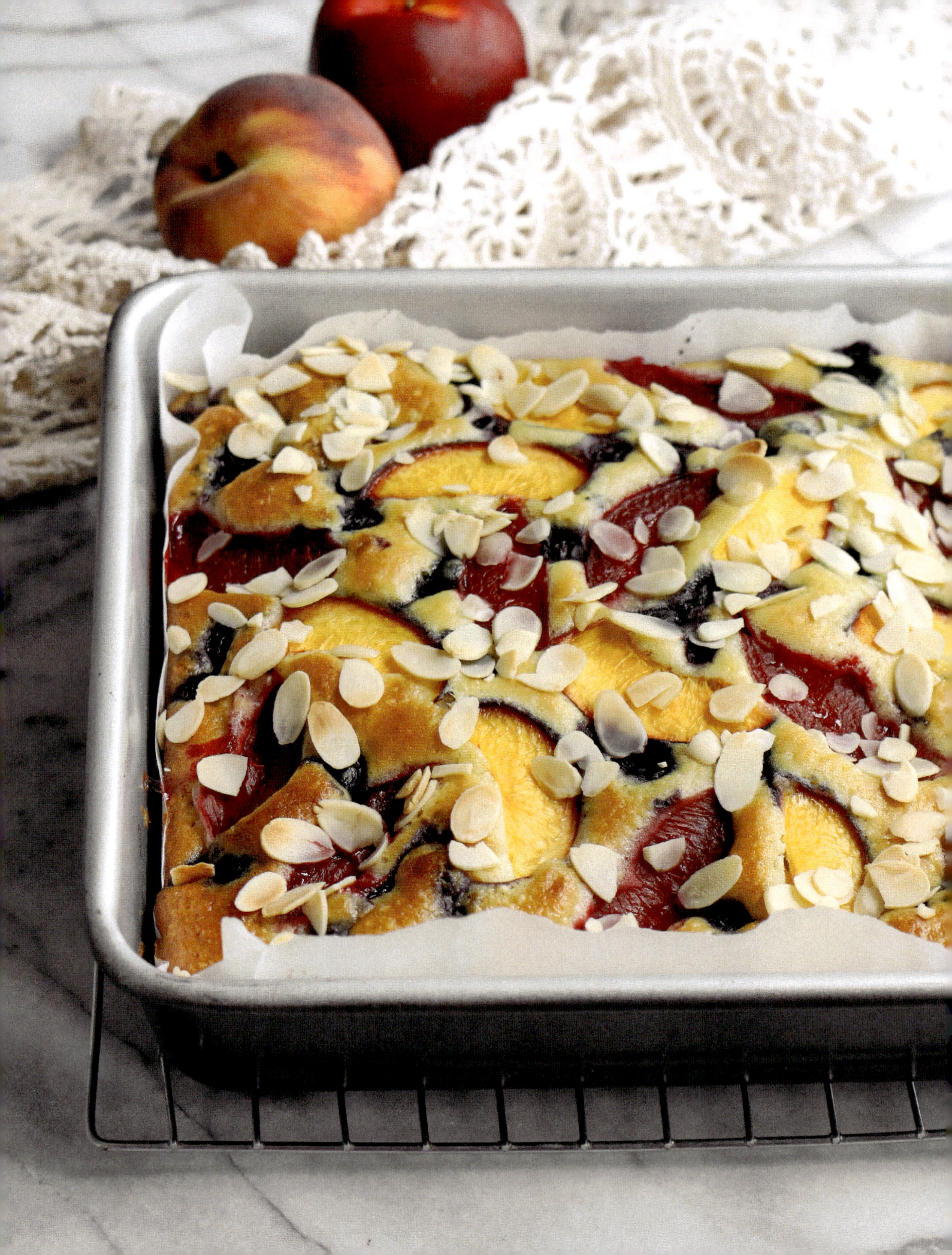

summer stone fruit almond & olive oil cake

makes about 9 servings

- 1 cup (240ml) whole milk
- ¾ cup plus 2 tbsp (175g) granulated sugar
- finely grated zest of 1 lemon
- 1 ½ cups (215g) all-purpose flour
- ½ cup (50g) blanched almond flour or ground blanched almonds
- 1 ½ tsp baking powder
- ¼ tsp baking soda
- ¼ tsp salt
- ⅓ cup (80ml) extra virgin olive oil
- 2 large eggs, at room temperature
- 3-4 stone fruits (a blend of red plums, peaches or nectarines), sliced into wedges
- ⅓ cup (35g) fresh or frozen blueberries
- sliced almonds for sprinkling

1. Preheat oven to 350°F. Line a 9x9-inch pan with parchment paper leaving a 2-inch overhang along each side.

2. Place milk, sugar and lemon zest in a medium saucepan over low heat for 3-4 minutes while stirring occasionally until the milk is warmed through and sugar is dissolved. Turn off the heat and let cool for 5-10 minutes.

3. Place flour, ground almonds, baking powder, baking soda and salt in a large bowl and whisk to blend evenly. Add olive oil and eggs and begin whisking to break up the yolks. Gradually add the milk mixture to the flour mixture while whisking until it forms a smooth batter.

4. Pour the batter into the prepared pan and spread it out evenly. Arrange sliced fruit on top in any way you like. Scatter blueberries between the slices and sprinkle with sliced almonds. Bake for 30-35 minutes until the cake is golden and a skewer inserted into the centre comes out clean. Transfer to a wire rack and let cool for 15 minutes. Lift the cake out of the pan and let cool on the rack for at least 1 hour before slicing.

Switch Up! Use any type of stone fruit for this recipe – I often make an Apricot Almond & Olive Oil Cake using 5-6 apricots cut into quarters.

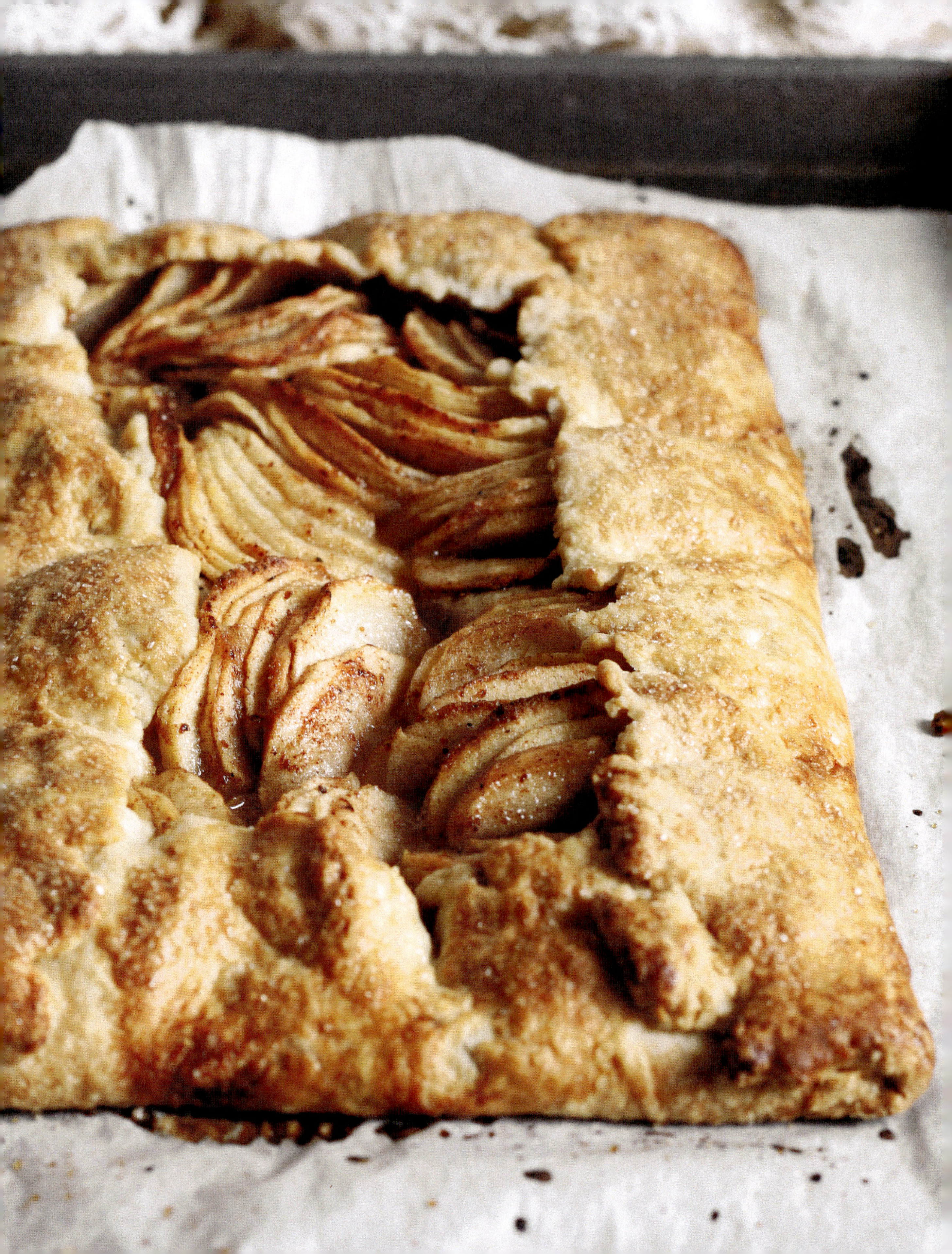

egg free

brandied brown butter apple galette
makes about 8 servings

Pastry:
- 1 ½ cups (215g) all-purpose flour
- 2 tbsp (25g) granulated sugar
- ½ tsp salt
- ½ cup plus 1 tbsp (125g) cold unsalted butter, in small pieces
- 3-4 tbsp (45-60ml) cold water

Topping:
- 3 tbsp (42g) butter
- 1 tbsp (15ml) Brandy liquor (or maple syrup if you are avoiding alcohol)
- 1 egg for brushing
- 2 tsp coarse sugar

Filling:
- 3 medium apples (any variety), peeled and cored
- 3 tbsp (40g) granulated sugar
- ½ tsp ground cinnamon
- ¼ tsp ground nutmeg
- 1 tsp (3g) corn starch

1. For the pastry, whisk together flour, sugar and salt in a large bowl. Add cold butter and rub it into the flour mixture using your fingertips until it resembles coarse crumbs with most of the fat well dispersed and some larger pea-sized pieces remaining. There should be no dusty flour in the bowl. Gradually sprinkle in the cold water, one tablespoon at a time, while gently tossing with a fork until the mixture is moistened and it just clings together in clumps. The dough will hold together when squeezed when it is ready, but it should not form a ball. It should be shaggy. Turn it out onto a clean surface and bring it together with your hands slightly cupped, pressing in loose bits until it is evenly moist and cohesive but not completely smooth. Flatten it into a rectangle, wrap well and refrigerate at least 2 hours or overnight.

2. Preheat oven to 400°F. Line a large baking sheet with parchment paper.

3. For the topping, melt butter in a small saucepan over medium-low heat and then continue to cook until it crackles and foams and turns golden brown with a nutty aroma. Remove from heat and carefully add brandy (or maple syrup if not using Brandy), swirling the pan to incorporate. It will sputter at this point, so keep a distance. Set aside to cool.

4. For the filling, thinly slice the apples into ⅛-inch pieces. Place them into a large bowl with sugar, cinnamon, nutmeg and corn starch. Toss it together so apples are evenly coated.

5. On a lightly floured work surface, roll the dough out to just over ⅛-inch thickness in the shape of a 14 x 10-inch rectangle. Rotate the dough as you are rolling and add more flour as necessary to prevent sticking. Carefully transfer it to the lined baking sheet. Neatly gather the apples together about 7-10 slices per bunch and arrange them across the dough ensuring there is about 2-inches of border space along each side. Or, arrange the apples in two consecutive rows down the centre of the pastry, overlapping them tightly like shingles.

6. Drizzle the brandied brown butter over the apples. Fold the pastry edges in over the apples to enclose them, brush the pastry lightly with beaten egg and sprinkle with coarse sugar. Bake for 35-40 minutes until the crust is deeply golden brown, the apples are tender and juices are bubbling. Transfer the baking sheet to a wire rack to cool for at least 20 minutes before slicing. Serve with softly whipped cream or vanilla ice cream!

raspberry maple crumble cheesecake bars

makes 9-12 bars

Base:
- 1 cup (90g) quick-cooking or minute oats
- ⅓ cup (50g) all-purpose flour
- ⅓ cup (35g) blanched almond flour
- 3 tbsp (45g) packed dark brown sugar
- ¼ tsp ground cinnamon
- ⅛ tsp salt
- ¼ cup (56g) unsalted butter, softened
- 3 tbsp (45ml) maple syrup

Filling:
- 1 block (250g) cream cheese, softened
- ¼ cup (50g) granulated sugar
- 1 large egg, at room temperature
- ½ tsp pure vanilla extract
- ¼ tsp pure almond extract
- 3 tbsp (45ml) maple syrup
- 1 cup (100g) fresh or frozen raspberries

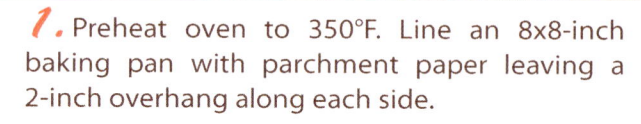

1. Preheat oven to 350°F. Line an 8x8-inch baking pan with parchment paper leaving a 2-inch overhang along each side.

2. For the base, combine oats, flour, ground almonds, brown sugar, cinnamon and salt in a large bowl. Mix to blend evenly and press out any lumps of brown sugar. Add soft butter and begin to mash it in with a fork or spatula. Add maple syrup and blend until evenly combined and it forms clumps – I use my hands for this. Reserve about ½ cup of the mixture for topping and press the rest evenly into the pan. Bake for 12-14 minutes until it feels set and dry to the touch. Transfer to a cooling rack.

3. For the filling, combine cream cheese and sugar in a medium bowl and beat with an electric hand mixer on medium speed until smooth and glossy. Beat in egg and extracts until well incorporated. Mix in maple syrup. Pour it over the base, scatter raspberries on top and crumble over the reserved base mixture.

4. Bake for 20-25 minutes until lightly golden and the filling is just set in the centre. Transfer pan to a wire rack and let cool completely. Refrigerate for at least 2 hours before dusting with icing sugar and slicing into squares.

raspberry turnovers

makes about 16 pastries

egg free

Pastry:
1 ½ cups (215g) all-purpose flour

3 tbsp (40g) granulated sugar

½ tsp salt

½ cup plus 1 tbsp (125g) cold unsalted butter, cut into small pieces

4-5 tbsp (60-75ml) cold water

Filling:
2 cups (227g) fresh or frozen raspberries

⅓ cup (65g) granulated sugar

2 tsp (10ml) freshly squeezed lemon juice

2 tsp (6g) all-purpose flour

1. For the pastry, whisk together flour, sugar and salt in a large bowl. Add butter and rub it in using your fingertips until it resembles a coarse, crumbly mixture with some pieces of butter the size of oat flakes. You can also use a stand mixer on medium-low to start breaking down the butter, then finish with your fingertips. Drizzle cold water over flour mixture one tablespoon at a time while gently tossing with a fork until the flour is moistened and it holds together in clumps. You may not need all of the water. It will hold together when squeezed when ready. Turn it out onto a work surface and bring it together with your hands, pressing in loose bits. Wrap well and refrigerate for at least 2 hours or overnight.

2. For the filling, combine raspberries and sugar in a small saucepan over medium-low heat and simmer for 5-7 minutes until it looks soupy. Stir in lemon juice and boil gently for 10-15 minutes until thick. Let cool completely and then refrigerate for 2 hours. The filling can be made 1 to 2 days in advance.

3. Roll the dough out into a large rectangle with ⅛-inch thickness on a lightly floured work surface. Slice it into 3 to 4-inch squares and transfer to parchment-lined baking sheets. Stir 2 teaspoons of flour into the chilled raspberry filling. Place a rounded teaspoon onto the centre of each square, fold the dough over from corner to corner to encase the filling in a triangle shape and press gently around the edges. Use the tines of a fork to crimp edges together and seal completely. It's ok if some filling squeezes out. Place baking trays in the fridge for 15 minutes until pastry is firm. Preheat oven to 375°F.

4. Lightly brush the tops of the pastries with beaten egg or milk and sprinkle with coarse sugar. Use a sharp knife to make 2 incisions on the tops and bake for 15-20 minutes until golden. Transfer to a wire rack to cool.

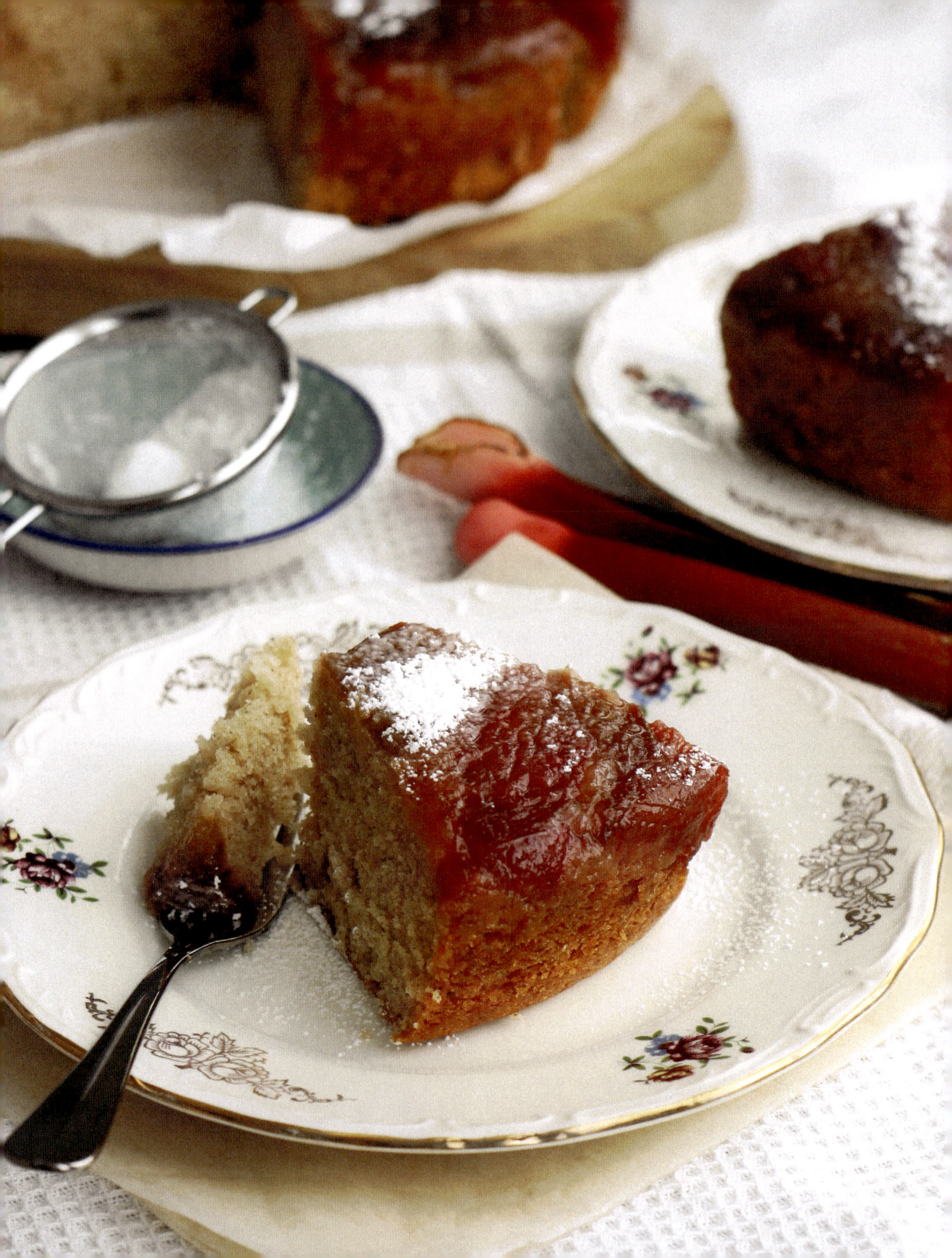

honey rhubarb melt cake

makes 8-10 servings

This cake is such a dream! I call it "melt" cake because it is SO soft that it just melts in your mouth!

Rhubarb topping:

½ lb (225g) trimmed rhubarb (about 4-5 stalks)

½ cup (100g) granulated sugar

2 tbsp (30ml) water

Cake batter:

1 ¼ cups (180g) all-purpose flour

1 tsp baking powder

¼ tsp baking soda

½ tsp ground cinnamon

¼ tsp ground cardamom

¼ tsp salt

6 tbsp (84g) unsalted butter, softened

⅔ cup (135g) granulated sugar

1 tsp (5ml) pure vanilla extract

1 large egg, at room temperature

3 tbsp (45ml) honey

½ cup (120ml) sour cream

¼ cup (60ml) whole milk

1. Preheat oven to 350°F. Line the base of an 8-inch round baking pan with parchment paper. Lightly grease the sides.

2. For the topping, slice rhubarb on a bias into 2-inch pieces. Add to a frying pan or skillet and toss with sugar in the pan. Drizzle water on top and place over medium-high heat. Cook while tossing occasionally until sugar dissolves into a syrup. Let boil for just a couple of minutes until the rhubarb softens slightly (but still holds its shape) and the syrup turns a pink hue. Transfer rhubarb to the base of your lined pan in an even layer. Pour syrup evenly over top (you should have about ¼ cup of syrup). If there is too much syrup, simmer it down slightly in the pan to reduce it.

3. For the cake batter, sift flour, baking powder, baking soda, spices and salt together in a medium bowl and whisk to blend evenly.

4. Beat butter with sugar and vanilla in a medium bowl using an electric hand mixer for 2 minutes on medium-high speed until pale and fluffy. Beat in egg until well incorporated and then mix in honey. Mix in sour cream. Add half of the flour mixture and beat on low speed until just combined. Add the milk and beat until evenly blended. Add remaining flour and mix just until combined and batter is smooth. Scrape down the sides and bottom of the bowl as necessary while mixing.

5. Dollop batter over the rhubarb in the pan and spread it out evenly to the sides. Bake for 40-50 minutes until the top is evenly browned, it springs back when pressed gently and a wooden skewer inserted into the centre comes out clean. Transfer pan to a wire rack and let cool completely. It will sink slightly as it cools, leaving you with a flat cake perfect for inverting. Once cooled, invert cake onto a serving plate and peel off the parchment. Dust with icing sugar immediately before serving.

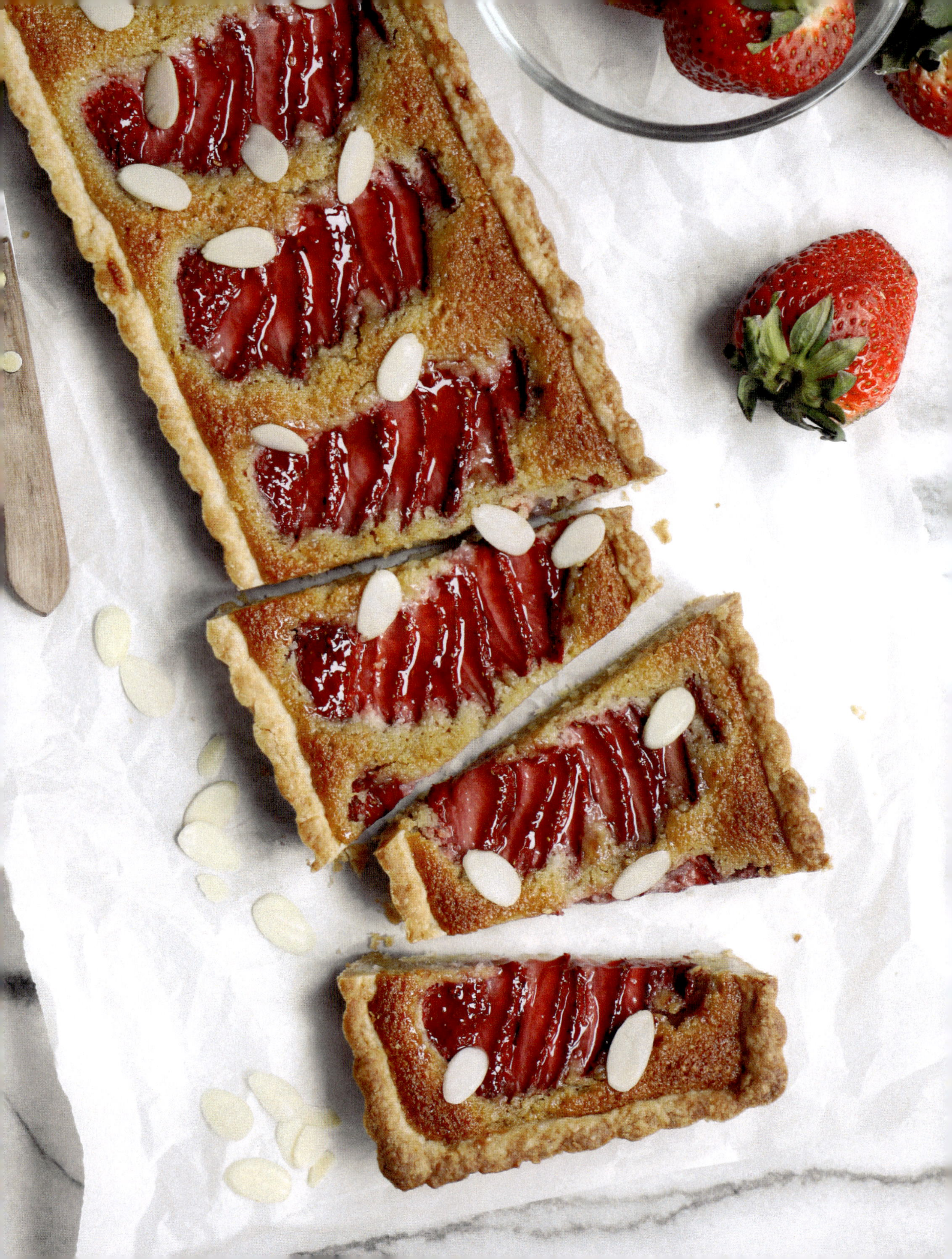

strawberry maple almond tart

makes 8-10 servings

Pastry:

1 cup plus 2 tbsp (160g) all-purpose flour

2 tbsp (25g) granulated sugar

¼ tsp salt

6 tbsp (84g) cold unsalted butter, cut into small pieces

1 large egg yolk

1 tbsp (15ml) ice cold water

Switch Up! Try using fresh raspberries when they are in season too – they taste lovely with maple! For a more polished look, melt some strawberry jam or jelly in a small saucepan over low heat and brush it over the berries while the tart is still warm.

Filling:

1 cup (100g) blanched almond flour or ground blanched almonds

¼ cup (55g) packed dark brown sugar

⅛ tsp salt

5 tbsp (70g) unsalted butter, softened

1 large egg, at room temperature

2 tbsp (30ml) maple syrup

½ tsp pure vanilla extract

4 tsp (12g) all-purpose flour

7-8 large strawberries, thinly sliced

icing sugar for dusting

1. For the pastry, combine flour, sugar and salt in a medium bowl. Add the pieces of cold butter and rub it thoroughly into the dry ingredients using your fingertips until well blended and the mixture resembles bread crumbs. Beat egg yolk with water in a small bowl and slowly drizzle it into flour mixture while tossing with a fork until it is evenly moistened. Bring it together with your hands slightly cupped, pressing in loose bits until it holds together. Fold it over itself a couple of times if necessary. Form the dough into a disk, wrap well and refrigerate for at least 2 hours or overnight.

2. Lightly dust your work surface with flour and roll the dough out to ⅛-inch thickness. Fit it into the base of a 14x5-inch rectangular (or 9-inch round) tart pan with removable bottom, pressing the dough into the edges and up the sides. Trim away excess dough. Cover with plastic wrap or foil and place it in the fridge while you make the filling.

3. Preheat oven to 375°F.

4. For the filling, place almond flour, brown sugar, salt and soft butter in the bowl of a food processor and pulse until smooth and creamy. Add egg and process until smooth. Blend in maple syrup and vanilla extract. Add flour and process until thick and creamy. Spoon mixture into chilled tart shell and spread it out evenly. Arrange sliced strawberries on top.

5. Bake for 10 minutes. Lower oven temperature to 350°F and bake for 20-25 minutes longer until the pastry is golden and the filling is puffed and nicely browned. The filling should still be slightly soft in the centre. Transfer tart to a wire rack and let cool for at least 1 hour before serving.

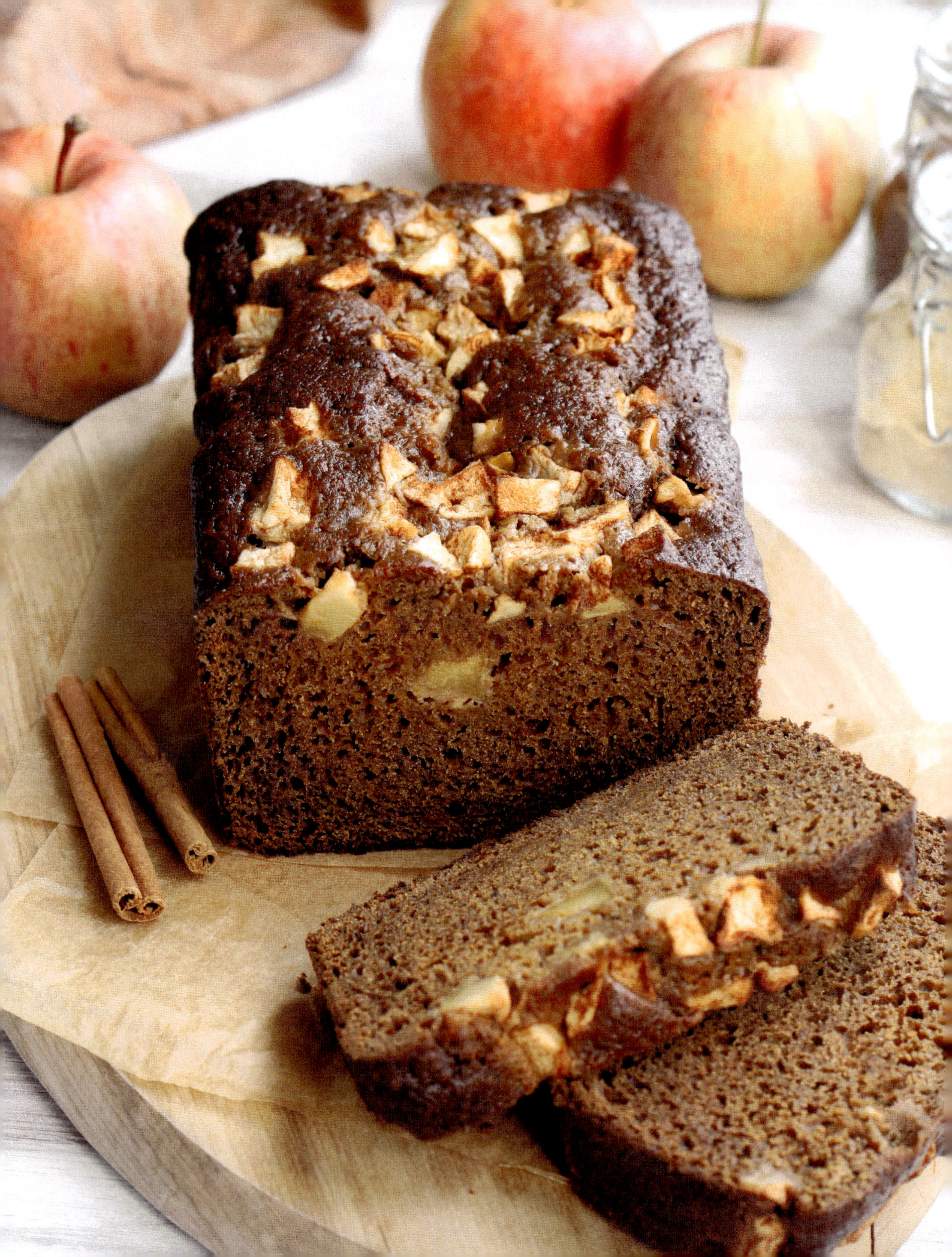

sticky apple ginger loaf

makes 8-10 servings

½ cup (113g) unsalted butter

½ cup (110g) packed dark brown sugar

½ cup (120ml) fancy (light) molasses*

1 ⅔ cups (235g) all-purpose flour

1 tsp baking soda

½ tsp baking powder

1 ¼ tsp ground ginger

1 tsp ground cinnamon, plus extra for coating the apples

¼ tsp <u>each</u> ground clove and allspice

½ tsp salt

2 large eggs, at room temperature

¾ cup (180ml) whole milk

1 large apple, peeled and cut into small ½-inch cubes (about 1 ½ cups chopped apple or 150g)

*For a lighter flavour you can replace half of the molasses (¼ cup) with maple syrup or honey.

1. Preheat oven to 350°F. Line a 9x5-inch loaf pan with parchment paper allowing it to come about 1 inch above the sides of the pan.

2. Place butter, brown sugar and molasses in a saucepan over medium-low heat and bring it just barely to a simmer while stirring until the butter is melted and the sugar is dissolved. Remove the pan from the heat and set aside to cool for 10 minutes.

3. Sift flour, baking soda, baking powder, spices and salt into a large bowl and whisk to blend evenly. Make a well in the centre of the dry ingredients and add the molasses mixture and eggs. Gradually begin to stir the ingredients together with a whisk, and once mostly incorporated, begin adding the milk while whisking as you go until the batter is smooth.

4. Pour the batter into the prepared pan and spread it out evenly. Toss chopped apples with ½ teaspoon of cinnamon and scatter them evenly over top. Bake for 45-55 minutes until the cake is firm and set in the middle and a toothpick inserted into the centre comes out clean.

5. Transfer pan to a wire rack to cool for 15 minutes, then lift the loaf out of the pan using the parchment overhang and let it cool completely on the rack before slicing.

quick bread vs cake

Quick breads are cakes with a simplified method and usually use less fat and sugar compared to birthday-style butter cakes. They require the undemanding technique of combining wet ingredients separate from dry ingredients and then mixing them both together to form a batter. It is meant to be fuss-free and fast, and produces a denser, open-textured crumb. It's the ingredient proportions that determine the quality of the loaf and less about the technique. Making tender butter cakes requires more technique and steps to build the batter. Some of these key stages include creaming butter with sugar, sifting flour and alternating the addition of liquid and dry ingredients to the creamed mixture.

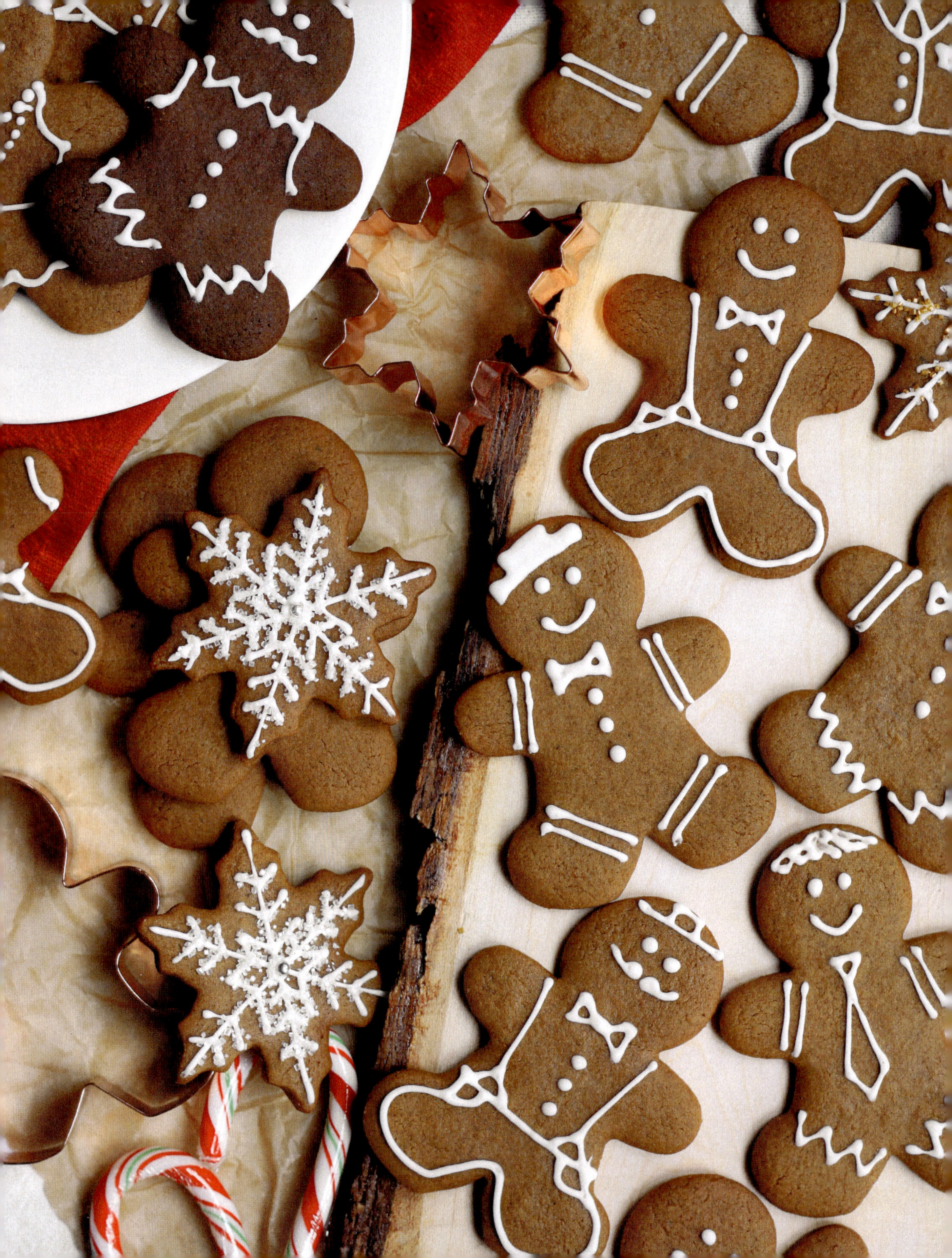

happy HOLIDAYS

Let's make all the classics! This chapter holds all of the recipes you'll need to celebrate your favourite holidays, even including Australia and New Zealand's Anzac Day! Expect hearty pies for Thanksgiving, colourful Easter treats, chocolate truffle cookies for your Valentine, orange and black pumpkin cheesecake squares for Halloween, boozy brownies for St. Patrick's Day and loads of traditional Christmas cookies to fill your dessert platter. So many of these recipes are filled with warm spices that are so indicative of the holiday season. And for me, Christmas isn't complete without a show-stopping Yule Log!

Here is a fun take on Strawberry Shortcake and a very Spring-like dessert that's perfect for Easter celebrations or to celebrate the beginning of berry season! The vanilla sponge cake recipe is very versatile and a great canvas for an array of flavourful fillings to make all kinds of delicious desserts. Try filling it with vanilla custard or lemon cream cheese frosting. You could slice it into rectangles or cut out circles and layer them with whipped chocolate ganache to make a simple layer cake.

strawberry shortcake swiss roll
makes 8-10 servings

Sponge cake:

4 large eggs, at room temperature*

⅔ cup (135g) granulated sugar

¼ tsp salt

2 tbsp (30ml) whole milk

2 tbsp (30ml) olive oil or sunflower oil

1 tsp (5ml) apple cider vinegar*

1 tsp (5ml) pure vanilla extract

1 cup (142g) all-purpose flour

½ tsp baking powder

Filling:

1 cup (120g) chopped hulled strawberries

2 tbsp (25g) granulated sugar

1 tsp (3g) corn starch

¼ cup (60ml) mascarpone

1 cup (240ml) 35% whipping cream

1 tsp (5ml) pure vanilla extract

*Room temperature eggs are important here since cold eggs do not whip as readily. You can also use lemon juice in place of cider vinegar.

1. Preheat oven to 350°F. Lightly grease a 16x12-inch jelly roll pan or rimmed baking sheet and line it with parchment paper.

2. Place eggs in the bowl of a stand mixer fitted with the whisk attachment (or in a large bowl if using a hand mixer) and beat on high speed for 3 minutes until very frothy and doubled in volume. Add sugar one tablespoon at a time and beat for 4-5 minutes until pale, thick and tripled in volume. The eggs should reach the "ribbon stage" where it can hold a figure "8" as it falls back onto itself when lifted with the beaters. Mix in salt.

3. Blend together milk, oil, vinegar and vanilla in a small bowl and gradually pour it into the egg mixture while mixing gently.

4. Sift flour and baking powder into a medium bowl and whisk to blend evenly. Sift it again over the mixer bowl with the beaten eggs and fold it in gently by hand using a balloon whisk or a wide spatula until just combined, scraping along the bottom of the bowl to incorporate the ingredients evenly.

5. Spread the batter evenly into prepared pan. Bake for 12-15 minutes until evenly golden and it springs back when pressed gently. Transfer pan to a wire rack to cool for a minute. Meanwhile, lay a tea towel or a large piece of parchment paper onto a work surface. Sift icing sugar generously over the warm cake to cover the surface and then carefully but swiftly invert it onto the towel/parchment so the sugared surface is facing down. Carefully peel off the paper. Tightly roll the cake up with the towel/parchment and let cool completely like this.

6. For the filling, combine strawberries and sugar in a small saucepan over medium heat. Bring to a boil while stirring occasionally, then cover and simmer for 5-10 minutes until soft and juicy. Combine corn starch with 1 tbsp (15ml) water in a small bowl and stir it into the strawberry sauce off the heat. Bring it back to a boil while stirring for a few seconds then refrigerate until chilled.

7. Combine mascarpone, cream and vanilla in a medium bowl and beat until it forms firm peaks. Fold in half of the strawberry mixture. Unroll the cooled cake and spread cream over the surface leaving about ½-inch border. Spoon remaining strawberry mixture randomly over the cream and swirl it in a bit. Roll up the cake with the filling and refrigerate for at least 1 hour before serving. Dust with icing sugar before slicing.

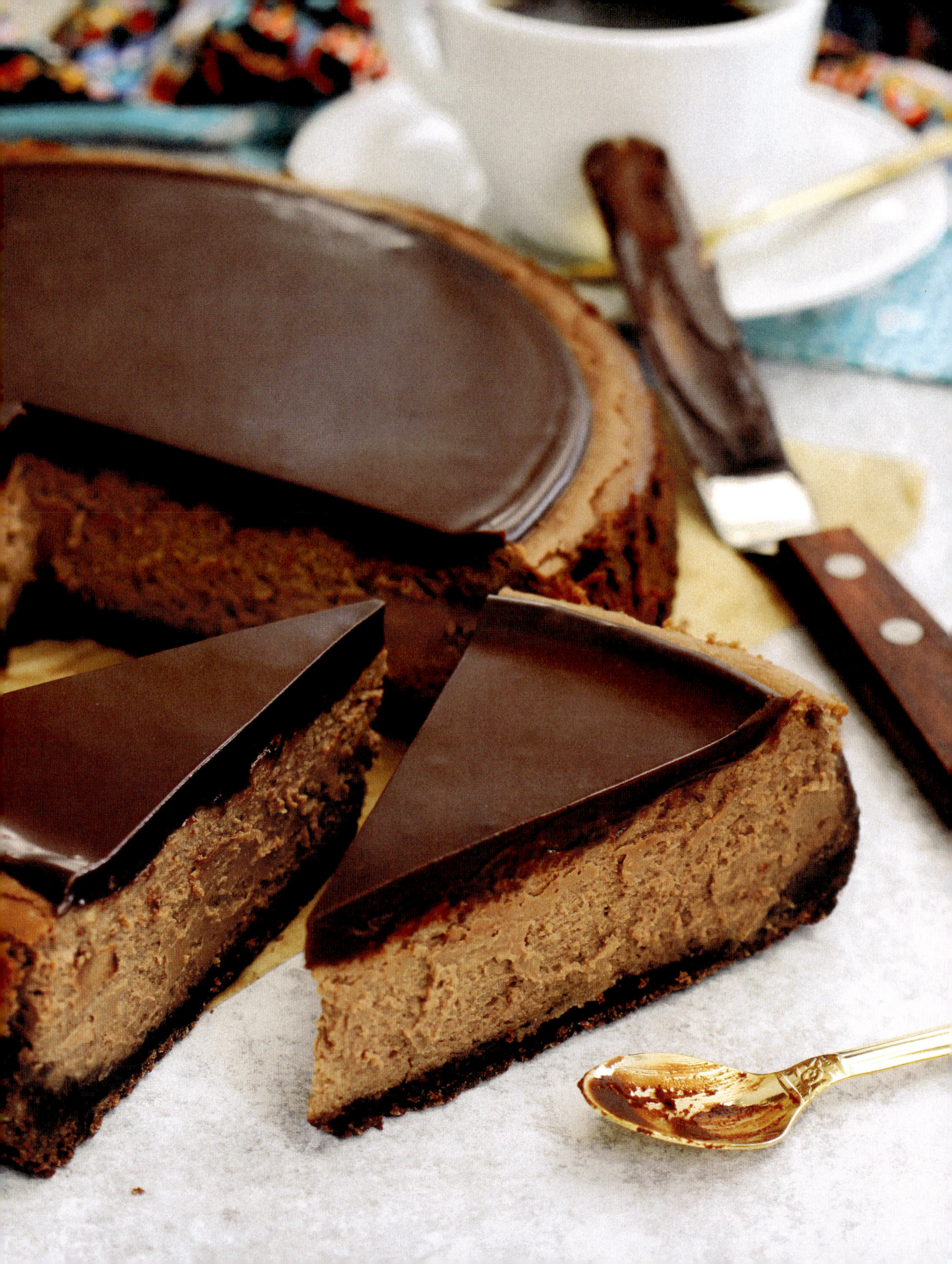

triple chocolate cheesecake

makes 8-10 servings

Base:
⅔ cup (95g) all-purpose flour

¼ cup (21g) cocoa powder

⅓ cup (70g) packed light brown sugar

¼ tsp espresso powder

¼ tsp salt

¼ cup (56g) unsalted butter, melted

Filling:
2 blocks (500g) cream cheese, softened

⅔ cup (135g) granulated sugar

1 tsp (5ml) pure vanilla extract

2 large eggs, at room temperature

⅓ cup (80ml) sour cream

4 oz (113g) dark chocolate, melted

Topping:
3 tbsp (45ml) water

2 tbsp (28g) unsalted butter

1 tbsp (15ml) honey

pinch of salt

4 oz (113g) bittersweet chocolate (70% cocoa)

---

1. Preheat oven to 350°F. Line the base of an 8-inch round springform pan with parchment paper.

2. For the crust, blend together flour, cocoa powder, brown sugar, espresso powder and salt in a medium bowl so there are no lumps of brown sugar. Stir in melted butter and use your fingertips to combine all ingredients so it forms damp crumbs. Turn the crumbly mixture out into prepared pan and press it down in an even layer, pushing it about ¾-inch up the sides to form an edge. Run the back of a spoon across the surface to smooth it out. Bake for 8-10 minutes until slightly puffed and feels dry to the touch. Transfer to a wire rack. Reduce oven to 300°F.

3. For the filling, beat cream cheese using an electric hand mixer in a large bowl until smooth. Add sugar and vanilla and beat until silky and glossy (you can also use a food processor). Beat in eggs one at a time and then mix in sour cream until evenly blended. Beat in melted chocolate. Pour the filling over the pre-baked crust and smooth out the surface. Bake for 35-45 minutes until set around the edges and slightly wobbly in the centre. Turn off the oven and leave it in for another 5-10 minutes. This gentle cooking produces the silkiest texture. Transfer to a wire rack to cool completely and then refrigerate for at least 2 hours.

4. For the topping, combine water, butter, honey and salt in a small saucepan over medium heat and bring to a simmer. Remove from heat and add chocolate. Let stand for 1 minute and then whisk until smooth and glossy. Pour it over the chilled cheesecake and spread it out evenly. Refrigerate until set before slicing with a hot dry knife.

Switch Up! Try replacing dark chocolate with an equal amount of milk chocolate for the cheesecake filling – it will have a slightly sweeter flavour and will be extra creamy. Also, for a super silky texture and to prevent the cheesecake from cracking as it bakes, cook it in a water bath. Wrap the base of the round springform pan with a double layer of aluminum foil. Place it onto a rimmed baking tray. Pour boiling water into the baking tray so that it comes about ½-inch up the sides of the foil-wrapped pan and bake as directed.

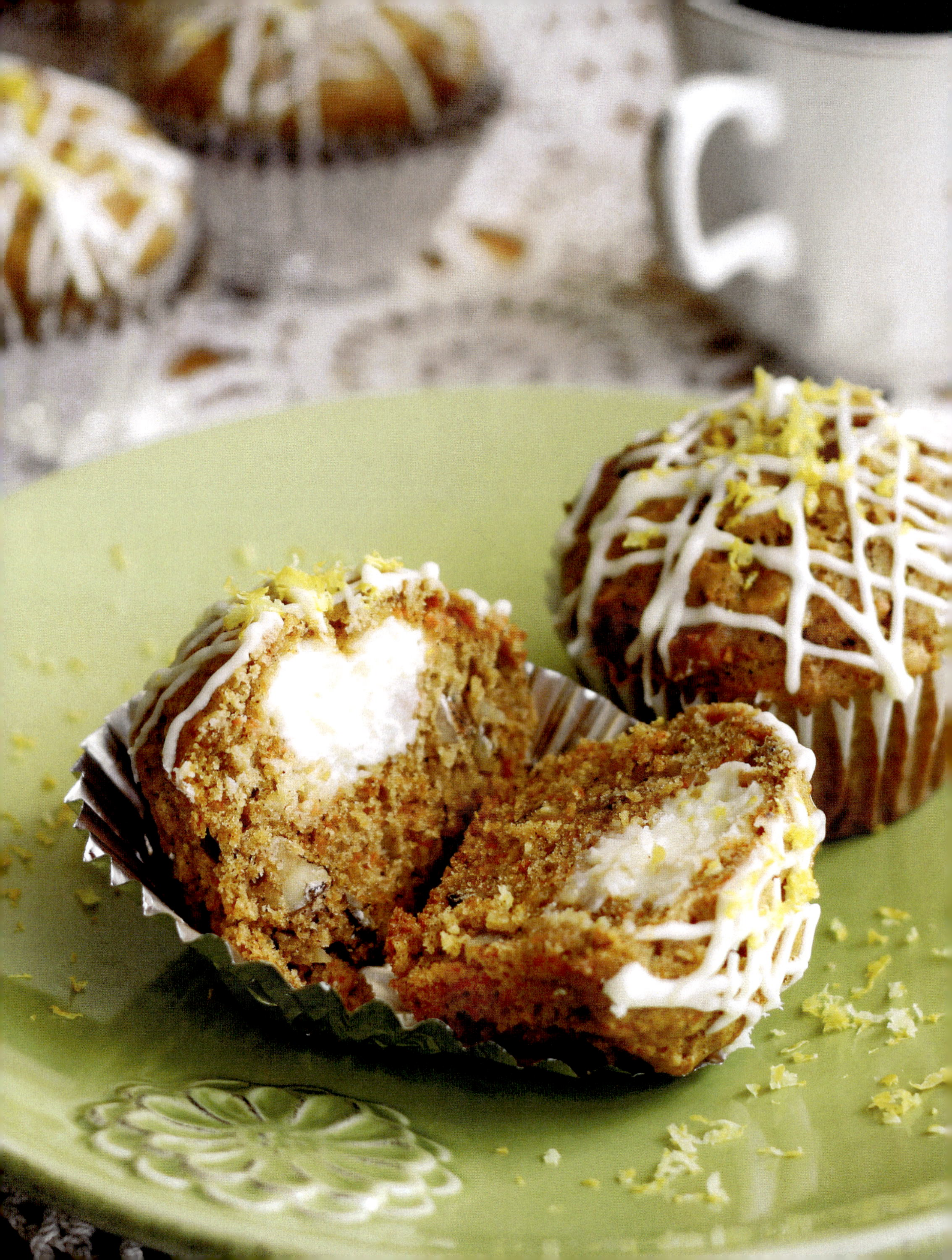

cream cheese-filled carrot cakes

makes 12 cupcakes

Cake batter:
1 ⅓ cups (190g) all-purpose flour
1 ¼ tsp baking powder
¼ tsp baking soda
1 tsp ground cinnamon
¼ tsp <u>each</u> ground allspice, coriander, nutmeg and ginger
¼ tsp salt
2 cups (227g) finely grated carrots (from about 2 large carrots)
½ cup (100g) granulated sugar
¼ cup (55g) packed light brown sugar
2 large eggs, at room temperature
¼ cup (60ml) full fat sour cream
⅓ cup (80ml) sunflower oil
⅓ cup (40g) coarsely chopped walnuts

Filling:
½ block (125g) cream cheese, softened
2 tbsp (25g) granulated sugar
2 tsp (10ml) honey

Glaze:
1 cup (125g) icing sugar
1-2 tsp (5-10ml) freshly squeezed lemon juice
lemon zest for topping

1. Preheat oven to 350°F. Line a standard 12-cup muffin pan with paper liners.

2. First make the filling. Beat cream cheese using an electric hand mixer on medium speed until smooth. Add sugar and honey and beat until glossy and creamy.

3. For the cake batter, sift flour, baking powder, baking soda, spices and salt into a medium bowl and whisk to blend evenly.

4. Combine grated carrots with both granulated sugar and brown sugar in a large bowl. Let it stand for no more than 3 minutes to allow the sugar to break down the carrots and help soften them slightly so that they don't become stringy bits in your cakes. Some of the carrot juice will be drawn out – do not discard this liquid. Whisk in eggs one at a time until well blended, then whisk in sour cream and oil. Add flour mixture and walnuts and fold gently using a spatula until mostly incorporated, but do not over-mix.

5. Divide about two-thirds of the batter evenly among paper liners filling them just half-way. Use the back of a small spoon to create a well in the centre of each portion of batter and place one teaspoon of cream cheese filling into the well. Divide remaining batter among muffin cups and spread it out to cover the filling. Bake for 18-20 minutes until firm to the touch. Transfer muffins to a wire rack to cool completely.

6. For the glaze, whisk together icing sugar with enough lemon juice so that it is thin enough to pour off a spoon and then drizzle over cooled cakes. Sprinkle finely grated lemon zest on top while the icing is tacky.

chocolate yolk cookies
makes 20 cookies

Filling:

¾ cup (100g) roasted hazelnuts

3 oz (85g) dark chocolate, roughly chopped

¼ cup (30g) icing sugar

pinch of salt

1 large egg white (reserve the yolk)

Cookie dough:

½ cup (113g) unsalted butter, softened

½ cup (60g) icing sugar

⅛ tsp salt

1 large egg yolk

1 tsp (5ml) pure vanilla extract

1 cup plus 1 tbsp (150g) all-purpose flour

2 oz (56g) melted dark chocolate

1. For the filling, grind hazelnuts in a food processor until very fine. Add chopped chocolate, icing sugar and salt and process until chocolate is broken down to small pieces. Add egg white and pulse until it comes together as a sticky paste and it forms a ball in the bowl. Scrape the mixture out onto a piece of plastic wrap, roll it into a log and refrigerate for 1 hour (or freeze for 30 minutes). Once firm, slice the log into 20 portions and roll them into smooth balls.

2. Preheat oven to 350°F. Line two large baking sheets with parchment paper.

3. For the cookie dough, beat butter, icing sugar and salt in a medium bowl with a wooden spoon until pale, fluffy and smooth. Stir in egg yolk and vanilla. Sift in the flour and fold it through until a smooth soft dough forms. Divide the dough into 20 portions and roll each one into smooth balls. Flatten dough balls into a disk shape in your palm – it will be soft so you can flour your hands to prevent sticking. Place a ball of chocolate filling in the centre of each dough disk, wrap the dough around the filling to encase it and roll it between your palms to smooth it out and form a sphere.

4. Place dough balls onto prepared baking sheets spacing them 1 to 2 inches apart. Bake for 15-16 minutes until bottoms are evenly browned and tops are lightly golden. Let cookies cool for 2 minutes on trays before transferring individually to a rack to finish cooling. Drizzle with melted chocolate.

peanut butter chocolate truffle cream cheese cookie bars

makes about 16 squares

egg free

Base:
- ⅓ cup (75g) salted butter, softened
- ¼ cup (55g) packed dark brown sugar
- 4 tbsp (60g) cream cheese, softened
- 2 tbsp (30ml) smooth peanut butter*
- ½ tsp pure vanilla extract
- 1 cup (142g) all-purpose flour

Topping:
- ⅓ cup (80ml) 35% whipping cream
- 5 oz (142g) semisweet chocolate (50-55% cocoa), finely chopped
- ⅓ cup (80ml) smooth peanut butter
- candy-coated mini chocolate eggs for topping

1. Preheat oven to 350°F. Line an 8x8-inch baking pan with aluminum foil leaving a 2-inch overhang along each side.

2. For the base, beat soft butter with brown sugar in a medium bowl until pale and creamy. Mix in cream cheese until well blended. Stir in peanut butter and vanilla. Add flour and fold it in until evenly combined to form a soft dough. Using either floured hands or a piece of plastic wrap, press the dough into an even layer into the bottom of the prepared pan.

3. Bake for 16-20 minutes until slightly puffed, golden on top and lightly browned around the edges. Let cool completely.

4. For the topping, heat cream in a small saucepan over medium heat until it comes to a gentle simmer. Do not boil. Remove from heat, add chopped chocolate and let stand for 2 minutes. Whisk gently from the centre and stirring out to the edges until melted, smooth and glossy. If it splits, stir in 1-2 teaspoons of cold cream or milk until it smooths out. Gently stir in peanut butter. Pour this mixture over the cooled base and spread it out evenly. Sprinkle chopped mini eggs on top. Refrigerate until set, then slice into squares.

*You can use either regular or natural peanut butter in this recipe. If yours is unsalted, add a pinch of salt in with the flour when making the base, and add a pinch to the chocolate topping as well!

ginger apple pie

makes about 8 servings

egg free

Pastry:
- 2 cups (284g) all-purpose flour
- 2 tbsp (25g) granulated sugar
- ¾ tsp salt
- ¾ cup (170g) very cold unsalted butter, cut into ¾-inch cubes
- ⅓ cup (80ml) ice cold water

Filling:
- 2 ½ lbs mixed tart and sweet apples (about 7-8, such as Granny Smith and Gala/Honey Crisp), peeled and cored
- ½ cup (110g) packed light brown sugar
- 1 tsp ground cinnamon
- ¼ tsp ground nutmeg
- 1 tbsp (9g) all purpose flour
- 1 ½ tbsp (12g) corn starch
- 2 tsp (10ml) freshly grated ginger
- 1 tsp (5ml) dark cooking molasses

Topping:
- 1 large egg (optional)
- 1 tbsp coarse sugar for sprinkling

1. For the pastry, combine flour, sugar and salt in a large bowl. Add 2 tbsp (28g) of butter and rub it into the flour mixture using your fingertips until it is evenly dispersed and the mixture resembles fine bread crumbs (you can also blend on medium-low speed in a stand mixer for 2 minutes). Add remaining cold butter and rub it in, pressing and smearing it between your thumbs and fingertips to flatten pieces of butter for an instant laminated effect (you can also use the mixer here, but finish with your hands to squeeze and flatten any large pieces of butter). Continue to rub in the fat until it resembles coarse crumbs with some larger oat flake-sized pieces remaining. There should be no dusty flour in the bowl. Gradually sprinkle in cold water, one tablespoon at a time, while gently tossing with a fork until the dough is moistened and it clings together in clumps. The dough will hold together when squeezed or pressed when it is ready and it will hold the impressions of your fingers, but it should not form a ball. You can add another tablespoon of water as needed if it is too dry. Do this part by hand and don't use the mixer once you add the water since it tends to over-mix in parts. Turn the shaggy mixture out onto a clean surface and bring it together with cupped hands, pressing in loose bits until it is cohesive. Divide it in two, flatten each portion into a disk, wrap well and refrigerate for at least 2 hours or overnight.

2. For the filling, slice apples to ⅛-inch thickness and place them into a large bowl. Stir together brown sugar, cinnamon, nutmeg, flour and corn starch in a small bowl. Add it to the bowl with the apples and toss everything together with a wide spatula until the apples are nicely coated. Stir in ginger and molasses.

3. Dust a work surface lightly with flour and roll one portion of dough out into a circle with ⅛-inch thickness. Rotate the dough and add more flour as necessary to prevent sticking. Transfer dough to an 8x2-inch round baking dish and fit it into the base and up the sides, letting excess hang over the edges. Refrigerate it while rolling the top crust. Roll the other half into a 12 to 13-inch circle and slice it into 1½-inch strips to make a wide lattice. Spoon apple mixture into chilled pie crust base, tucking them in neatly to fill all the spaces (this will prevent your pie from shrinking too much as it cools). Weave the strips over the filling, letting the ends hang over the edge and press them down to seal against the edge pastry from the bottom crust. Trim excess dough and roll it up to create a thick border. Place the pie in the freezer for 10 minutes while you preheat the oven to 425°F.

4. Beat egg until blended in a small bowl and lightly brush the top and edges of the chilled pie with egg wash. Sprinkle liberally with sugar. Place pie on a rimmed baking sheet and bake for 20 minutes. Reduce oven temperature to 350°F and bake for 45-50 minutes longer until pastry is nicely browned and juices have been bubbling for at least 5 minutes.

This is a classic Apple Pie with an elevated flavour from fresh ginger and a touch of molasses for a rich caramel-like taste. Just a simple rolled edge crust makes a beautiful pie, but you can crimp or fork the edges as well.

Switch Up! Make a Berry Apple Pie (image, right). Prepare the filling as directed using 5 cups (600g) of mixed cherries, blackberries and strawberries (hulled and quartered) with about 3 peeled and cored apples (450g), diced. Omit the ginger and molasses.

sifting *vs* whisking

Sifting dry ingredients (flour, cocoa powder, baking powder, soda, etc.) is good practice for most recipes but may not be required in cases where a dense texture is desired such as in brownies and chewy cookies. Sifting mainly serves to break up lumps and evenly distribute fine particles into the batter to help them incorporate readily without having to mix excessively. It also aerates the ingredients. The process of adding dry ingredients to a cake batter alternately with liquid usually serves the purpose of evenly incorporating ingredients with minimal mixing. As a general rule, sift dry ingredients for sponge cakes, butter cakes, tender sugar cookies and whenever using cocoa powder or corn starch to remove lumps. For pastry, chewy drop cookies and brownies it is only necessary to whisk dry ingredients together to blend well.

hand mixer *vs* stand mixer

You can make the most delicious desserts with just a sturdy spatula, a whisk and a mixing bowl. However, electric mixers certainly make things easier and provide more power than our arms can normally produce. Stand mixers with the paddle (flat beater attachment) are excellent for "creaming" or beating butter with sugar to introduce lots of tiny air pockets into fat as the foundational step to making cookie dough and cake batters. They are also ideal for whipping eggs and sugar with the whisk attachment for sponge cakes and swiss meringue buttercream. Hand mixers with two beaters can perform all of these functions too and when I'm working in small batches, I actually prefer them. The interweaving beaters do a great job of incorporating air into cake batter and emulsifying eggs into creamed butter and sugar. If using a stand mixer, I recommend switching to the whisk attachment after the creaming step to make airy cakes.

salted *vs* unsalted butter

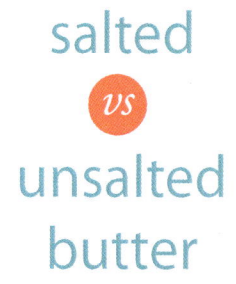

As much as recipes tend to call for unsalted butter, salted butter really makes tasty baked goods! I typically develop most recipes with unsalted butter so that I can control how much salt is used since it varies depending on the type of recipe and ingredients. For example, I prefer unsalted butter for cakes. However, I love to use salted butter for cookies and brownies! It really makes a difference in the flavour, adding a more complex richness and less overall sweetness. Salted butter usually contains 1.5-2% salt. As a general rule, for every ½ cup (113g) of unsalted butter in a recipe, you can substitute salted butter and then reduce the added salt by half. For example if a standard cookie dough recipe calls for ½ cup unsalted butter and then ½ tsp of salt, you can use ½ cup salted butter and ¼ tsp salt.

Irish cream coffee brownies

makes 16 brownies

Brownie base:

5 oz (142g) dark chocolate (50-60% cocoa), coarsely chopped

6 tbsp (84g) unsalted butter

¾ cup (150g) granulated sugar

2 large eggs, at room temperature

2 tsp espresso powder

½ tsp salt

2 tbsp (12g) cocoa powder, sifted

½ cup (71g) all-purpose flour

Topping:

⅔ block (170g) cream cheese, softened

¼ cup plus 1 tbsp (60g) granulated sugar

1 large egg, at room temperature

½ tsp pure vanilla extract

3 tbsp (45ml) Irish cream liquor

¾ cup (180ml) 35% whipping cream

cocoa powder for dusting

1. Preheat oven to 350°F. Line an 8x8-inch baking pan with parchment paper leaving a 2-inch overhang along each side.

2. For the brownie base, melt chocolate and butter in a heatproof bowl set over a saucepan with ½-inch of barely simmering water and stir until smooth (or melt in the microwave). Whisk in sugar. Whisk in eggs one at a time, adding espresso powder in with the last egg. Beat until it tightens up and the batter looks thick and glossy. Whisk in salt and cocoa powder, then stir in flour until combined. Scrape the batter into the prepared pan and spread it out in an even layer. Set aside.

3. For the topping, beat cream cheese with sugar until smooth. Beat in egg and vanilla until incorporated. Mix in liquor. Pour mixture slowly over the brownie batter and spread it out evenly. Bake for 27-30 minutes until a toothpick inserted in the centre comes out mostly clean with a few sticky brownie bits attached. Transfer pan to a wire rack and let brownies cool completely in the pan.

4. Whip cream in a medium bowl with a whisk or hand mixer until it reaches firm peaks and spread it over cooled brownies in the pan. Refrigerate for at least 1 hour and dust with cocoa powder before slicing.

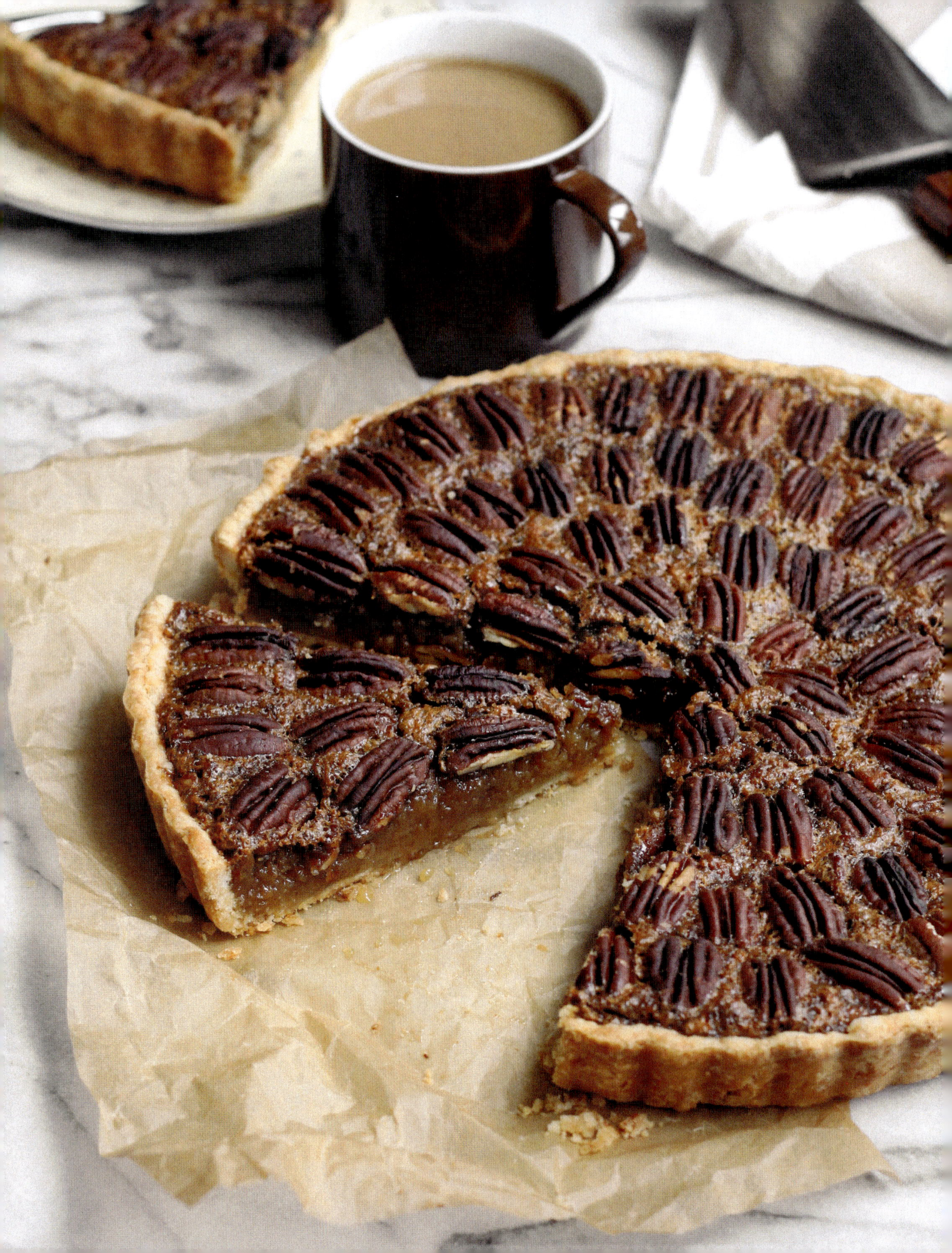

maple brown butter bourbon pecan pie

makes 8-10 servings

Pastry:

1 ⅓ cups (190g) all-purpose flour

2 tbsp (25g) granulated sugar

¼ tsp salt

½ cup (113g) cold unsalted butter, cut into ½-inch cubes

3-4 tbsp (45-60ml) ice cold water

Filling:

¼ cup (56g) unsalted butter

1 cup (220g) packed light brown sugar

⅓ cup (80ml) light corn syrup

⅓ cup (80ml) maple syrup

1 tbsp (15ml) Bourbon whiskey

1 tsp (5ml) pure vanilla extract

1 tsp (5ml) white vinegar

¼ tsp salt

3 large eggs, lightly beaten

1 tsp (3g) all-purpose flour

½ cup (60g) coarsely chopped pecans

1 cup (110g) pecan halves

1. For the pastry, place flour, sugar and salt in a large bowl and whisk to blend (or pulse in a food processor). Add cold butter and rub it in with your fingertips (or pulse in short bursts) until it resembles coarse crumbs. The butter should be well dispersed with some larger, oat flake-sized pieces remaining and there should be little dusty flour left in the bowl. Drizzle in cold water one tablespoon at a time while tossing gently with a fork (or pulsing the food processor) until the flour is moistened and it holds together in clumps, but it should not form a ball. If the dough still feels dry, sprinkle in another tablespoon of water. Turn the shaggy dough out onto a clean work surface and bring it together in a ball with your hands slightly cupped, turning it frequently and pressing in loose bits until it is cohesive. Flatten and shape it into a disk, wrap well and refrigerate for at least 2 hours or overnight.

2. Preheat oven to 350°F. Roll dough out to ⅛-inch thickness on a lightly floured work surface and fit it into a 10-inch round fluted tart pan with removable bottom. Fold excess pastry over the sides to build an edge crust. Place it in the fridge while making the filling.

3. For the filling, first brown the butter. Place butter in a small saucepan over medium-low heat and stir until melted. Increase heat and let it come to a boil while stirring. It will bubble and crackle as water evaporates. Continue to cook, stirring frequently, until the crackling noises fade and the bubbles subside. A dense golden foam will form at the surface as the last bit of water squeezes out and the colour will progress from golden yellow to brown. This takes around 8-10 minutes. Once you smell that nutty aroma and begin to see little brown bits as you stir, take the pan off the heat and immediately pour the brown butter into a heatproof bowl to cool for 5 minutes.

4. Combine brown sugar, corn syrup, maple syrup, brown butter, bourbon, vanilla, vinegar and salt in a medium bowl. Whisk in eggs and then flour. Stir in chopped pecans. Pour the filling into chilled pastry case and arrange pecan halves on top in concentric circles. Place tart pan on a rimmed baking tray and bake for 45-55 minutes until the filling puffs and the pastry is evenly browned. Cover with foil if browning too fast. Transfer to a wire rack to cool completely before serving.

anzac fudge bars

makes 16 squares

Anzac cookie base:

⅔ cup (60g) quick-cooking or minute oats

½ cup (45g) medium unsweetened shredded coconut

½ cup (71g) all-purpose flour

½ cup (110g) packed light brown sugar

¼ tsp baking soda

¼ tsp salt

5 tbsp (70g) unsalted butter, melted

2 tbsp (30ml) maple syrup

Fudge layer:

3 tbsp (42g) unsalted butter

4 oz (113g) dark chocolate (60-70% cocoa)

1 large egg, at room temperature

⅓ cup plus 1 tbsp (80g) granulated sugar

½ tsp pure vanilla extract

¼ tsp salt

¼ cup (35g) all-purpose flour

1. Preheat oven to 350°F. Line an 8x8-inch pan with parchment paper, leaving a 2-inch over hang along each side.

2. For the base, combine oats, coconut, flour, brown sugar, baking soda and salt in a medium bowl. Press out any lumps of sugar. Add melted butter and maple syrup and mix together until evenly blended. Press the mixture in an even layer into the prepared pan and bake for 8-10 minutes until lightly golden brown on top. Transfer to a wire rack while you make the fudge layer. Reduce oven to 325°F.

3. For the fudge layer, melt together butter and chocolate in a heatproof bowl set over a saucepan with ½-inch of simmering water or in the microwave in short bursts with frequent stirring. Whisk together egg, sugar, vanilla and salt in a large bowl until smooth. Whisk in warm chocolate mixture. Sprinkle flour over top and stir it in until combined. Spread it over the baked cookie base and bake again for 15-20 minutes until the fudge layer is just set and slightly cracked around the edges but still soft in the centre. Transfer to a wire rack to cool completely before slicing.

pumpkin chocolate cheesecake bars

makes 12-16 bars

Base:

⅔ cup (95g) all-purpose flour

¼ cup (21g) cocoa powder

⅓ cup (70g) packed light brown sugar

¼ tsp salt

¼ cup (56g) unsalted butter, melted

Filling:

3 oz (85g) dark chocolate, chopped

¾ block (190g) cream cheese, softened

½ cup (100g) granulated sugar

1 large egg, at room temperature

¼ cup (60ml) 35% whipping cream

¾ cup (180ml) pure pumpkin purée

1 tsp (3g) all-purpose flour

½ tsp <u>each</u> ground cinnamon and ginger

⅛ tsp <u>each</u> ground nutmeg and allspice

1. Preheat oven to 350°F. Line an 8x8-inch baking pan with parchment paper leaving a 2-inch overhang along each side.

2. For the base, combine flour, cocoa powder, brown sugar and salt in a medium bowl until evenly blended (or pulse in a food processor). Add melted butter and stir to combine. Use your fingertips to blend the mixture until it forms clumps. Turn it out into the prepared pan and press it down in an even layer. Run the back of a spoon over the surface to smooth it out. Bake for 10-12 minutes until slightly puffed and feels somewhat dry. Transfer to a wire rack to cool. Reduce oven temperature to 325°F.

3. For the filling, gently melt chocolate in a heat-proof bowl set over a saucepan with ½-inch of barely simmering water or melt it in the microwave in short bursts with frequent stirring until smooth.

4. Beat cream cheese with sugar in a medium bowl using an electric hand mixer until smooth and glossy (or blend in a food processor). Beat in egg until well combined. Mix in cream. Add pumpkin purée, flour and spices and beat on low until evenly combined. Add ½ cup (120ml) of pumpkin batter to the melted chocolate and stir to blend well. Pour remaining pumpkin batter over cooled crust and spread it out evenly. Dollop chocolate mixture over pumpkin layer and swirl together with the back of a knife or a wooden skewer.

5. Bake for 20-25 minutes until the filling is just set and matte on the surface. Transfer to a wire rack to cool completely, then cover and refrigerate for 2 hours before slicing.

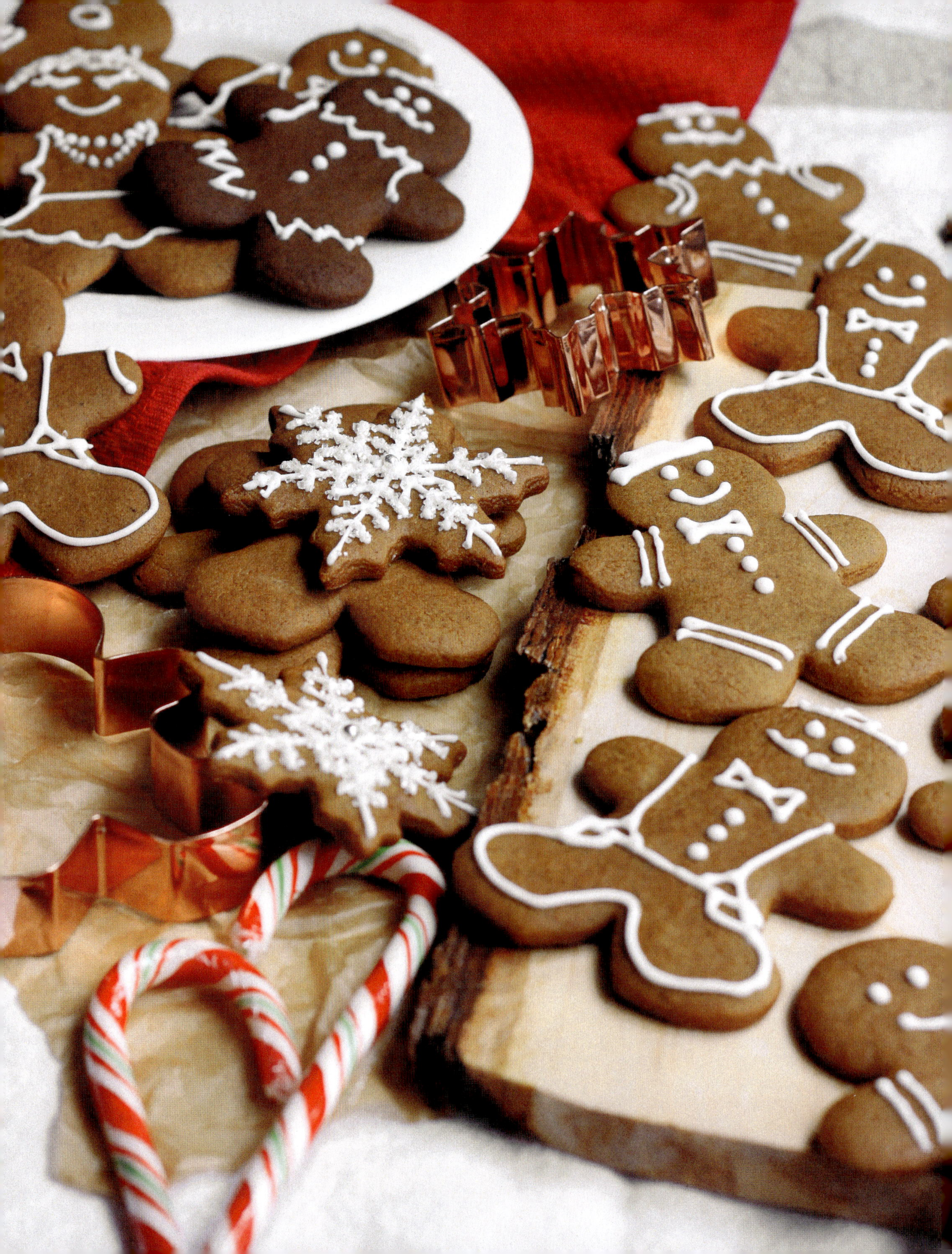

classic gingerbread cookies

makes 32-36 cookies

3 cups (425g) all-purpose flour

1 tbsp ground ginger

1 ½ tsp ground cinnamon

½ tsp ground allspice

¼ tsp ground clove

¼ tsp freshly grated nutmeg

½ tsp baking soda

½ tsp baking powder

½ tsp salt

½ cup plus 1 tbsp (125g) unsalted butter, softened

⅔ cup (145g) packed light brown sugar

1 large egg, at room temperature

⅔ cup (160ml) fancy (light) molasses*

1. Combine flour, spices, baking soda, baking powder and salt in a large bowl and whisk to blend evenly. Set aside.

2. Beat butter with brown sugar in the bowl of an electric stand mixer fitted with the paddle attachment (or in a large bowl if using a hand mixer) for 2 minutes on medium-high speed until pale and fluffy. Add egg and beat until well incorporated. Beat in molasses until combined. Gradually add the flour mixture while mixing on low speed until incorporated.

3. Divide the dough in half, wrap each portion in plastic wrap or parchment paper and refrigerate for at least two hours or overnight.

4. Preheat oven to 350°F. Line two large baking sheets with parchment paper.

5. On a lightly floured surface, roll dough out to ¼-inch thickness. Use a cookie cutter of your choice to stamp out different shapes. Gently transfer cut-outs onto prepared baking sheets using an offset spatula. Leave about 1 inch of space between them.

6. Bake for 8-12 minutes (depending on the size of the cookies) until lightly browned around the edges. Small cookies will take about 8 minutes while larger ones will need about 12 minutes. Transfer baking sheets to a wire rack and let cookies cool completely on the trays before decorating with Royal Icing (recipe in the pink box below).

*You can also make this with robust "cooking" molasses. In this case, follow the directions as written, except increase brown sugar to ¾ cup (165g), increase egg to 2 whole eggs, and reduce molasses quantity to ⅓ cup (80ml).

ROYAL ICING

1 tbsp (7g) meringue powder*

1 ¼ cups (155g) icing sugar, sifted

2-3 tbsp (30-45ml) warm water

Combine meringue powder, icing sugar and water in the bowl of a stand mixer fitted with the whisk attachment (or use an electric mixer) on high speed for 10-12 minutes until thick like marshmallow and it forms firm peaks. This thick icing is great for outlines and detailing, but then thin out the icing with water as needed for flooding and filling.

Spoon icing into a piping bag fitted with a small plain tip to decorate. Let cookies dry for 2 hours until icing hardens before storing.

You can use one large fresh egg white in place of meringue powder, and then omit the added warm water.

egg free

florentine medallions

makes about 24 medallions

1 cup (100g) sliced almonds

¾ cup (95g) dried cherries, roughly chopped

¼ cup (35g) all-purpose flour

⅓ cup (80ml) 35% whipping cream

½ cup (100g) granulated sugar

2 tbsp (30ml) honey

1 ½ tbsp (20g) butter

pinch of salt

4 oz (113g) bittersweet chocolate, chopped

1. Coarsely chop half of the sliced almonds, then combine all of the almonds together with the chopped dried cherries and flour in a medium bowl and mix well.

2. Combine cream, sugar, honey, butter and salt in a small saucepan over medium heat and bring to a boil while stirring. Boil for 1 minute. Remove from heat and pour it over the almond mixture. Stir until well combined, then set aside to thicken as the oven heats.

3. Preheat oven to 325°F. Generously grease two standard nonstick 12-cup muffin pans with soft butter -- be sure to use butter and not oil or these will be more likely to stick.

4. Spoon level tablespoons of the mixture into the muffin pan cups and bake for 14-16 minutes until evenly golden brown and bubbling around the edges. Transfer pans to a wire rack to cool and set for 5-10 minutes. Once they are firm but still flexible, use a small offset spatula or butter knife to release the edges of each medallion from the pan and then gently peel them up. Transfer to a wire rack to finish cooling and set completely.

5. Melt chocolate gently in a heatproof bowl set over a saucepan with ½-inch of simmering water or in a microwave in short bursts with frequent stirring. Dip the bottoms of each medallion into melted chocolate and transfer to a baking sheet lined with waxed paper to set. Once the chocolate hardens, transfer to an airtight container for storage.

These Florentines are thicker and chewier than the traditional lace cookie, which transforms them into a decadent confection more so than a cookie and I love them! See page 174 for tips on how to make the traditional lace cookie as well.

soft spicy gingerbread cake

makes 9-12 servings

Traditional gingerbread is made with hot water which intensifies both the colour of the crumb and the flavour of the spices. Try making the variation in the pink box for my sweet Milky version too!

1 ½ cups (215g) all-purpose flour

¾ tsp baking soda

¼ tsp salt

1 tsp <u>each</u> ground ginger and cinnamon

¼ tsp ground allspice

⅛ tsp <u>each</u> ground nutmeg and clove

½ cup (113g) unsalted butter, softened

⅔ cup (145g) packed light brown sugar

1 large egg, at room temperature

⅓ cup (80ml) fancy (light) molasses*

⅔ cup (160ml) hot water

1 x Butterscotch Sauce recipe (page 172)

> *You can substitute robust "cooking" molasses (NOT blackstrap) for fancy molasses in this recipe, but it will yield a darker colour and stronger flavour. If you only have blackstrap molasses on hand, you can still make this recipe by blending equal proportions of blackstrap molasses and honey to make up ⅓ cup.

> **Switch Up!** Milky Gingerbread Cake: I also make this recipe using ¾ cup (180ml) evaporated milk in place of hot water. The batter will be thicker and the result is a lighter tan-coloured crumb, a firmer texture and a sweet milky flavour that balances the intense spices. It's not traditional but it is delicious! Also, try dividing the batter between to 8-inch round pans and bake for 20-25 minutes to create a beautiful layer cake with your favourite cream cheese frosting!

1. Preheat oven to 350°F. Line an 8x8 or 9x9-inch baking pan with parchment paper, leaving a 2-inch overhang along each side. Bring a kettle of water to a boil and then let stand until ready to use.

2. Sift flour, baking soda, salt and spices into a medium bowl and whisk to blend.

3. Beat butter with brown sugar for 2-3 minutes in a large bowl using an electric hand mixer until pale and fluffy. Add egg and beat until smooth. Beat in molasses until blended and mixture is somewhat fluffy and creamy-looking. With mixer on low, gradually add flour mixture. It will be thick. Once it is mostly combined, add hot water and beat until batter is smooth.

4. Spread batter evenly into prepared pan and bake for 30-35 minutes until a skewer inserted into the centre comes out clean. Transfer pan to a wire rack to cool. Serve with butterscotch sauce.

double chocolate hazelnut biscotti

makes about 24 cookies

1 ⅔ cups (235g) all-purpose flour	½ cup (110g) packed dark brown sugar
¾ tsp baking powder	¼ cup (50g) granulated sugar
½ tsp baking soda	1 tsp (5ml) pure vanilla extract
¼ tsp salt	⅓ cup (75g) unsalted butter, melted
½ cup (42g) cocoa powder	½ cup (65g) whole roasted hazelnuts
½ cup (85g) dark chocolate chips	½ cup (60g) dried cranberries
2 large eggs, at room temperature	

1. Preheat oven to 350°F. Line a large baking sheet with parchment paper.

2. Combine flour, baking powder, baking soda and salt in a large bowl. Sift in cocoa powder and whisk to blend evenly. Stir in chocolate chips.

3. Vigorously whisk eggs with both sugars and vanilla in a medium bowl until smooth, thick and lightened by a shade. Whisk in melted butter. Make a well in the centre of the dry ingredients and pour in the egg mixture. Stir gently with a spatula or wooden spoon until most of the flour is absorbed. Fold in hazelnuts and dried cranberries until evenly distributed. The dough will be stiff and a bit sticky but not wet. Use your hands to incorporate the cranberries if necessary.

4. Divide dough in half and roll each half into a 10-inch log. Place them onto prepared baking sheet and flatten them to about 2 inches wide. Bake for about 25 minutes until puffed and slightly cracked at the surface. Transfer baking sheet to a rack and let cool on the pan for at least 30 minutes until cool enough to handle. Reduce oven to 300°F.

5. Transfer logs to a cutting board and slice them diagonally on a sharp angle at about ¾-inch increments with a gentle sawing motion. Place cookies back onto the baking sheet right-side-up and bake for 10-15 minutes until dry and crisp.

chewy gooey double ginger molasses cookies

makes about 20 cookies

10 tbsp (140g) unsalted butter, softened
1 cup (220g) packed light brown sugar
1 large egg, at room temperature
¼ cup (60ml) fancy (light) molasses
2 cups (284g) all-purpose flour
1 ¼ tsp baking soda
½ tsp salt
2 tsp ground ginger
1 tsp ground cinnamon
⅛ tsp ground clove
½ cup (70g) chopped crystallized ginger
½ cup (100g) granulated sugar for rolling

1. Beat butter with brown sugar in the bowl of a stand mixer fitted with the paddle attachment on medium speed for 2 minutes until smooth, creamy and a bit fluffy. Beat in egg until evenly incorporated, scraping down the sides of the bowl as necessary. Add molasses and beat until combined.

2. Combine flour, baking soda, salt, ginger, cinnamon and clove in a medium bowl and whisk to blend evenly. Add it to the butter mixture with the crystallized ginger and mix on low speed just until incorporated.

3. Wrap the dough well (or cover the dough in the bowl) and refrigerate for at least 2 hours or up to 8 hours.

4. When ready to bake, preheat the oven to 350°F. Line two large baking sheets with parchment paper.

5. Roll heaped tablespoons of dough into smooth balls and then roll in granulated sugar to coat evenly. Place onto prepared baking sheets with at least 2 inches of space between each one (flatten slightly if you prefer flatter cookies). Bake for 9-11 minutes until evenly browned, puffed and cracked at the surface. Transfer baking sheets to a wire rack and let cookies cool for 2 minutes before transferring individually to the rack to finish cooling.

vanilla sugar cookies

makes 35-40 cookies

2 cups (284g) all-purpose flour

½ tsp baking powder

½ tsp salt

¾ cup (170g) unsalted butter, softened

¾ cup (150g) granulated sugar

1 ½ tsp (7mL) pure vanilla extract

1 large egg, at room temperature

Switch Up! For a festive flavour, add ½ tsp ground cardamom or cinnamon and ⅛ tsp ground nutmeg in with the dry ingredients. These cookies keep for up to 3 weeks and their texture and flavour improves with age.

1. Sift flour, baking powder and salt into a large bowl. Whisk to blend evenly and set aside.

2. Place butter into the bowl of a stand mixer fitted with the paddle attachment (or in a large bowl if using an electric hand mixer) and beat on medium speed until smooth and creamy. Slowly stream in sugar while mixing and then beat on medium-high speed for 3-4 minutes until very pale and fluffy. Scrape down the sides and bottom of the bowl midway through this creaming stage. Beat in vanilla and egg until well incorporated. Gradually add flour mixture while mixing on low speed, then finish mixing by hand with a spatula so that you don't over-mix.

3. Wrap dough well and refrigerate for 30 minutes.

4. Preheat oven to 350°F. Line 2 large baking sheets with parchment paper.

5. Roll the dough out to just under ¼-inch thickness on a lightly floured work surface. Stamp out as many shapes as you can using any 2 to 3-inch round cutter (or any cookie cutter shape of your choice). Place cut-outs onto prepared baking sheets, spacing them 1 inch apart. Bake for 10-14 minutes until edges are lightly golden around the edges. Under-baking sugar cookies will mean that they will just taste doughy, so make sure to let them brown lightly. Transfer baking sheets to a wire rack to cool for 2 minutes before transferring cookies individually to the racks to finish cooling. Decorate with royal icing (recipe on page 61) and sprinkles if desired!

pistachio cherry & chocolate biscotti

makes 30-35 cookies

1 ¾ cups (250g) all-purpose flour

2 tsp baking powder

½ tsp salt

½ cup (85g) dark chocolate chips

½ cup (65g) roasted unsalted pistachios

2 large eggs, at room temperature

¾ cup (150g) granulated sugar

zest of one orange

⅓ cup (75g) unsalted butter, melted and cooled

½ tsp pure almond extract

½ cup (60g) dried tart cherries

1 egg, well beaten for brushing

coarse sugar for sprinkling

1. Preheat oven to 350°F. Line a large baking sheet with parchment paper.

2. Combine flour, baking powder and salt in a large bowl and whisk to blend evenly. Stir in chocolate chips and pistachios.

3. Combine eggs, sugar and orange zest in a medium bowl and whisk vigorously until thickened and lightened in colour like custard. Whisk in melted butter and almond extract.

4. Make a well in the centre of the flour mixture and pour in egg mixture. Stir with a wooden spoon or spatula until most of the flour is absorbed. Add dried cherries and fold them through to distribute evenly. The dough will be a bit sticky.

5. Divide dough in half and place it onto a lightly floured work surface. With lightly floured hands, gently roll each portion into an 11 to 12-inch log and then transfer the logs onto the prepared baking sheet spacing them about 3 inches apart. Flatten logs with your hands so that they are about 2½ inches wide and ¾-inch high.

6. Brush flattened logs lightly with beaten egg and sprinkle with sugar. Bake for about 25 minutes until golden brown. Transfer baking sheet to a wire rack and cool for at least 30 minutes so that the cookie logs no longer feel soft and are firm enough to slice neatly. Reduce oven temperature to 300°F.

7. Use a sharp serrated knife to slice logs diagonally into ½-inch pieces and place them back onto the baking sheet so they are standing right-side-up. Bake for another 10-15 minutes until dry and crisp. Serve with espresso!

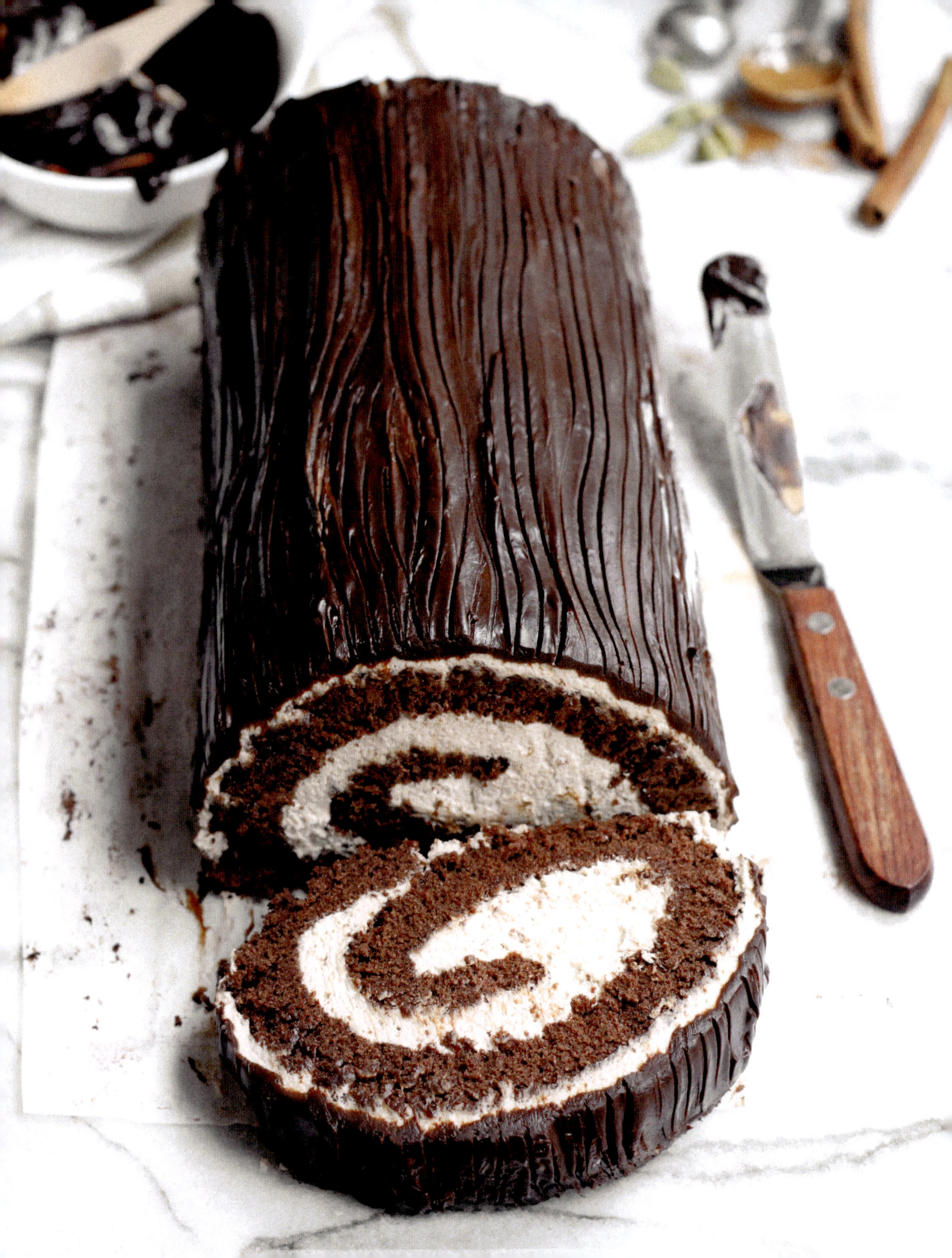

chocolate chai yule log

makes 8-10 servings

Sponge cake:

4 large eggs, at room temperature

⅔ cup (145g) packed light brown sugar

1 tsp espresso powder

½ tsp pure vanilla extract

¼ tsp salt

½ cup (71g) all-purpose flour

¼ cup (21g) Dutch process cocoa powder

2 tbsp (28g) unsalted butter, melted*

> *For the sponge cake, you can also replace the melted butter with an equal amount of vegetable oil to produce an even more flexible cake for rolling. But, butter has better flavour!

Filling:

1 ¼ cups (300ml) 35% whipping cream

2 tbsp (30g) packed dark brown sugar

1 tsp (2g) cocoa powder

¼ tsp <u>each</u> ground cinnamon and ginger

⅛ tsp <u>each</u> ground clove and cardamom

Glaze:

½ cup (120ml) 35% whipping cream

1 tsp (5ml) honey

4 ½ oz (130g) dark chocolate (60% cocoa), finely chopped

1. Preheat oven to 350°F. Lightly spray a 13x9-inch rimmed baking sheet or jelly roll pan with cooking spray and line the base with parchment paper. You can also use a 16x12-inch sheet pan and the cake will be thinner.

2. For the sponge cake, beat eggs in the bowl of an electric stand mixer fitted with the whisk attachment (or in a large mixing bowl if using an electric hand mixer) for 3 minutes on high speed until frothy and pale. Gradually add brown sugar and beat for 3-4 minutes longer until it triples in volume and is very pale and thick. Beat in espresso powder, vanilla and salt. Sift flour and cocoa powder into a medium bowl. Whisk to blend evenly and then sift it again gently over the egg mixture in the bowl. Use a large rubber spatula or big wire whisk to carefully fold the dry ingredients into the whipped eggs. Once mostly incorporated, slowly add the cooled melted butter and finish folding just until evenly combined.

3. Pour batter into prepared pan and spread it out evenly in a thin layer right to the edges. Bake for 9-12 minutes until it springs back when pressed gently. If using a 16x12-inch pan, bake for 8-10 minutes. Transfer pan to a wire rack and let cool for 1-2 minutes so it is easier to handle. Dust the surface of the sponge cake evenly with extra cocoa powder. Run a knife around sides to loosen it from the pan. Invert cake onto a clean kitchen towel or another large piece of parchment paper and gently peel off the parchment.

4. While the cake is still warm, gently roll it into a snug log starting from one short side and incorporating the kitchen towel or parchment as you are rolling. Let the cake cool completely in this rolled shape.

5. For the filling, combine cream, brown sugar, cocoa and spices in a medium bowl and beat on medium speed using an electric hand mixer until it reaches firm peaks.

6. Gently unroll the cooled sponge cake and spread about three-quarters of the filling evenly over it leaving a ½-inch border all around. Roll the cake back up to encase the filling starting at a short end. Transfer the rolled cake to a serving plate and refrigerate for at least 30 minutes. Spread remaining filling over the chilled cake to cover it and refrigerate again for 30 minutes while you make the glaze.

7. For the glaze, combine cream and honey in a small saucepan and bring to a simmer over medium heat. Remove from heat and add chopped chocolate. Let stand for a minute before stirring gently until smooth and glossy. Spoon this over the chilled cake and then quickly spread it along the length of the log using an offset spatula, trying not to go over the same area twice or it will pick up the cream filling and smear it into the chocolate glaze (this still looks nice though, just not as tidy). Run the tings of a fork along the length of the log to resemble wood grain. Refrigerate for 1 hour before slicing and serving.

chocolate truffle sandwich cookies

makes about 15-20 cookies

5 oz (142g) dark chocolate (50-60% cocoa), finely chopped

⅓ cup (80ml) 35% or 10% cream

1 tsp (5ml) honey

1. Follow the recipe for Vanilla Sugar Cookies on page 66. Use a small 1 to 2-inch round or heart-shaped cutter to stamp out shapes. Bake for 8-12 minutes (depending on size) until lightly golden around the edges. Let cool.

2. For the filling, add chopped chocolate to a bowl. Heat cream with honey in a small saucepan until it simmers then pour it over the chocolate. Stir gently until smooth and glossy and then spread it between two cookies. Drizzle with extra melted dark chocolate and top with sprinkles!

chocolate snowflake crinkle cookies

makes 22-24 cookies

7 oz (200g) bittersweet chocolate (70% cocoa), chopped
¼ cup (56g) unsalted butter
2 large eggs, at room temperature
¾ cup (150g) granulated sugar
1 tsp (5ml) pure vanilla extract
½ tsp salt
1 cup (142g) all-purpose flour
½ tsp baking powder
¼ tsp baking soda
½ cup (100g) granulated sugar for rolling
1 cup (125g) icing sugar for rolling

1. Combine chocolate and butter in a heatproof bowl set over a saucepan with ½-inch of simmering water and stir until completely melted and smooth (or melt in the microwave in short 20 second bursts with frequent stirring). Set aside.

2. Combine eggs, sugar and vanilla in the bowl of a stand mixer fitted with the paddle attachment (or in a large bowl if using a hand mixer) and beat for 3-4 minutes on medium-high speed until pale and thick. Mix in salt. Add warm melted chocolate mixture and mix on low until well blended.

3. Combine flour, baking powder and baking soda in a medium bowl and whisk to blend evenly. Add this to the chocolate mixture and fold it in with a spatula until just combined. Scrape down the sides and bottom of the bowl and mix by hand to incorporate all ingredients. Do not over-mix.

4. Cover the dough in the bowl and refrigerate for 20 minutes just until the dough is firm enough to shape. Meanwhile, preheat the oven to 350°F. Line two large baking sheets with parchment paper.

5. Scoop tablespoons of chilled dough and roll into smooth balls. Roll each ball evenly in granulated sugar, then roll in icing sugar so they are generously coated and you can no longer see the dough. Place onto prepared baking sheets, spacing them 2 inches apart. Bake for 8-10 minutes until cracked at the surface and still soft in the middle. Let cookies cool for 3 minutes on the pan, then transfer individually to a rack to finish cooling.

gianduja rocher crescent cookies

makes about 24 cookies

Cookie dough:

½ cup (113g) unsalted butter, softened

¾ cup (90g) icing sugar

½ tsp pure vanilla extract

¼ tsp salt

1 large egg yolk

¾ cup (105g) all-purpose flour

⅓ cup (28g) cocoa powder

½ cup (65g) roasted hazelnuts, finely ground

For dipping:

3 oz (85g) bittersweet chocolate, melted

¼ cup (30g) roasted hazelnuts, finely chopped

1. Combine butter, icing sugar, vanilla and salt in a medium bowl and beat with a wooden spoon or spatula until very pale and fluffy. Beat in egg yolk. Sift flour and cocoa over the butter mixture and fold it in until evenly combined. Fold in hazelnuts.

2. Roll level tablespoons of dough into balls and then roll them under your fingertips on a clean work surface into smooth logs with tapered ends. Shape each one into a crescent by curving the ends inward and place them onto parchment-lined baking sheets. Space them about 2 inches apart. Place baking sheets in the freezer for 10 minutes. Meanwhile, preheat oven to 350°F.

3. Bake for 10-12 minutes until cookies appear dry and slightly cracked at the surface. Transfer baking sheets to a wire rack and let cookies cool completely on trays.

4. Once cool, dip one end of each cookie into melted chocolate and then dip into chopped hazelnuts. Transfer cookies back to cooled, lined baking sheets to set.

chocolate chai spice cookies

makes 20-22 cookies

½ cup (113g) unsalted butter, softened
¾ cup (165g) packed light brown sugar
2 tbsp (30ml) light (fancy) molasses
1 large egg, at room temperature
1 ⅓ cups (190g) all-purpose flour
3 tbsp (18g) cocoa powder
¾ tsp baking soda
1 tsp ground cinnamon
¾ tsp ground ginger
¼ tsp ground cardamom
⅛ tsp ground nutmeg
⅛ tsp ground clove
pinch of ground black pepper
½ tsp salt
1 cup (142g) dark chocolate chunks
½ cup (100g) granulated sugar for rolling

1. Combine butter and brown sugar in the bowl of a stand mixer fitted with the paddle attachment (or in a large bowl if using an electric hand mixer) and beat for 2-3 minutes on medium speed until smooth and a bit fluffy. Mix in molasses. Scrape down the sides and bottom of the bowl. Beat in egg until well incorporated and the mixture is pale and creamy.

2. Sift flour, cocoa powder, baking soda, spices and salt into a medium bowl. Whisk to blend evenly. Add flour mixture to the butter mixture and mix on low speed until mostly combined, then fold in chocolate chunks by hand. Cover and chill for 30 minutes.

3. Preheat oven to 350°F. Line two large baking sheets with parchment paper.

4. Roll heaped tablespoons of dough into smooth balls (with about 1 ½-inch diameter) and then roll them evenly in sugar. Place dough balls onto prepared baking sheets spacing them 2 inches apart and bake for 8-10 minutes until puffed and cracked at the surface, but still soft in the middle. Transfer baking sheets to a wire rack and let cool for 2 minutes before transferring cookies individually to the racks to finish cooling.

egg free

chocolate chip pecan butter balls & batons

makes about 34 cookies

⅔ cup (150g) unsalted butter, softened

½ cup (60g) icing sugar

1 tsp pure vanilla extract

¼ tsp salt

2 tsp (10ml) water

1 cup (110g) pecan halves

1 ½ cups (215g) all-purpose flour

⅔ cup (100g) finely chopped dark chocolate

3 oz (85g) dark chocolate for dipping

chocolate sprinkles or chopped nuts

1. Preheat oven to 325°F. Line two large baking sheets with parchment paper.

2. Beat butter with icing sugar for 3-5 minutes on medium-high speed in the bowl of a stand mixer fitted with the paddle attachment until very pale and fluffy. Scrape down the bowl several times during mixing. Beat in vanilla, salt and water.

3. Pulse pecans in a food processor until finely ground. Combine with flour and chocolate chips in a medium bowl and add it to the butter mixture. Mix on low speed until evenly combined.

4. Roll level tablespoons of dough into 2-inch logs and place onto baking sheets spacing them just 2 inches apart (they don't spread much). Alternatively you can roll them into balls and flatten slightly. Bake for 18-20 minutes or until edges are golden and bottoms are lightly browned. Transfer cookies to a wire rack to cool.

5. Dip in melted chocolate and then top with chocolate sprinkles or chopped nuts.

peppermint crème chocolate sandwich cookies

makes about 15 sandwich cookies

Cookie dough:

½ cup (113g) unsalted butter, softened
¾ cup (150g) granulated sugar
1 tsp (5ml) pure vanilla extract
1 large egg, at room temperature
½ tsp salt
1 cup (142g) all-purpose flour
⅓ cup (28g) Dutch process cocoa powder
½ tsp baking soda

Filling:

2 oz (56g) pure white chocolate, finely chopped
2 tbsp (30ml) 35% whipping cream
⅓ cup (75g) unsalted butter, softened
1 cup (125g) icing sugar, sifted
½ tsp pure peppermint extract
½ tsp pure vanilla extract
pinch of salt
4 oz (113g) dark chocolate, melted

1. Combine butter and sugar in a medium bowl and beat with a hand mixer on high speed for 2 minutes until pale and fluffy. Add vanilla, egg and salt and beat until well incorporated. Sift in flour, cocoa and baking soda and fold it in gently until a soft dough forms. Cover and refrigerate for 30 minutes.

2. Preheat oven to 350°F. Line two large baking sheets with parchment paper.

3. Roll tablespoons of dough into balls and place onto baking sheets spacing them 2 inches apart. Flatten with the palm of your hand so they are ½-inch thick. Bake for 8-9 minutes until matte on the surface and edges are set. Transfer trays to a wire rack to cool.

4. For the filling, stir together white chocolate and cream in a small saucepan over low heat and until melted and smooth (or melt in the microwave). Let cool completely until set.

5. Beat butter in a medium bowl using an electric hand mixer on medium speed until smooth. Sift in icing sugar and beat until creamy and fluffy. Beat in extracts and salt. Add cooled white chocolate cream and beat until whipped, light, creamy and fluffy.

6. Spread or pipe filling between two cookies, dip them in melted dark chocolate and finish with sprinkles if desired!

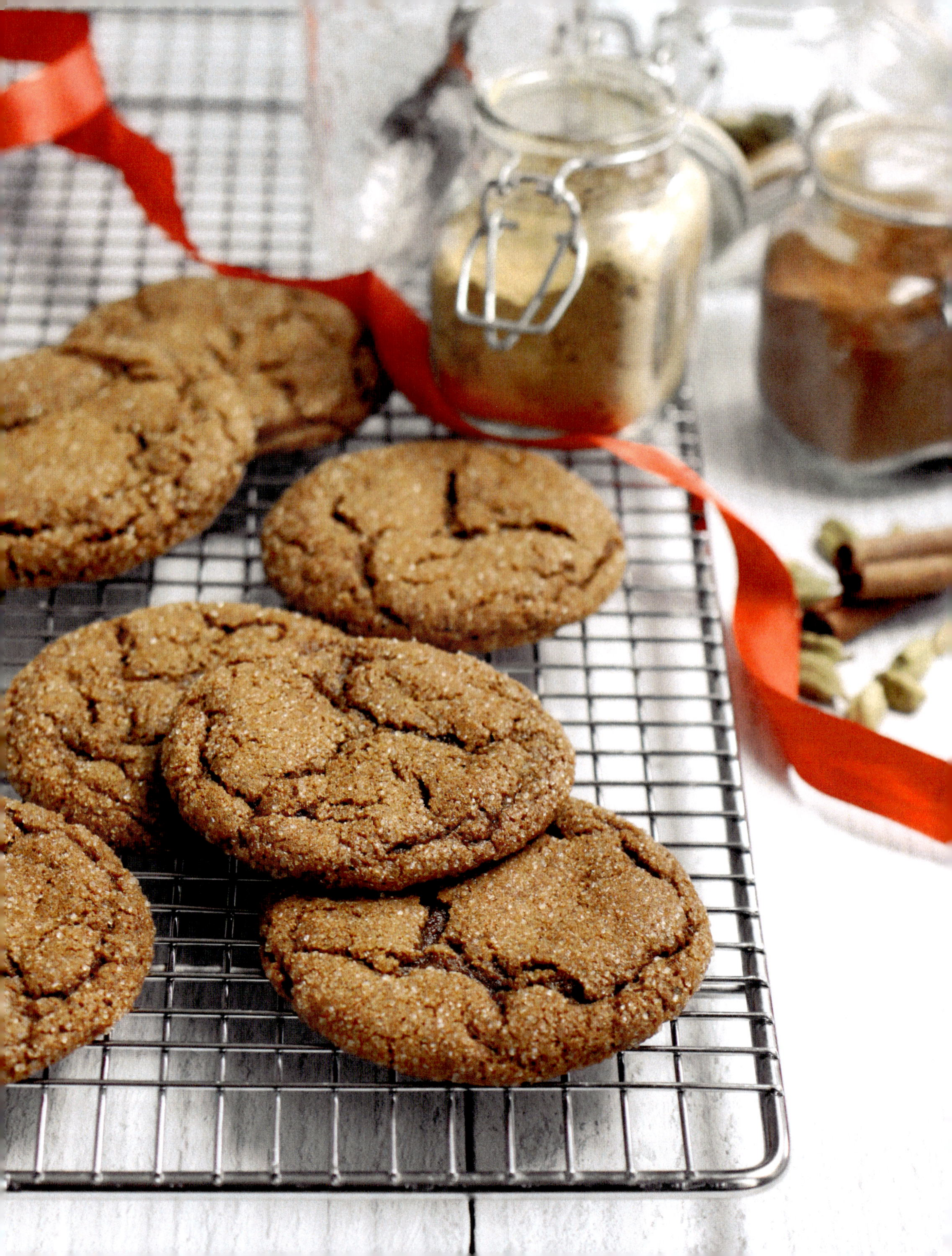

soft & chewy molasses spice crinkle cookies

makes 20-22 cookies

1 ½ cups (215g) all-purpose flour

1 tsp baking soda

1 tsp ground ginger

1 tsp ground cinnamon

¼ tsp ground cardamom

¼ tsp ground allspice or clove

⅛ tsp ground nutmeg

½ tsp salt

½ cup (113g) unsalted butter, softened

¾ cup (150g) granulated sugar

2 tbsp (30ml) dark "robust" cooking molasses (not blackstrap)

1 large egg, at room temperature

1 tbsp (15ml) whole milk

½ cup (100g) granulated sugar for rolling

1. Combine flour, baking soda, spices and salt in a medium bowl and whisk to blend evenly.

2. Combine butter and sugar in the bowl of a stand mixer fitted with the paddle attachment and beat on medium speed for 2 minutes until smooth and somewhat fluffy (alternatively, you can use an electric hand mixer). Beat in molasses until well combined. Add egg and beat until well incorporated and the mixture looks fluffy and lightened in colour. Beat in milk. Scrape down the sides of the bowl with a rubber spatula several times during mixing.

3. Add half of the flour mixture and beat on low speed until mostly combined. Add remaining dry ingredients and beat just until evenly blended. Do not over-mix. Cover the bowl well and refrigerate the dough for 2 to 4 hours.

4. Preheat oven to 350°F. Line two large baking sheets with parchment paper. Remove dough from refrigerator and let stand at room temperature for about 15 minutes before rolling to make it easier to work with.

5. Place granulated sugar in a small bowl. Roll heaped tablespoons of dough into balls and then roll them around in sugar to coat evenly. Transfer dough balls to baking sheets, spacing them 2-3 inches apart. Bake for 10-12 minutes until cracked on the surface and lightly browned around the edges. Let cool for 1 minute on baking sheets before transferring individually to a wire rack to finish cooling.

When planning for the holidays, try making this cookie dough in advance to bake later. To do this, roll the dough into balls, roll them in sugar, place them onto a lined baking tray and freeze them as individual balls. Once frozen solid, transfer balls to a freezer bag, seal it well and keep frozen for up to 3 months. You can bake straight from frozen in a 375°F preheated oven for 12-15 minutes. Or, let thaw for 15 minutes then bake at 350°F for 12-15 minutes.

vanilla walnut crescent cookies

makes 25-30 cookies

Cookie dough:

¾ cup (90g) coarsely chopped walnuts

1 ¼ cups (180g) all-purpose flour

½ cup (113g) unsalted butter, very soft

½ cup (100g) granulated sugar

⅛ tsp salt

1 large egg yolk

1 tsp (5ml) pure vanilla extract

For rolling:

¾ cup (90g) icing sugar

2 tbsp (25g) granulated sugar

1. Place walnuts with 1 tablespoon of the flour in a food processor and process until finely ground. Combine ground walnuts with remaining flour in a medium bowl.

2. Combine butter with sugar, salt, egg yolk and vanilla in a large bowl and beat with a wooden spoon or spatula until pale and fluffy. Add the flour mixture and fold it in gently until a smooth dough forms. It will be crumbly at first so use your hands to bring it together if necessary. Wrap the dough with plastic or parchment paper and refrigerate for 1 hour.

3. Preheat oven to 375°F. Line two large baking sheets with parchment paper.

4. Divide dough into three portions and roll each piece into a log with about ¾-inch diameter. Slice each log into about 9 pieces and then roll each piece under your fingertips, adding more pressure at the ends to form tapered crescent shapes. If the dough feels dry, squeeze it in your hand – the warmth will help shape the dough. Place each piece onto prepared baking sheets leaving about 2 inches of space between them. Bake for 10-14 minutes until lightly golden. Transfer the baking sheets to a wire rack and let the cookies cool for 5 minutes.

5. Stir together icing sugar and granulated sugar in a medium bowl. Gently roll the warm cookies individually in the sugar to coat them generously. Transfer cookies to a wire rack and let cool completely.

pfeffernusse German spice cookies

makes about 35 cookies

Cookie dough:

2 cups (284g) all-purpose flour

¾ tsp baking soda

½ tsp <u>each</u> ground cinnamon, cardamom, ginger, and anise or fennel seed

¼ tsp <u>each</u> ground nutmeg, clove, allspice and black pepper

¼ tsp salt

⅓ cup (80ml) honey

⅔ cup (145g) packed light brown sugar

¼ cup (56g) unsalted butter, melted

1 large egg

1 large egg yolk

1 tbsp (15ml) 10%, 18% or 35% cream

1 cup (125g) icing sugar for rolling

Glaze:

1 cup (125g) icing sugar

4-5 tsp (20-25ml) milk or light cream

1. Sift flour, baking soda, spices and salt into a large bowl and whisk to blend evenly.

2. Combine honey, brown sugar and butter in a medium saucepan over low heat and whisk until butter is melted. Remove from heat and whisk in whole egg, egg yolk and cream. Add it to the flour mixture and stir until evenly blended. The batter will be dense and wet at this point. Cover the bowl tightly and refrigerate for 1 hour.

3. Preheat oven to 325°F. Line two large baking sheets with parchment paper.

4. Use a small scoop or a spoon to measure about 2 teaspoons of cookie dough and roll into smooth balls. Place them onto prepared baking sheets spacing them about 2 inches apart and bake for 14-16 minutes until lightly browned. Transfer baking sheets to a wire rack to cool completely.

5. For the glaze, whisk together icing sugar and milk or cream until the icing is thick and opaque but flowing and then spoon it over each cookie on a wire rack to let the excess icing drip down. Let the cookies set until icing is hardened before storing. These cookies keep for 2 weeks in an airtight container.

Switch Up! For a simpler option (if you don't have time to make the icing), you can just roll the cooled cookies generously in icing sugar until they are evenly coated.

chocolate silk pie with press-in gingerbread crust

makes 8-10 servings

Crust:

¾ cup (105g) all-purpose flour

¼ cup (55g) packed dark brown sugar

½ tsp ground ginger

½ tsp ground cinnamon

⅛ tsp ground clove

¼ tsp salt

¼ cup (56g) unsalted butter, softened

Filling:

4 ½ oz (125g) semisweet chocolate (55% cocoa), chopped

½ cup (120ml) 35% whipping cream

1 tbsp (15ml) honey

pinch of salt

1 large egg, at room temperature

1 tbsp (15ml) Bourbon whiskey (optional)

1. Preheat oven to 350°F.

2. For the crust, combine flour, brown sugar, spices and salt in a medium bowl and blend well to remove any lumps of sugar. Cut the soft butter into small pieces and rub it into the dry ingredients thoroughly using your fingertips until the mixture resembles soft bread crumbs. Tip it out into an 8-inch round tart pan with removable bottom (or springform pan). Press it firmly and evenly into the bottom and ¾-inch up the sides. Bake for 10-15 minutes until golden. Transfer to a wire rack and reduce oven to 300°F.

3. For the filling, place chocolate in a heatproof bowl and set aside. Heat cream in a small saucepan over medium heat until it comes to a simmer. Remove it from the heat, pour it over the chocolate and let stand for 2 minutes. Whisk until melted, smooth and glossy. Stir in honey and salt then whisk in egg so it is thick and glossy. Stir in whiskey (if using) and pour the filling into the cooled crust. Tilt the pan around so that the filling spreads out evenly to the edges to fill the base.

4. Bake for 15-20 minutes until it looks shiny and set around the edges with a slightly wobble in the centre. It will continue to set as it cools. Transfer pan to a wire rack to cool to room temperature and then refrigerate to set completely. Dust with cocoa powder before serving.

double chocolate gingerbread cookies

makes about 20 cookies

Follow the Chocolate Chai Spice Cookies recipe on page 73 and make the following substitutions:

1. Replace fancy molasses with robust cooking molasses for a more intense flavour.

2. For the spices, use 1 tsp ground ginger, ¾ ground cinnamon, ¼ tsp ground allspice, ¼ tsp ground nutmeg and ⅛ tsp ground clove.

3. Bake as directed, then dip cookies in melted dark chocolate and sprinkle with crushed candy cane.

chocolate peppermint-dipped graham crackers

egg free

makes about 24 cookies

Follow the recipe for Homemade Graham Crackers on page 111.

1. Finely chop 5 oz (142g) of dark chocolate and melt it gently. See page 205 for a simple tempering technique so that the chocolate sets shiny and streak-free.

2. Dip the corners of each graham cracker in melted dark chocolate and sprinkle with crushed peppermint candy.

3. Use these to make the most delicious and festive S'mores!

funfetti fudge brownies, page 85

happy BIRTHDAYS

Here you'll find simple and delectable desserts with all the textures – soft, fudgy, gooey, chewy! There are layer cakes for every birthday celebration big and small from plush classic yellow vanilla cake to ultra moist chocolate fudge cake and colourful funfetti brownies. The best part is how simple they all are to make – you'll never buy a box mix again! There are many more party bites like chocolate chip cookies, magic bars, s'mores cookies and butter tarts, with no shortage of peanut butter treats too.

secret sauce chocolate chip cookies

makes 16-18 cookies

- ½ cup (113g) salted butter
- 1 cup (220g) packed dark brown sugar
- 1 large egg, at room temperature
- 1 tsp (5ml) pure vanilla extract
- 1 tsp (5ml) soy sauce*
- ¾ tsp baking soda
- 1 ½ cups (215g) all-purpose flour
- 1 cup (142g) dark chocolate chunks

*This recipe has a secret ingredient: soy sauce! Trust me, it replaces added table salt and adds a savoury quality that makes them irresistible.

1. Place butter in a saucepan over low heat just until about half melted, then stir off the heat until completely melted, thick and creamy-looking like custard. Or, heat in the microwave for 20-30 seconds in a heatsafe bowl. If it over-heats, let it cool for 5 minutes until thickened. Transfer to a mixing bowl, add brown sugar and beat with a spatula until pale and fluffy, or use an electric mixer and beat for 2-3 minutes on medium speed. Beat in egg, vanilla, soy sauce and baking soda until smooth, thick and creamy. Mix in flour until just combined. Fold in chocolate. Cover the bowl and chill for 20 minutes.

2. Preheat oven to 350°F. Line 2 baking sheets with parchment.

3. Roll about 2 tablespoons of dough into smooth balls and place onto prepared baking sheets spacing them 3 inches apart. Flatten dough balls slightly and bake for 10-12 minutes until golden brown around the edges. Let cookies cool for 3 minutes on the baking sheets, then transfer individually to the rack to finish cooling.

funfetti fudge brownies

makes 16 brownies

Brownie batter:

5 oz (142g) bittersweet chocolate (70% cocoa), coarsely chopped

⅓ cup (75g) unsalted butter

¾ cup (150g) granulated sugar

2 large eggs, at room temperature

¼ tsp salt

⅓ cup plus 1 tbsp (60g) all-purpose flour

Funfetti layer:

½ block (125g) cream cheese, softened

¼ cup (50g) granulated sugar

2 tbsp (28g) unsalted butter, softened

1 tsp (5ml) pure vanilla extract

1 large egg, at room temperature

2 tsp (6g) all-purpose flour

4 tsp rainbow 100's & 1000's sprinkles

1. Preheat oven to 350°F. Line an 8x8-inch baking pan with parchment paper, leaving a 2-inch overhang along each side.

2. For the brownie batter, melt chocolate and butter in a heatproof bowl set over a saucepan with ½-inch of simmering water (or melt it in the microwave in short bursts with frequent stirring). Remove from heat and stir in sugar. Whisk in eggs one at a time until it tightens up and looks thick and glossy. Stir in salt and flour. Spread batter evenly into prepared pan. Chill for 5 minutes to firm up.

3. For the funfetti layer, beat soft cream cheese with sugar in a small bowl using an electric hand mixer until smooth. Add soft butter and beat until creamy and glossy. Beat in vanilla and egg until well combined, then mix in flour.

4. Drizzle half of the cream cheese mixture evenly over brownie batter and spread it out gently in an even layer. Sprinkle 2 teaspoons of rainbow sprinkles evenly over top. Drizzle remaining vanilla mixture back and forth over the sprinkles trying to drizzle evenly to cover as much surface as you can, then gently spread it out to fill the corners. Try not to spread back over the same area or the sprinkles will smear into the batter. Add remaining sprinkles on top and bake for 25-28 minutes until puffed and the surface looks matte. Transfer to a rack to cool then refrigerate for at least 1 hour before slicing.

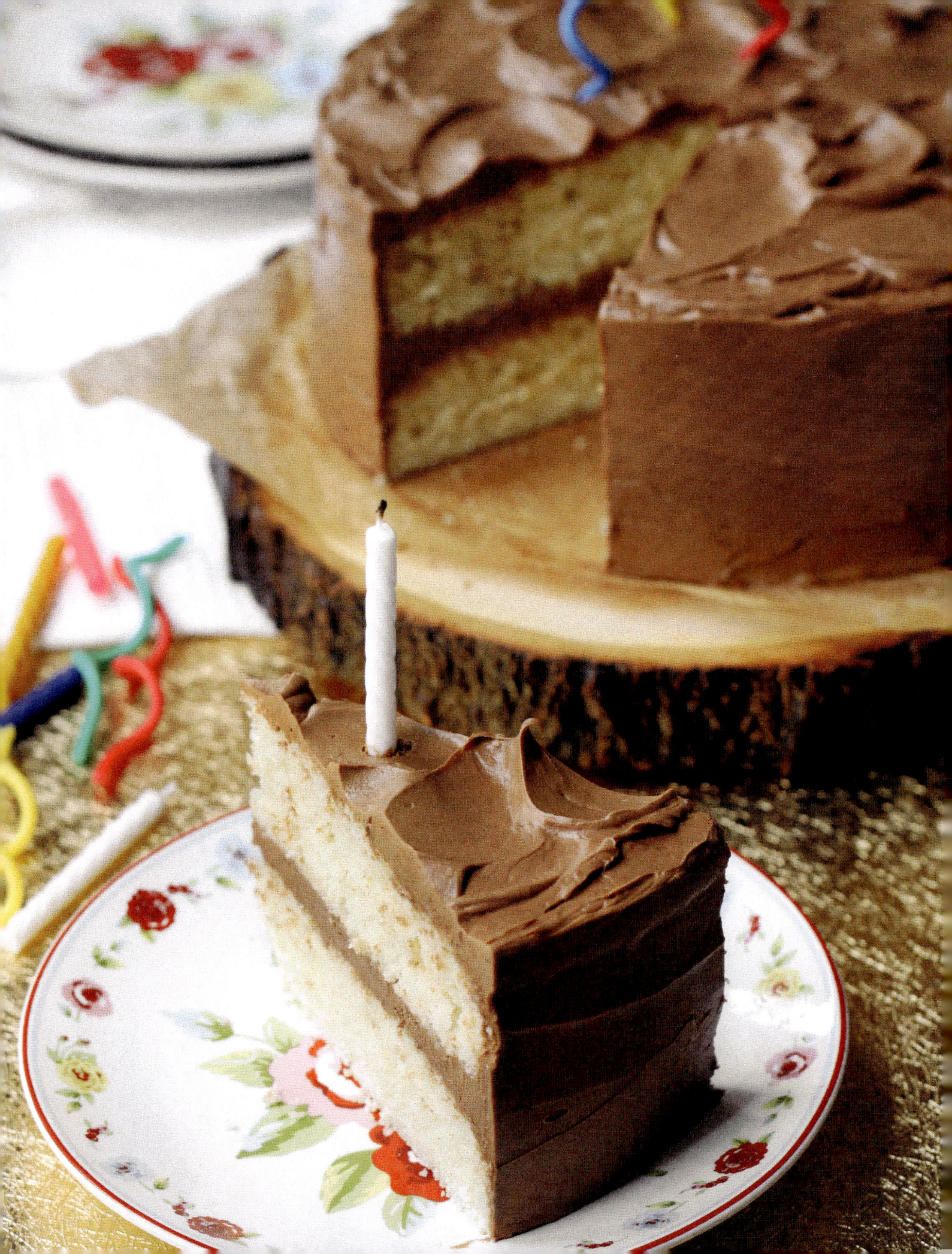

best vanilla birthday cake

makes 10-12 servings

2 ½ cups (355g) all-purpose flour

2 tbsp (16g) corn starch

2 tsp baking powder

½ tsp baking soda

¾ tsp salt

½ cup (113g) unsalted butter, softened

3 tbsp (45ml) vegetable oil

2 tsp (10ml) pure vanilla extract

1 ½ cups (300g) granulated sugar

3 large eggs, at room temperature

½ cup (120ml) sour cream

1 cup (240ml) whole milk

1 x Creamy Chocolate Buttercream recipe (page 97)

1. Preheat oven to 350°F. Grease and flour two 9x3-inch or 8x3-inch round cake pans and line the bases with parchment paper.

2. Sift flour, corn starch, baking powder, baking soda and salt into a medium bowl and whisk to blend evenly.

3. Combine butter, oil and vanilla in the bowl of a stand mixer fitted with a paddle attachment (or in a large bowl if using an electric hand mixer) and beat for 30 seconds on medium speed to blend well. Gradually add sugar and then increase to medium-high speed and beat for 3-4 minutes longer until pale and fluffy, stopping twice to scrape down the sides and bottom of the bowl. Beat in eggs one at a time, blending well after each addition and scraping the bowl. At this point I like to switch to the whisk attachment if using a stand mixer to incorporate the dry ingredients more evenly. Add one-third of the flour mixture and mix on low to combine. Mix in sour cream. Mix in the remaining flour mixture in two parts alternating with additions of milk. Once combined, mix on high speed for just 5 seconds to emulsify the batter. Scrape down the bowl to ensure all ingredients are evenly incorporated.

4. Divide batter evenly between prepared pans and spread it out smoothly. Bake for 23-26 minutes for 9-inch pans and 30-35 minutes for 8-inch pans until evenly golden and a skewer inserted into the centre comes out clean. It is important not to over-bake these cakes. They will spring back when pressed gently when ready. Transfer pans to a wire rack and let cool for 15 minutes before turning out of the pan to cool completely. Frost the cooled cakes with Creamy Chocolate Buttercream.

I love this classic cake for its perfect balance of textures – it's soft, tender and just moist enough without being gummy or dry.

fluffy golden vanilla cupcakes
with whipped chocolate ganache frosting

makes about 24 cupcakes

These cupcakes are the closest thing to boxed yellow cake mix with that classic sweet vanilla aroma and springy, fluffy texture except even better because they're homemade! The flavour is custardy and the crumb is so perfectly fine and uniform – this isn't your typical dense buttercake recipe. The aroma as they bake is so nostalgic, you'll feel like a kid again!

Cake batter:
- 1 cup (240ml) whole milk
- ¼ cup (56g) unsalted butter
- ¼ cup (60ml) sunflower oil
- 2 tsp (10ml) pure vanilla extract
- 1 ⅔ cups (235g) all-purpose flour
- 1 tbsp (8g) corn starch
- 2 tsp baking powder
- ¾ tsp salt
- 3 large eggs, at room temperature
- 1 large egg yolk
- 1 ½ cups (300g) granulated sugar

1. Preheat oven to 350°F. Line 24 cups from two standard muffin pans.

2. Combine milk, butter, oil and vanilla in a saucepan over medium-low heat until butter is melted and the mixture feels hot, but do not let it boil. You can also heat it gently in the microwave. Set aside.

3. Sift flour, corn starch, baking powder and salt into a bowl. Whisk to blend evenly.

4. Beat eggs and yolk on high speed for 2 minutes in the bowl of a stand mixer fitted with the whisk attachment until very frothy. Gradually stream in sugar and continue to beat on high for 6-8 minutes until very pale, thick and tripled in volume. It will fall in ribbons when lifted with the beaters. Gradually add flour mixture while mixing on low until just combined. Do not over-mix. Stir up the warm milk mixture to incorporate the melted butter, then slowly pour it into the bowl while mixing on low until combined and silky smooth. Scrape down the sides and bottom of the bowl and whisk by hand to remove any lumps.

5. Spoon batter into lined cupcake wells so they are three-quarters full. Bake for 18-22 minutes until lightly golden and a toothpick inserted into the cakes comes out clean. Transfer pans to a wire rack to cool.

Switch Up! This recipe makes two incredibly soft, fluffy 8-inch round yellow cake layers that rise nice and flat for stacking (page 89). Line the pans with parchment paper, lightly grease the sides and bake for 28-32 minutes until evenly golden. Let cool in the pans for 10 minutes, run a knife around the edges and invert onto a rack to cool.

happy birthdays 89

egg free *gluten free*

whipped chocolate ganache
makes about 3 cups

1 cup (240ml) 35% whipping cream

2 tbsp (30ml) corn syrup or honey

pinch of salt

8 oz (227g) semisweet chocolate (50-55% cocoa), finely chopped

Switch Up! For a dense fudge frosting, do not whip it. Instead, follow step 1, then refrigerate the ganache until very thick and spreadable. It is super glossy and pipes like a dream!

1. Combine cream, corn syrup or honey and salt in a saucepan over medium-low heat until it simmers. Meanwhile, place chopped chocolate in a heatproof bowl. Pour hot cream over the chocolate and let stand for 3 minutes. Whisk from the centre and working your way out to the edges making concentric circles until it is completely melted, smooth and glossy.

2. Let the ganache cool completely at room temperature until it is thick and silky, but not firm. It should look like soft chocolate pudding. This will take 1 to 2 hours. If your climate is very hot, you can refrigerate until thickened, but be sure to stir every 5 minutes so that it cools evenly and it is uniformly thickened. It is important that the ganache is not warm at all, nor cold or firm when you whip it. If it is still warm, it will not whip quick enough or it may split. If it is cold it will become too stiff and grainy to pipe or spread on your cake.

3. Beat the cooled ganache with an electric hand mixer or using the whisk attachment of a stand mixer on medium speed for 1 ½ to 2 minutes until lightened in colour like creamy milk chocolate. Do not over-beat or it can become grainy. If you use the refrigerator method and left it for too long that it became cold, it will whip very quickly within 30 seconds. In this case it is best to leave it at room temperature for 20 minutes before whipping. Use it immediately to cover a cake or cupcakes.

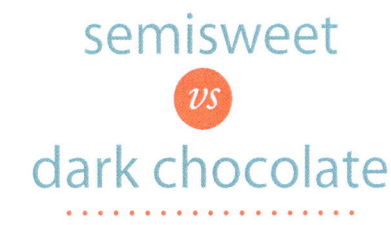

semisweet *vs* dark chocolate

"Dark" is a classification of chocolate that generally refers to any chocolate with more than 45% cocoa solids and does not contain milk ingredients. It is an all-encompassing term that includes semisweet (50%) and bittersweet (70%) chocolate. However, differences in cocoa content translate to differences in sugar content and this is crucial in some recipes since it can affect the texture of the final dessert. So, it is important to acknowledge the cocoa content. Where the type of chocolate impacts the final outcome, I specify the cocoa content in the recipe. Semisweet chocolate contains 50-55% cocoa, dark chocolate contains 60-70% cocoa, and bittersweet chocolate contains 70-75%.

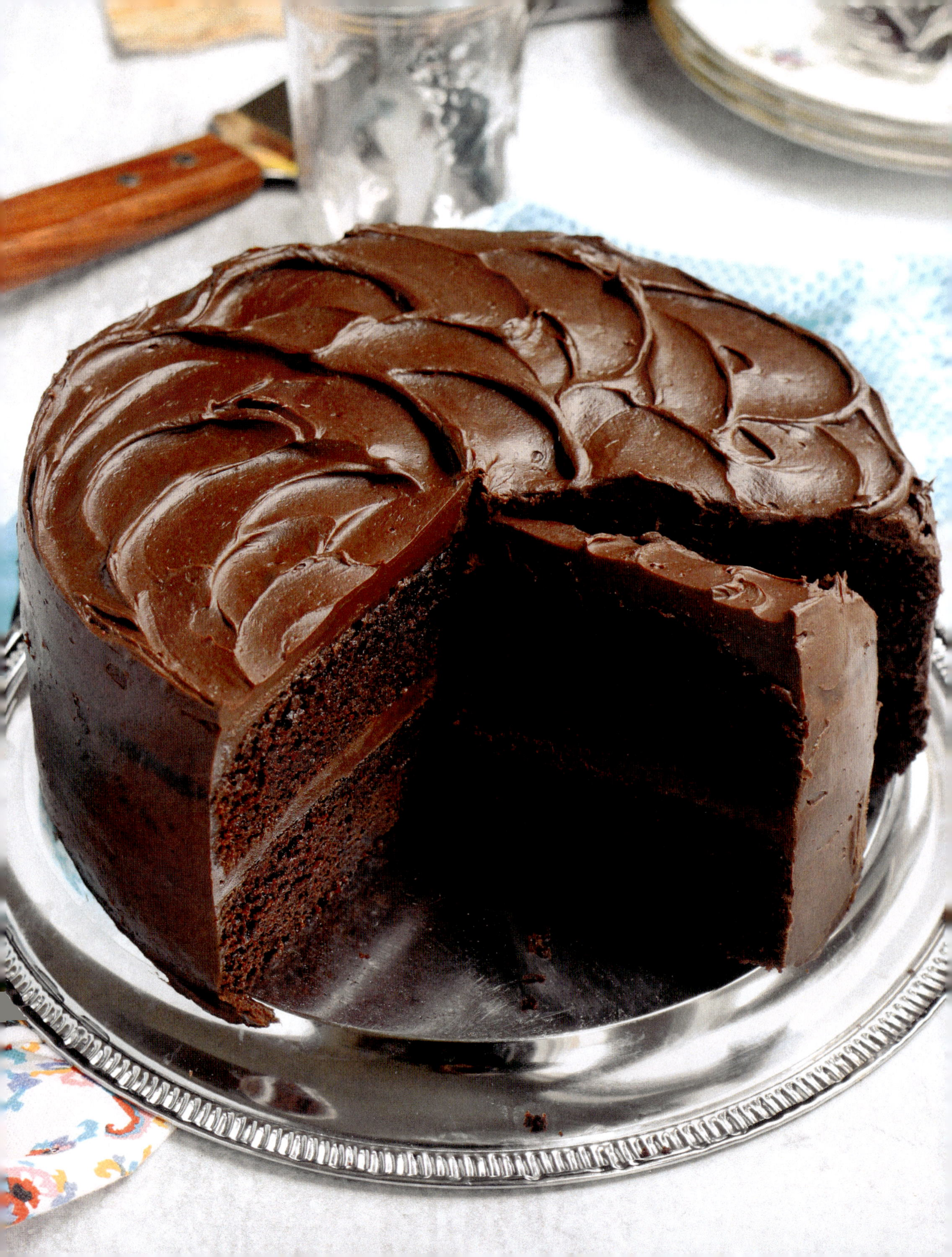

double dark chocolate cake
makes 10-12 servings

Cake:

1 ½ cups (215g) all-purpose flour

⅔ cup (56g) Dutch process cocoa powder

1 tsp baking powder

¾ tsp baking soda

1 ⅓ cups (265g) granulated sugar

½ tsp salt

2 large eggs, at room temperature

½ cup (120ml) sunflower oil

½ cup (120ml) sour cream

¾ cup (180ml) milk, at room temperature

1 tsp (5ml) pure vanilla extract

Chocolate Fudge Frosting:

8 oz (227g) dark chocolate (60% cocoa), coarsely chopped

¾ cup (180ml) 35% whipping cream

3 tbsp (45ml) honey

2 tbsp (12g) cocoa powder, sifted

½ cup (120ml) sour cream

You'll be shocked at how incredible this cake is with so little effort and such simple ingredients! It's soft with a clean, classic chocolate flavour. The recipe on the next page for "Ultra Moist Chocolate Fudge Cake" uses a unique method with hot coffee and a combination of butter and oil to produce a luxurious moist texture and rich chocolate flavour!

1. Preheat oven to 350°F. Lightly grease and flour two 8-inch round cake pans and line the base of each with parchment paper.

2. For the cake, sift flour, cocoa, baking powder and baking soda into a large bowl. Add sugar and salt and whisk well to blend evenly. Beat the eggs well in a small bowl and add them to the dry ingredients. Add oil and sour cream and begin to mix on low speed with an electric mixer. Once it's mostly combined, gradually add the milk with vanilla while mixing and beat on medium speed for about 1 minute just until smooth.

3. Divide batter evenly between prepared pans and bake for 20-25 minutes until a skewer inserted into the centre comes out clean. Transfer pans to a wire rack and let cool for 15 minutes before inverting the cakes to cool completely.

4. For the frosting, combine chocolate, cream and honey in a saucepan over low heat and stir until completely melted, smooth and glossy. Pour it into a bowl and whisk in cocoa powder. Add sour cream and whisk it through. Chill for 15 minutes then beat with a whisk for about 15 seconds until thick and lightened a bit. Use immediately as it will continue to thicken as it cools.

5. To assemble, place one cake layer onto a serving plate or stand. Spread about 1 cup of frosting evenly on top. Place on the other cake layer. Spread remaining frosting all over the top and sides of the cake. The best way to do this is to first spread a thin layer over the entire surface – this is called a "crumb coat" as it catches any loose crumbs. Refrigerate the cake for 15 minutes and then cover with remaining frosting using an offset spatula, creating swooshes and swirls.

double dark chocolate cake pg 91

ultra moist chocolate fudge cake

makes 10-12 servings

Cake:

1 cup (240ml) strong hot coffee

1 ⅔ cups (235g) all-purpose flour

⅔ cup (56g) cocoa powder

1 tsp baking powder

1 tsp baking soda

1 cup (200g) granulated sugar

½ cup (110g) packed dark brown sugar

¾ tsp salt

⅔ cup (160ml) sour cream

2 large eggs, at room temperature

¼ cup (60ml) sunflower oil

¼ cup (56g) unsalted butter, melted

1 tsp (5ml) pure vanilla extract

1 x Chocolate Fudge Frosting recipe (page 91)

This variation on chocolate cake is extra moist and the photo below shows just how fudgy it is! The hot coffee swells the starch in the flour and locks moisture in the batter before it bakes. You can use plain hot water if you avoid coffee.

1. Preheat oven to 350°F. Lightly grease and flour two 8-inch round cake pans and line the base of each with parchment paper.

2. Prepare the coffee. Brew a pot or make instant coffee – measure out 1 cup of boiling water and stir in 1 tablespoon of instant coffee or 2 teaspoons of espresso powder.

3. Sift flour, cocoa, baking powder and baking soda into a large bowl. Add both sugars and salt and whisk to blend very well, pressing out any lumps of brown sugar. Combine sour cream, eggs, oil, melted butter and vanilla in a medium bowl and whisk to blend and break up the eggs. Add it to the dry ingredients and mix with an electric hand mixer on low speed until mostly blended. It will be quite thick. Add hot coffee gradually in three stages to minimize clumps forming and beat until evenly combined and the batter is smooth. Scrape down the sides and bottom of the bowl once during mixing.

4. Divide batter evenly between prepared pans and bake for 30-33 minutes until a skewer inserted into the centre of the cakes comes out clean. Transfer to a rack and cool in the pans for 15 minutes before inverting the cakes onto the rack to cool completely.

5. Prepare the Chocolate Fudge Frosting as directed on page 91 and spread it over the cake layers as directed.

sweet & salty magic bars

makes 16 squares

Base:

¾ cup (105g) all-purpose flour

¼ cup (55g) packed light brown sugar

⅛ tsp baking powder

⅛ tsp salt

¼ cup (56g) unsalted butter, melted

Topping:

1 cup (240ml) sweetened condensed milk

½ cup (45g) medium unsweetened shredded coconut, toasted

⅔ cup (95g) bittersweet chocolate chunks

⅔ cup (80g) whole roasted cashews

8-10 soft toffee caramels, unwrapped and cut into quarters

sea salt flakes

1. Preheat oven to 350°F. Line an 8x8-inch baking pan with parchment paper leaving a 2-inch overhang along each side.

2. For the base, combine flour, brown sugar, baking powder and salt in a medium bowl and blend well, pressing out any lumps of brown sugar. Stir in melted butter and work it in with your fingertips to incorporate evenly. Tip the mixture into the prepared pan and press it down in an even layer using the back of a spoon to smooth it out. Bake for 10-14 minutes until lightly golden. Transfer to a wire rack to cool for about 10 minutes. Reduce oven temperature to 325°F.

3. For the topping, pour ½ cup (120ml) of sweetened condensed milk over the crust and spread it out evenly with an offset spatula. Scatter half of the coconut and chocolate chunks on top. Next, scatter the cashews and chopped caramels on top followed by the remaining coconut and chocolate. Drizzle the rest of the sweetened condensed milk over top with a spoon and then sprinkle with sea salt flakes.

4. Bake for 20-25 minutes until the condensed milk is bubbling and golden at the edges. Transfer to a rack and let cool completely. Use the parchment paper to lift the slab out of the pan and cut into squares. They can be individually wrapped in parchment and frozen to make a chewy sweet treat straight from the freezer!

4 ingredient chocolate cake

makes about 8 servings

gluten free

8 oz (227g) dark chocolate (60-70% cocoa)

7 tbsp (100g) salted butter

4 large eggs, at room temperature

5 tbsp (60g) granulated sugar

1. Preheat oven to 400°F. Lightly grease the sides of an 8-inch round springform pan with butter and line the base with parchment paper. Wrap the bottom of the pan with a double layer of foil to prevent water from seeping in as it bakes in a water bath.

2. Coarsely chop the chocolate and place it in a saucepan with the butter or cream (see note to the right) over low heat. Stir until completely melted and smooth, then pour it into a large clean bowl and set aside to cool for at least 10 minutes until it reaches room temperature.

3. Place eggs and sugar in the bowl of a stand mixer fitted with the whisk attachment and beat for 1 minute on medium speed until blended. Increase speed to medium-high and beat for 6 minutes longer until very pale, thick, fluffy and voluminous. The eggs will be billowy and should fall off the beater in folds. Add one-third of the whipped eggs to the cooled chocolate mixture and fold it in using a wide spatula. Fold in remaining eggs in two parts. Reach down to the bottom of the bowl to lift up the dense chocolate mixture and try not to over-mix as it will knock the air out.

4. Pour batter into prepared pan and then place the pan onto a rimmed baking tray. Pour boiling water into the baking tray so that it comes about ½ inch up the sides of the cake pan before carefully placing it in the oven. Bake for 5 minutes. Reduce oven temperature to 350°F and bake for 25-30 minutes until the cake is puffed and slightly cracked on the surface. It will feel a bit firm, but trust that it will be tender. Transfer cake pan onto a wire rack to cool completely. It will sink on cooling.

5. Run a knife around the edges of the pan and release the sides. Dust with cocoa and serve with whipped cream if desired. This cake is best served at room temperature. Slice with a hot dry knife.

This cake is essentially baked chocolate mousse. The batter bakes in a water bath or "bain marie" which helps it cook evenly and it creates a moist environment to prevent it from drying out. I have a modified version with a simplified method that uses cream instead of butter. Cream adds moisture directly in the form of water since it is just 35% fat and it eliminates the need for a water bath. In this method, follow the recipe except replace butter with ¾ cup (180ml) 35% whipping cream, add a pinch of salt and bake without the water bath. Either way, this cake has the most luxurious texture that melts in your mouth. It may crumble when you slice it, but it's never dry – you'll be surprised at how tender it is!

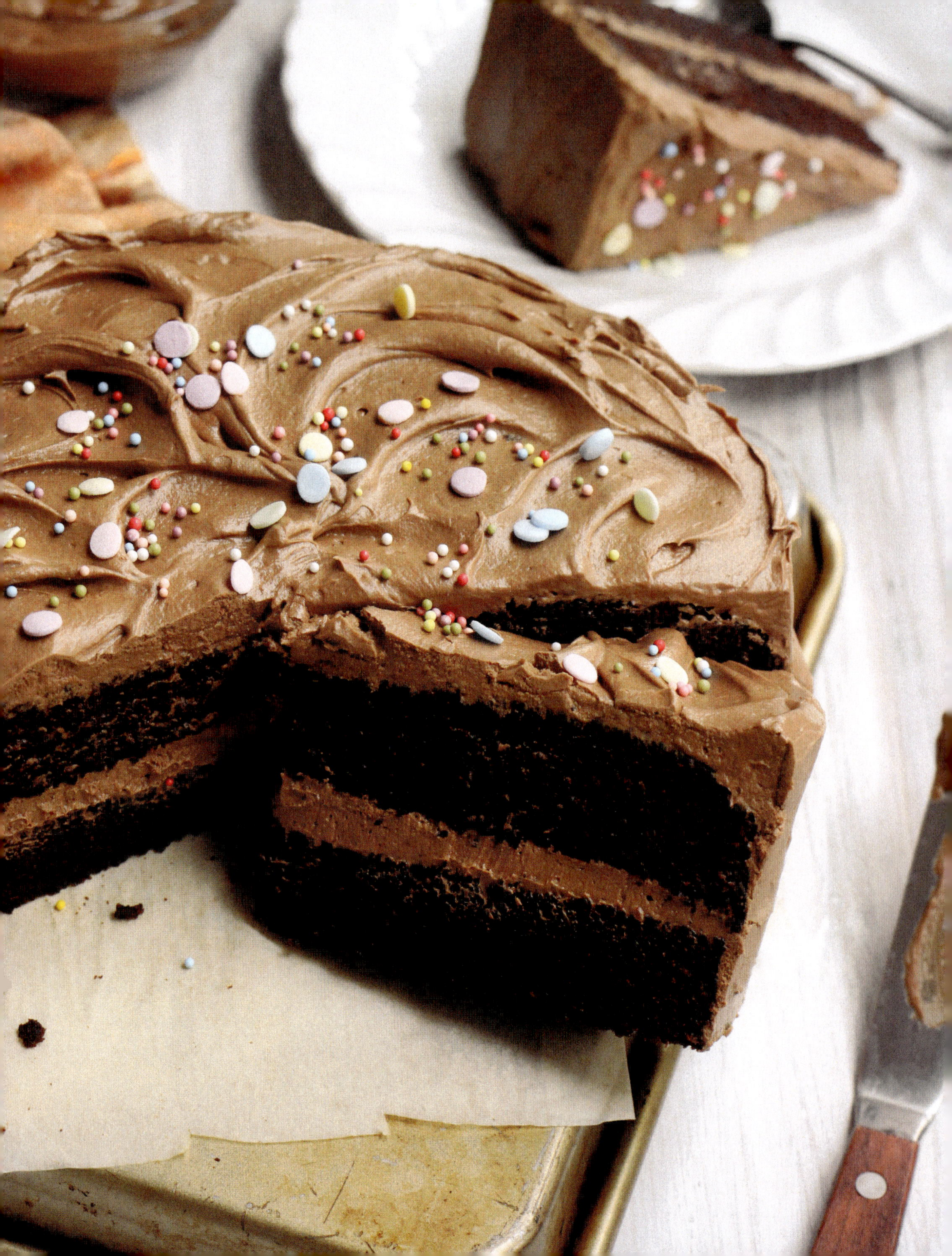

chocolate celebration cake

makes 10-12 servings

This recipe is great to celebrate any occasion big or small because it's less fussy. Instead of making two cake layers, just make the Sour Cream & Honey Chocolate Cake on page 192 which bakes up quite tall. Slice it in half to make two layers and slather this creamy frosting all over it. The frosting is versatile too – I prefer a blend of milk and dark chocolate here, but you can use all 5 oz of milk chocolate or all dark chocolate if that's what you have on hand. It will change the level of sweetness slightly, but either way it will be great!

1 x Sour Cream & Honey Chocolate Cake recipe (page 192)

Creamy Chocolate Buttercream:

3 tbsp (27g) all-purpose flour

½ cup plus 2 tbsp (125g) granulated sugar, divided

⅔ cup (160ml) whole milk

½ cup (113g) unsalted butter, softened

1 tsp (5ml) pure vanilla extract

2 oz (56g) pure milk chocolate, coarsely chopped

3 oz (85g) bittersweet chocolate (70% cocoa), coarsely chopped

1. Prepare the Sour Cream & Honey Chocolate Cake as directed on page 192. Allow it to cool completely and then slice it in half using a large serrated knife.

2. For the buttercream, whisk together flour and 2 tbsp (25g) sugar in a small saucepan. Slowly whisk in milk until blended. Place over medium-low heat and cook while whisking constantly for 7-10 minutes until thickened like pudding. Do not stop whisking. It will be like a thick white paste. Pour it into a bowl, place plastic wrap directly over the surface and let cool to room temperature. You can refrigerate it to speed it up, but don't let it get cold.

3. Beat the soft butter until creamy in the bowl of a stand mixer fitted with the whisk attachment (or in a large bowl if using a hand mixer). Add remaining ½ cup (100g) sugar and vanilla and beat for 2-3 minutes until pale and fluffy. Gradually add cooled flour/pudding mixture in 4 or 5 additions, beating well after each addition until creamy, fluffy and light. Combine both types of chocolate and melt gently in the microwave or in a heatproof bowl set over a saucepan of simmering water. Stir until completely melted and smooth and let cool for about 5 minutes so that it is no longer warm, then beat it into the frosting until blended.

4. To assemble the cake, place one half onto a serving plate or stand. Spread about 1 cup of frosting on this first layer. Place the other cake half on top. Spread remaining frosting all over the top and sides of the cake. The best way to do this is to first spread a thin layer over the entire surface – this is called a "crumb coat" as it catches any loose crumbs. Refrigerate the cake for 15 minutes. Then, cover with remaining frosting using an offset spatula, creating swooshes and swirls. Decorate with sprinkles if you wish.

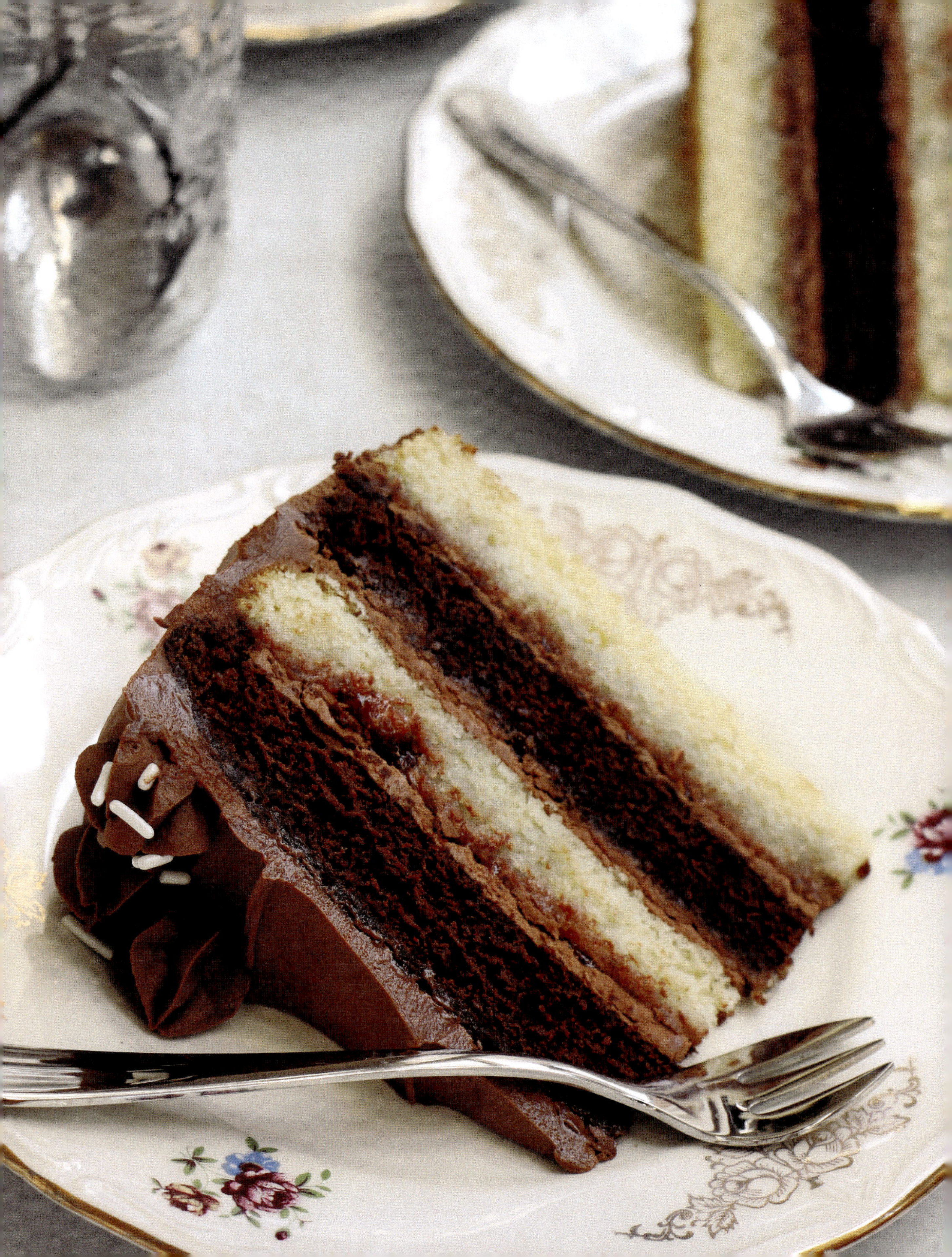

neapolitan layer cake

makes 10-12 servings

This impressive layer cake is great for so many occasions – birthdays, anniversaries, wedding showers, baby showers, graduations and engagement parties! And, who doesn't like the classic combination of chocolate, vanilla and strawberry? You will only need one of the layers from the Best Vanilla Birthday Cake which you will slice in half horizontally to make two thinner layers. Thin layers make the cake look more sophisticated. You can wrap and freeze the other layer for another day and it will keep for up to 3 months. In fact, you can make both the vanilla and chocolate cake recipes in advance and freeze them until you are ready to assemble this Neapolitan Layer Cake!

1 x Best Vanilla Birthday Cake recipe (page 87)

1 x Sour Cream & Honey Chocolate Cake recipe (page 192)

Dark Chocolate Frosting:

¼ cup (35g) all-purpose flour

¾ cup (165g) packed light brown sugar, divided

¾ cup (180ml) whole milk

¾ cup (170g) unsalted butter, softened

2 tbsp (12g) cocoa powder, sifted

6 oz (170g) dark chocolate (60% cocoa), melted and cooled

Filling:

⅔ cup (160ml) strawberry jam

1. Bake the Best Vanilla Birthday Cake as directed on page 85 in two 9-inch pans. Let cool completely. You will only need one layer for this recipe. Slice it in half horizontally.

2. Bake the Sour Cream & Honey Chocolate Cake as directed on page 192 for 35-45 minutes in a 9-inch springform pan. Let cool completely and level off the top with a serrated knife to create a flat surface. Then, slice the cake in half horizontally.

3. For the frosting, whisk together flour and 3 tbsp (45g) brown sugar in a small saucepan. Slowly whisk in milk until blended. Place over medium heat and cook, whisking constantly, for 7-10 minutes until it becomes paste-like and thickens like pudding. Pour it into a bowl, cover with plastic wrap directly on the surface and refrigerate until cooled to room temperature. Beat soft butter with remaining sugar in a bowl using a hand mixer for 3 minutes until pale and fluffy. Add cooled flour mixture in 4 or 5 additions, beating well after each addition until creamy, fluffy and light. Mix in cocoa. Gradually beat in cooled melted chocolate.

4. To assemble, place one of the vanilla layers onto a serving plate or stand. Spread half of the strawberry jam (⅓ cup) evenly over it leaving a ½-inch border. Spread a thin layer of frosting over the jam. Place a layer of chocolate cake on top and cover with a thin layer of frosting. Lay the other vanilla cake layer on top and spread with remaining jam. Spread a thin layer of frosting over it and top with the last chocolate cake layer. Spread remaining frosting all over the top and sides of the cake. You can reserve about 1 cup of frosting to pipe decorations on top with a star tip. Decorate with sprinkles if you wish.

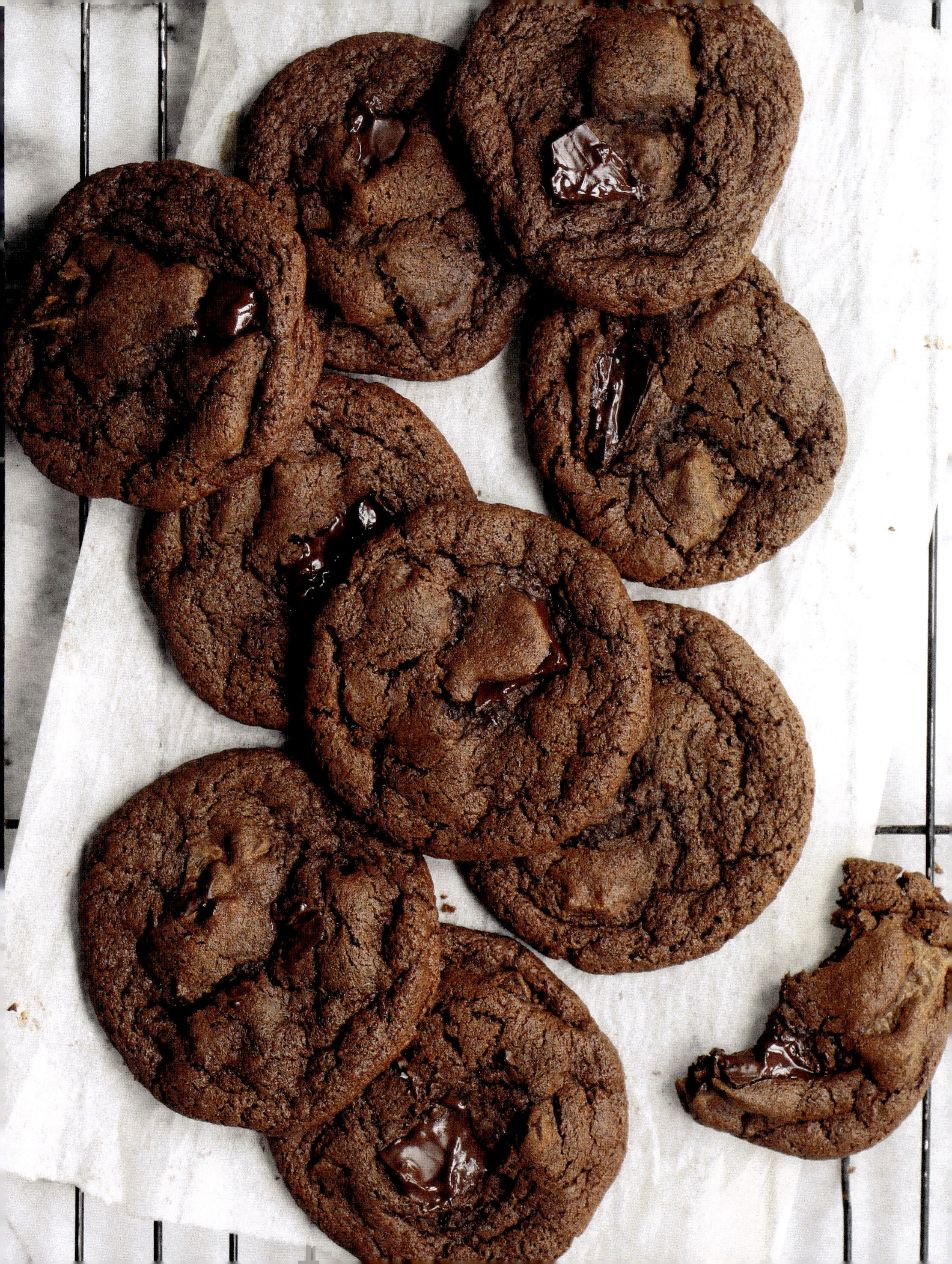

chewy gluten-free double chocolate chunk cookies

makes about 22 cookies

gluten free

½ cup (113g) unsalted butter

½ cup (100g) granulated sugar

¼ cup (55g) packed dark brown sugar

1 large egg, at room temperature

1 tbsp (15ml) honey

1 tsp (5ml) pure vanilla extract

1 cup (125g) tapioca or arrowroot starch

⅓ cup (55g) fine white rice flour

½ cup (42g) cocoa powder (I prefer natural cocoa)

½ tsp baking soda

¼ tsp salt

1 ¼ cups (175g) dark or bittersweet chocolate chunks

The baking time is important for these cookies. Check on them after 8 minutes – they should be puffed and set around the edges but still quite soft in the middle. If they are over-baked, they will have a slightly more crumbly texture, but when these are baked perfectly, they are fudgy and incredible!

1. Combine butter with both sugars in the bowl of a stand mixer fitted with the paddle attachment and beat for 2 minutes until smooth and a bit fluffy. It will look like damp sand. Scrape down the sides and bottom of the bowl with a spatula as needed. Add egg and beat until well incorporated. Beat in honey and vanilla until combined.

2. Sift tapioca or arrowroot starch, rice flour, cocoa powder and baking soda into a medium bowl. Add salt and whisk to blend evenly. Add these dry ingredients to the bowl with the creamed butter/sugar mixture and mix on low speed at first to prevent dusty starch from covering your kitchen. Scrape down the sides of the bowl with a spatula and then mix in most of the chocolate chunks, reserving a few for topping just before baking. Mix until the dry ingredients are incorporated. Cover the bowl and let rest for 30 minutes (if your kitchen is hot, place it in the fridge while you preheat the oven).

3. Preheat oven to 350°F. Line two large baking sheets with parchment paper.

4. Roll heaped tablespoons of dough into smooth balls and place onto prepared baking sheets spacing them 2 ½ inches apart. You should get at least 22 dough balls from this batch, otherwise the portions will be too big and the cookies might spread to wide. Flatten dough balls slightly.

5. Bake for 8-10 minutes until set around the edges, puffed and cracked at the surface. They will still be quite soft in the middle. It is important not to over-bake these. Transfer baking sheets to a wire rack and let cookies cool completely on the trays. They will be delicate while warm, but will set as they cool.

gluten free

thick & chewy flourless chocolate chunk peanut butter cookies

makes about 12 cookies

⅔ cup (160ml) regular (or natural*) smooth peanut butter

⅓ cup (70g) packed light brown sugar

1 large egg, at room temperature

1 tsp (5ml) honey

½ tsp pure vanilla extract

¼ tsp baking soda

⅓ cup (35g) large flake rolled oats

½ cup (70g) dark chocolate chunks

1. Preheat oven to 350°F and line a large baking sheet with parchment paper.

2. Combine peanut butter, brown sugar, egg, honey and vanilla in a medium bowl and mix well with a spatula or wooden spoon until evenly combined and smooth. The dough will stiffen up once the egg is incorporated. Mix in baking soda. Add oats and chocolate chunks and mix until evenly distributed.

3. Scoop heaped tablespoons of dough onto prepared baking sheet spacing them about 2 inches apart. Flatten dough mounds slightly with the palm of your hand (or leave them round if you prefer even thicker cookies). Bake for 9-12 minutes until golden. Let cookies cool for 5 minutes on the baking sheet before transferring to a wire rack to finish cooling.

*Cookies made with regular (emulsified) peanut butter will spread more than cookies made with natural peanut butter (the kind that you need to stir) since it has added oil and sugars, so I recommend to flatten the dough balls if you use the natural kind. Also, if you use unsalted natural peanut butter (made from just peanuts), then add ⅛ tsp salt to this recipe.

soft & gooey cream cheese caramel cashew cookie bars

egg free

makes 16 squares

Base:

⅓ cup (75g) unsalted butter, softened

¼ cup (50g) granulated sugar

1 tsp (5ml) pure vanilla extract

pinch of salt

4 tbsp (60g) cream cheese, softened

1 cup (142g) all-purpose flour

Topping:

¾ cup (150g) granulated sugar

3 tbsp (42g) unsalted butter

¼ cup (60ml) 35% whipping cream

3 tbsp (45g) cream cheese, softened

½ tsp pure vanilla extract

¼ tsp salt

1 cup (120g) roasted cashews

1. Line an 8x8-inch baking pan with foil and lightly butter the bottom surface.

2. For the base, beat together butter, sugar, vanilla and salt in a medium bowl using a wooden spoon. Beat in cream cheese until smooth. Sprinkle in flour and fold it in until combined. Use floured hands or a piece of plastic wrap to press the dough evenly into the bottom of prepared pan, pressing it up the sides a bit to create an edge. Refrigerate for 30 minutes while the oven preheats.

3. Preheat oven to 350°F. Bake the base for 20-24 minutes until puffed and golden.

4. For the filling, pour the sugar in an even layer in a wide heavy-bottomed saucepan and place over medium-high heat. As the sugar around the edges begins to melt and liquefy, move it from the edges to the centre of the pan to help it melt evenly and encourage the rest of the sugar crystals to melt. Continue moving the sugar like this from the edges to the middle until it is all evenly melted and turns into a clear amber syrup. The sugar will clump up at first but will melt eventually. Press out any lumps of sugar with the back of a wooden spoon to get a clear syrup before adding the other ingredients. Remove from heat and whisk in butter. Carefully whisk in cream, then whisk in cream cheese one tablespoon at a time, making sure each tablespoon is incorporated smoothly before adding the next.

5. Return pan to heat and simmer for 1 minute while whisking. Stir in vanilla, salt and cashews. Pour it over the baked crust and spread it out. Bake again for 8-10 minutes until caramel is bubbling. Transfer to a rack and to cool completely in the pan. Sprinkle with sea salt flakes and refrigerate for at least 2 hours before slicing.

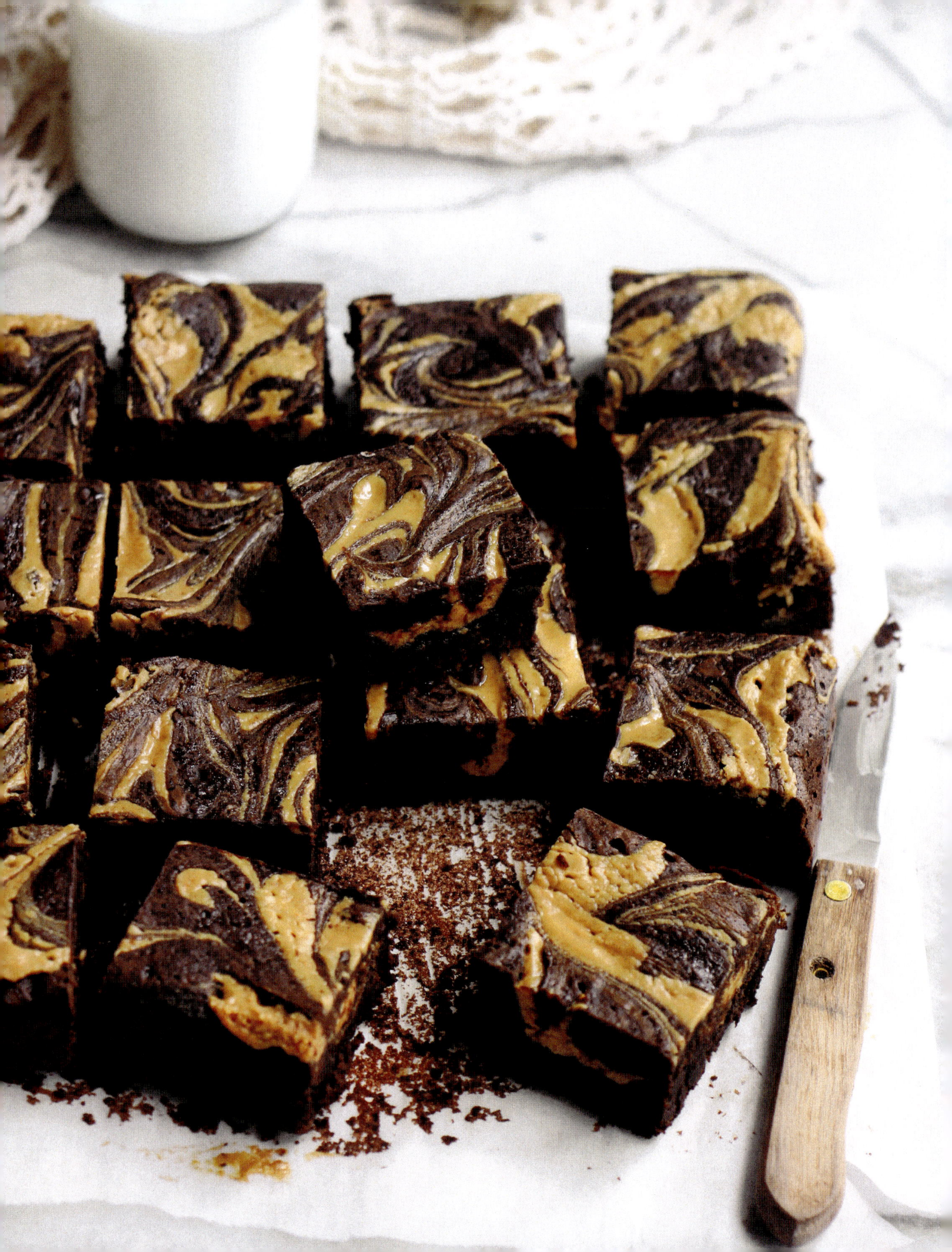

gluten free

flourless peanut butter swirl brownies

makes 16 brownies

5 ¼ oz (150g) bittersweet chocolate (70% cocoa), chopped

⅓ cup (75g) unsalted butter

3 large eggs, at room temperature

¾ cup (165g) packed light brown sugar

1 tsp (5ml) pure vanilla extract

¼ tsp salt

⅓ cup (35g) blanched almond flour or ground blanched almonds

⅓ cup (28g) cocoa powder

½ cup (120ml) smooth natural unsalted peanut butter

1. Preheat oven to 350°F. Line an 8x8-inch pan with parchment paper leaving a 2-inch overhang along each side.

2. Combine chocolate with butter in a medium saucepan over low heat and stir until melted and smooth, or melt in the microwave with short 20 second bursts and frequent stirring.

3. Beat eggs with brown sugar, vanilla and salt in a large bowl using a whisk (or use an electric hand mixer) for a minute or two until it is very frothy and the sugar is dissolved. Add melted chocolate mixture and whisk until well incorporated. The batter will tighten up and look glossy. Add almond flour and sift in cocoa powder, then stir until evenly combined.

4. Pour the batter into prepared pan and spread it out evenly. Dollop tablespoons of peanut butter randomly over the batter and swirl it through with the back of a knife or a skewer to create a marbled effect.

5. Bake for 23-26 minutes until slightly puffed and just set in the middle. Transfer pan to a wire rack and let cool completely in the pan. For best results, refrigerate for 1 hour before slicing with a hot dry knife and wipe the knife clean before each cut.

baking pan vs baking dish

Baking pans are metal-based and conduct heat more efficiently. Baking dishes are composed of glass or ceramic and are slower to conduct heat. Baking in dishes often requires that you add another 10 minutes to the baking time. I prefer to bake cakes, brownies and cookies in metal bakeware for immediate heat transfer and even browning. Glass is great for baking pies because it cooks the filling slowly and the clarity allows you to check for a nicely browned bottom crust. Ceramic retains heat well making it great to prepare desserts that are served warm such as fruit crumbles, crisps and cobblers.

triple chocolate fudge cupcakes

makes 13-15 cupcakes

¾ cup (105g) all-purpose flour

½ cup (42g) cocoa powder

½ tsp baking soda

½ tsp baking powder

½ tsp salt

2 large eggs, at room temperature

⅓ cup (70g) packed light brown sugar

½ cup (100g) granulated sugar

1 tsp (5ml) pure vanilla extract

3 tbsp (42g) unsalted butter

3 tbsp (45ml) sunflower oil

½ cup (120ml) buttermilk*

White Chocolate Tahini Glaze

Milk Chocolate Glaze (see pink box for recipes)

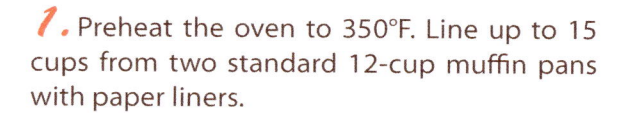

1. Preheat the oven to 350°F. Line up to 15 cups from two standard 12-cup muffin pans with paper liners.

2. Sift flour, cocoa powder, baking soda and baking powder into a medium bowl. Add salt and whisk to blend well.

3. Beat eggs with brown sugar in a medium bowl using a hand mixer on high speed for 2 minutes until frothy. Slowly stream in granulated sugar and continue beating for 2 more minutes until pale, thick and doubled in volume. Mix in vanilla. Melt together butter with oil in a saucepan over low heat or in the microwave and beat into egg mixture. With mixer on low, gradually beat in half of the dry ingredients until just combined. Beat in buttermilk. Mix in remaining dry ingredients until evenly incorporated. Do not over-mix.

4. Fill the paper cup liners just halfway with batter (this is crucial – only fill halfway to avoid cupcakes from spilling over the edges or sinking in the middle). Bake for 18-20 minutes until they spring back when pressed gently and a toothpick inserted in the centre comes out clean. Transfer to a wire rack to cool completely before glazing (see below).

For the White Chocolate Tahini Glaze, combine 4 oz (113g) chopped white chocolate with 2 ½ tbsp (37ml) 35% whipping cream in a small saucepan over very low heat. Stir until melted and smooth. Remove from heat and stir in 2 tbsp (30ml) tahini. Let stand until thick and spreadable, then spoon 1 heaped teaspoon onto each cupcake. Refrigerate until set.

For the Milk Chocolate Glaze, combine 4 oz (113g) chopped milk chocolate with 3 tbsp (45ml) 35% whipping cream and a pinch of salt in a small saucepan over very low heat. Stir until melted and smooth, then let stand until it cools down a bit but is still runny. Gently spread it over the white chocolate glaze to cover it and refrigerate immediately until set.

*You can substitute buttermilk with ½ cup of stirred low fat plain yogurt.

sea salt s'mores cookies

makes 20-22 cookies

½ cup (113g) unsalted butter, softened
¾ cup (165g) packed light brown sugar
2 tbsp (30ml) honey
1 large egg, room temperature
1 tsp (5ml) pure vanilla extract
1 cup (142g) all-purpose flour
¾ cup (96g) whole wheat flour
¾ tsp baking soda
½ tsp cinnamon
½ tsp salt
5 oz (142g) bittersweet chocolate, chopped into chunks plus extra for topping
¾ cup (40g) mini marshmallows*
sea salt flakes for sprinkling

1. Beat butter with brown sugar on medium speed for 2 minutes in the bowl of a stand mixer fitted with the paddle attachment (or in a large bowl using a wide spatula) until smooth, creamy and somewhat fluffy. Beat in honey, egg and vanilla until well incorporated.

2. Combine both flours, baking soda, cinnamon and salt in a medium bowl and whisk to blend evenly. Add the flour mixture to the creamed butter mixture and mix until just incorporated. Add chocolate chunks and marshmallows and fold them through the dough. Scoop heaped tablespoons of dough onto parchment-lined baking sheets and refrigerate for 30 minutes.

3. Preheat oven to 350°F.

4. Squish extra chunks of dark chocolate on top of cookie dough balls if desired and sprinkle sea salt over each one. Bake for 10-12 minutes until evenly golden and still soft in the middle. Let cookies cool and set completely on the baking sheets since the marshmallows that ooze out are very sticky while warm.

*Toss marshmallows with a bit of the flour mixture so they are evenly coated before adding to the cookie dough. This helps to prevent them from sticking together and hold their shape better in the dough.

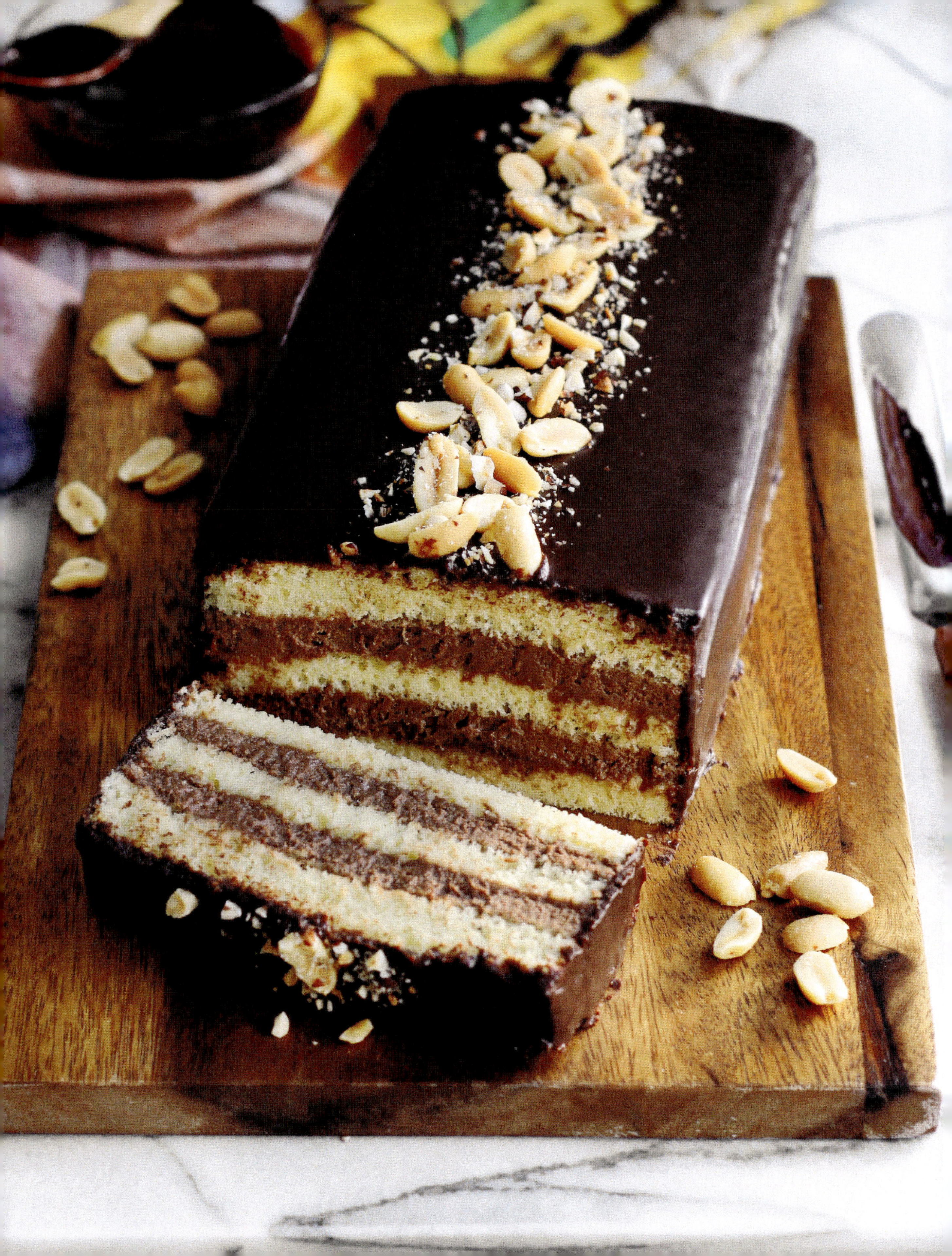

chocolate peanut butter mousse cake

makes 8-10 servings

Sponge cake:

4 large eggs

⅔ cup (135g) granulated sugar

1 tsp (5ml) pure vanilla extract

¼ tsp salt

¾ cup (105g) all-purpose flour

2 tbsp (28g) unsalted butter

1 tbsp (15ml) whole milk

Filling:

2 large egg yolks

¼ cup (50g) granulated sugar

⅓ cup (80ml) whole milk

2 oz (56g) bittersweet chocolate

2 oz (56g) milk chocolate

¼ cup (60ml) smooth peanut butter

¾ cup (180ml) 35% whipping cream

Glaze:

4 oz (113g) dark chocolate, chopped

1 tbsp (14g) unsalted butter

⅓ cup (80ml) whole milk

2 tsp (10ml) honey

2 tbsp (30ml) smooth peanut butter

¼ cup (30g) chopped roasted peanuts

1. Preheat oven to 350°F. Line a 16x12-inch rimmed baking sheet with parchment.

2. For the sponge, combine eggs and sugar in the bowl of a stand mixer. Place over a saucepan with 1-inch of simmering water and whisk constantly for 2-3 minutes until thickened and sugar is dissolved. Transfer bowl to mixer with the whisk attachment and beat on high for 5 minutes until pale, thick and fluffy. Mix in vanilla and salt.

3. Sift flour over the whipped eggs and fold it in gently. Melt butter with milk in a small saucepan or in the microwave and dribble it into the batter while folding gently until evenly combined. Spread batter evenly into prepared pan. Bake for 10-12 minutes until evenly golden and it springs back when pressed. Transfer to a rack and let cool completely. Invert cake, peel off parchment and trim the edges. Slice it into three equal rectangles (about 4½ x 11 inches).

4. For the mousse, beat egg yolks with sugar in a medium bowl for about 3 minutes on high speed using a hand mixer until pale and thick. Gently heat milk in a saucepan until steaming then slowly whisk it into the egg yolk mixture until blended. Pour it back into the saucepan and cook for 2-3 minutes over medium heat while stirring frequently until thickened. It should coat the back of a spoon like thick cream. Pour it into a bowl with both chocolates and stir until melted and smooth. Stir in peanut butter, cover and refrigerate until thoroughly chilled.

5. Whip cream with a whisk or electric hand mixer until it holds firm peaks, then gently fold it into the cooled custard.

6. Spread the mousse over two cake layers, dividing it evenly. Stack these layers, then place the plain one on top and smooth out the sides where some filling has squeezed out. Refrigerate for at least 30 minutes.

7. For the glaze, combine chocolate, butter, milk and honey in a saucepan over medium-low heat and stir until smooth and glossy. Remove from heat and stir in peanut butter. Pour it all over the chilled cake and quickly spread it evenly over the surface and around the sides. Sprinkle roasted peanuts on top and chill until ready to serve.

shiny top fudge brownies

makes 16 brownies

6 oz (170g) bittersweet chocolate (70% cocoa)
6 tbsp (84g) salted butter*
2 large eggs, at room temperature
½ cup (100g) granulated sugar
⅓ cup (70g) packed light brown sugar

1 tsp (5ml) pure vanilla extract
¼ tsp salt
½ tsp espresso powder (optional)
⅓ cup (50g) all-purpose flour
1 tbsp (6g) cocoa powder

*I prefer salted butter for this brownie recipe because it adds a richness that elevates the chocolate flavour intensity, but if you choose to use unsalted butter then increase the added salt in the recipe to ½ teaspoon. Try baking at 325°F for 25-30 minutes if you prefer a soft & chewy texture through and through!

1. Preheat oven to 350°F. Line an 8x8-inch baking pan with parchment paper, leaving a 2-inch overhang along each side.

2. Chop the chocolate and place it in a heatproof bowl set over a saucepan with ½-inch of simmering water. Add butter and stir until completely melted, smooth and glossy. Or, melt the chocolate with butter in the microwave in short 20 second bursts with frequent stirring.

3. Combine eggs with both sugars and vanilla in the bowl of a stand mixer fitted with the whisk attachment and beat on high for 4-5 minutes until pale, thick and fluffy. When you lift up the beater, the egg foam will fold in ribbons back onto itself as it falls back into the bowl. Beat in salt and espresso (if using it) then mix in the warm melted chocolate mixture until evenly blended. Combine flour and cocoa in a small bowl to press out any lumps, sprinkle it over the batter and fold it in until evenly incorporated.

4. Spread batter into prepared pan and bake for 20-25 minutes until a skewer inserted into the centre comes out with a few moist crumbs attached. Transfer pan to a wire rack and let cool completely in the pan. Refrigerate for 1 hour before slicing into squares.

homemade graham crackers

makes about 40 crackers

egg free

- 1 ¼ cups (160g) whole wheat flour
- 1 cup (142g) all-purpose flour
- ½ cup (110g) packed light brown sugar
- ½ tsp ground cinnamon
- ½ tsp baking soda
- ¼ tsp baking powder
- ¼ tsp salt
- ½ cup (113g) cold unsalted butter, cut into small pieces
- 2 tbsp (30ml) honey
- 1 tsp (5ml) fancy molasses
- 3-4 tbsp (45-60ml) whole milk
- ½ tsp pure vanilla extract

1. Place both flours, brown sugar, ground cinnamon, baking soda, baking powder and salt in the bowl of a food processor and pulse to blend. Add cold butter and process until it looks like coarse crumbs. (You can also use a stand mixer with the paddle attachment on low for 3-4 minutes). Stir together honey, molasses, 3 tablespoons (45ml) milk and vanilla in a small bowl and add to flour mixture. Pulse until it starts to clump together. It will look dry but should hold together when squeezed in your hand. If it is really dry, mix in another 1 tbsp milk.

2. Turn the dough out onto a work surface and bring it together in a ball so that it is cohesive. Divide dough in half, wrap each one well and refrigerate for 30 minutes.

3. Preheat oven to 350°F. Roll each portion of dough out to an even ⅛-inch thickness between two sheets of parchment paper. Use some elbow grease to ensure it is evenly rolled and the middle isn't thicker than the edges. Remove the top layer of parchment paper. Using a ruler and a knife, score the dough to make 2¼-inch wide strips. Then, score across each strip to create 2¼-inch squares. You should have about 20 squares per sheet. Do not trim away excess dough along the edges. Slide the parchment with the rolled dough onto a 16x12-inch baking sheet. Use a toothpick or fork to make small holes down the centre of each square.

4. Bake the sheets of dough for 15-20 minutes until evenly browned. Let them get nicely golden in the centre because under-baking will make soft cookies. The edges might get dark before the centre squares are cooked enough, but that's ok. The longer you bake, the more crisp they will be. Transfer baking sheets to a wire rack to cool completely (they will crisp up as they cool) and then break away squares along the score lines. Store in an airtight container for about a week.

Switch up! The moisture from the cream in the ganache filling will migrate to the cookies and transform them into plush, soft sandwiches which makes for a pleasant bite. If you prefer the cookies to stay crunchy, make a firmer filling by gently melting together 5 oz (142g) dark chocolate and 2 tbsp (28g) of butter.

peanut butter & chocolate sandwich cookies

makes 20-25 sandwich cookies

Cookie dough:

1 ¾ cups (250g) all-purpose flour

¼ tsp baking soda

¼ tsp salt

6 tbsp (84g) unsalted butter, softened

⅔ cup (145g) packed light brown sugar

¾ cup (180ml) regular smooth peanut butter

2 tbsp (30ml) honey

1 large egg, at room temperature

Filling:

4 oz (113g) dark chocolate (60% cocoa solids), finely chopped

⅓ cup (80ml) 35% whipping cream

For dipping:

3 oz (85g) dark chocolate, chopped

1 tbsp (14g) coconut oil

crushed roasted peanuts

1. Combine flour, baking soda and salt in a medium bowl and whisk to blend evenly.

2. Combine butter and brown sugar in the bowl of a stand mixer fitted with the paddle attachment (or in a large bowl if using an electric hand mixer) and beat on medium speed for 2 minutes until smooth and a bit fluffy. Mix in peanut butter and honey. Scrape down the bowl and then beat in egg until well combined. Add flour mixture and mix gently until well incorporated. The dough will be soft. Turn the dough out onto a large piece of plastic wrap or parchment paper and shape it into a 12-inch log. Smooth and square off the sides (I use a ruler to do this). Wrap well and refrigerate for at least 1 hour until firm (or freeze for about 30 minutes).

3. Preheat oven to 350°F. Line two large baking sheets with parchment paper.

4. Slice the chilled log into thin squares about ⅛-inch to ¼-inch thickness. Transfer squares to baking sheets and space them 1 inch apart. Bake for 9-11 minutes until lightly browned around the edges and evenly golden on top. Let cookies cool for a minute on baking sheets before transferring individually to a wire rack to cool completely.

5. For the filling, place chopped chocolate in a heatproof bowl. Heat cream in a saucepan over medium heat or in the microwave until it comes to a simmer. Remove from heat and then pour it over the chopped chocolate in the bowl, cover and let stand for a minute before stirring until smooth and glossy. Spoon about 1 teaspoon of chocolate ganache onto the underside of half of the cookies and place another cookie on top. Press gently to sandwich the cookies together and repeat.

6. For dipping, combine dark chocolate and coconut oil in a heatproof bowl set over a saucepan with ½-inch of simmering water and stir until melted and smooth (or melt in the microwave with short bursts and frequent stirring). Dip the sandwich cookies halfway into melted chocolate. Transfer to trays lined with parchment or waxed paper and sprinkle with chopped peanuts before the chocolate sets.

gooey butter tarts

makes 12 tarts

Pastry:
- 1 ⅓ cups (190g) all-purpose flour
- 2 tbsp (25g) granulated sugar
- ¼ tsp salt
- ½ cup (113g) cold unsalted butter, cut into small pieces
- 3-4 tbsp (45-60ml) ice cold water

*For an EXTRA gooey runny filling, replace 2 tbsp (30ml) of brown sugar with golden corn syrup.

Filling:
- ¼ cup (56g) unsalted butter, very soft
- 1 cup (220g) packed dark brown sugar*
- 1 large egg
- ¼ cup (60ml) 35% whipping cream
- 1 tsp (5ml) white vinegar
- ½ tsp pure vanilla extract
- ¼ tsp salt
- ½ tsp all-purpose flour

1. For the pastry, whisk together flour, sugar and salt in a large bowl. Add cold butter and cut or rub it into the flour mixture using a pastry cutter or your fingertips until it resembles coarse crumbs (you can also use a food processor for this step). The butter should be well dispersed so that there is no dusty flour left in the bowl.

2. Drizzle water into the flour mixture 1 tablespoon at a time while gently tossing with a fork until moistened and it holds together in clumps. You may not need all of the water. Turn the crumbly dough out onto a work surface and gather it together in a ball with your hands slightly cupped, turning it and squeezing in loose bits until it is cohesive. Roll the dough into a log, wrap it tightly and refrigerate for at least 2 hours or overnight.

2. Slice dough log into 12 equal portions. Roll out each portion to ⅛-inch thickness on a lightly floured surface. Fit dough rounds into the wells of a standard 12-cup muffin pan, pressing it into the corners and up the sides. Place pan in the fridge for 30 minutes.

3. Preheat oven to 375°F. For the filling, mix together soft butter and brown sugar in a medium bowl until it looks like a smooth paste. Whisk in egg until blended, the stir in cream, vinegar, vanilla, salt and flour. Spoon it into chilled pastry shells, dividing it evenly. Bake for 15 minutes. Reduce oven to 325°F and bake for 5 minutes more until the pastry is browned and filling is bubbling. Transfer pan to a rack to cool for 5 minutes. Use a knife to loosen the edges of the tarts especially if the filling has bubbled up over the sides and then transfer them to the rack to finish cooling.

Here's the debate: do you like gooey, runny butter tarts, or squishy, custardy ones? I'm giving you both! This recipe makes the gooey kind, and the maple version on the next page (page 115) makes the firmer-set version.

maple raisin butter tarts

makes 12 tarts

¼ cup (56g) unsalted butter, melted

¾ cup (165g) packed dark brown sugar

2 large eggs, at room temperature

⅓ cup (80ml) pure maple syrup

1 tsp (5ml) white vinegar

½ tsp pure vanilla extract

¼ tsp salt

1 tsp (3g) all-purpose flour

¼ cup (30g) raisins

Follow the recipe for Gooey Butter Tarts on page 114, combining all of the above ingredients (except raisins) for the filling. Sprinkle 5-6 raisins into each pastry shell, then fill and bake as directed.

pb & jelly sandwich cookies

makes 20-25 sandwich cookies

Follow the recipe for Peanut Butter & Chocolate Sandwich Cookies on page 113.

As you are shaping and squaring off the cookie dough to form a log, round off the top side and make a slight groove along the centre to resemble a loaf of bread. The sliced cookies will look like a piece of toast!

Spread your favourite raspberry or strawberry jam between two cookies instead of the chocolate filling.

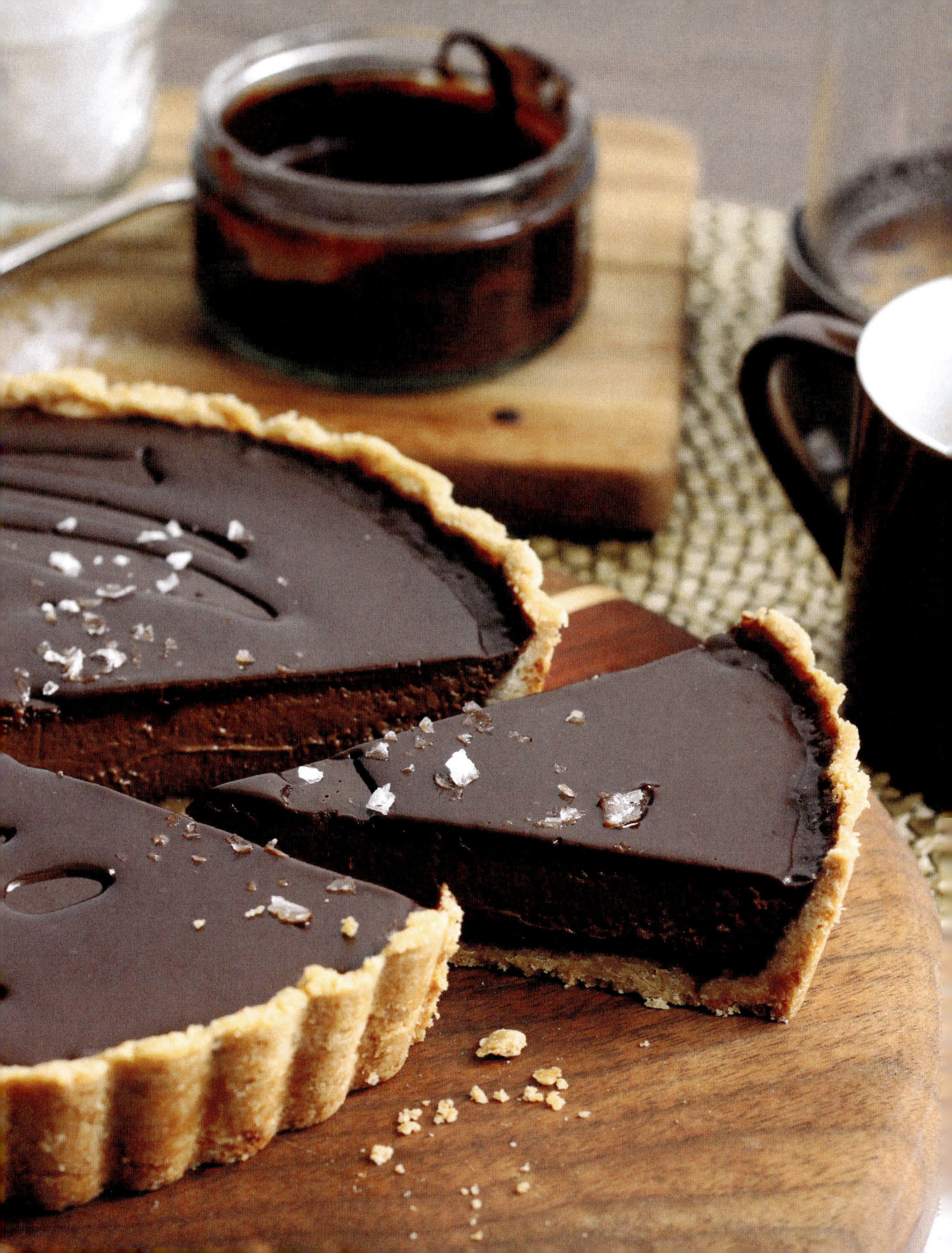

salted chocolate cream pie

makes 8-10 servings

Pastry:

1 cup plus 2 tbsp (160g) all-purpose flour

2 tbsp (30g) packed light brown sugar

¼ tsp salt

6 tbsp (84g) cold unsalted butter

1 large egg yolk

1 ½ tbsp (22ml) cold water

Filling:

⅔ cup (160ml) 35% whipping cream

⅔ cup (160ml) whole milk

3 tbsp (40g) granulated sugar

1 tbsp (15ml) honey

5 oz (142g) dark chocolate (60-70% cocoa), coarsely chopped

1 large egg, at room temperature

⅛ tsp salt

Glaze:

2 oz (56g) bittersweet chocolate (70% cocoa), coarsely chopped

¼ cup (60ml) hot water

1 tbsp (12g) granulated sugar

1 tbsp (14g) unsalted butter

sea salt flakes for topping

1. For the pastry, combine flour, brown sugar and salt in a medium bowl and rub together to combine evenly and remove any lumps of sugar. Cut the cold butter into small pieces and rub it into the dry ingredients using your fingertips until well blended and the mixture resembles coarse crumbs. Beat egg yolk with cold water using a fork in a small bowl and slowly drizzle into the flour mixture while tossing with the fork until it is evenly moistened. Turn the crumbly mixture onto a work surface and bring it together with your hands until it holds together, folding it over itself a couple of times. Form the dough into a disk, wrap well and refrigerate for 2 hours.

2. Preheat oven to 375°F. Roll the dough out to ⅛-inch thickness on a lightly floured work surface and fit it into a 9-inch round tart pan with removable bottom. Place it in the freezer for 10 minutes to firm up, then prick the pastry several times with a fork. Bake for 10 minutes, reduce oven to 350°F and bake for another 10-15 minutes until evenly golden. Transfer to a rack to cool.

3. For the filling, combine cream, milk, sugar and honey in a small saucepan over medium-low heat and bring it to a simmer. Remove from heat and add chocolate. Let stand off the heat for 2 minutes, then whisk until completely melted, smooth and glossy. Beat egg well with salt in a medium bowl. Gradually pour in the chocolate/cream mixture bit by bit while whisking to temper the egg and make a smooth custard. Pour the chocolate custard into the pre-baked crust and bake for 10 minutes. Turn off the oven and leave the tart inside for another 10 minutes to cook gently until the edges are set with just a slight wobble in the centre. Transfer to a wire rack to cool completely and then refrigerate for at least 2 hours.

4. For the glaze, combine chocolate, hot water and sugar in a small saucepan over medium heat and whisk until melted and smooth. Whisk in butter so it becomes thick and glossy. Pour the warm glaze over the cooled tart, tilting the pan to coax the glaze out to the edges. Let it set for 30 minutes, then top with sea salt flakes before serving.

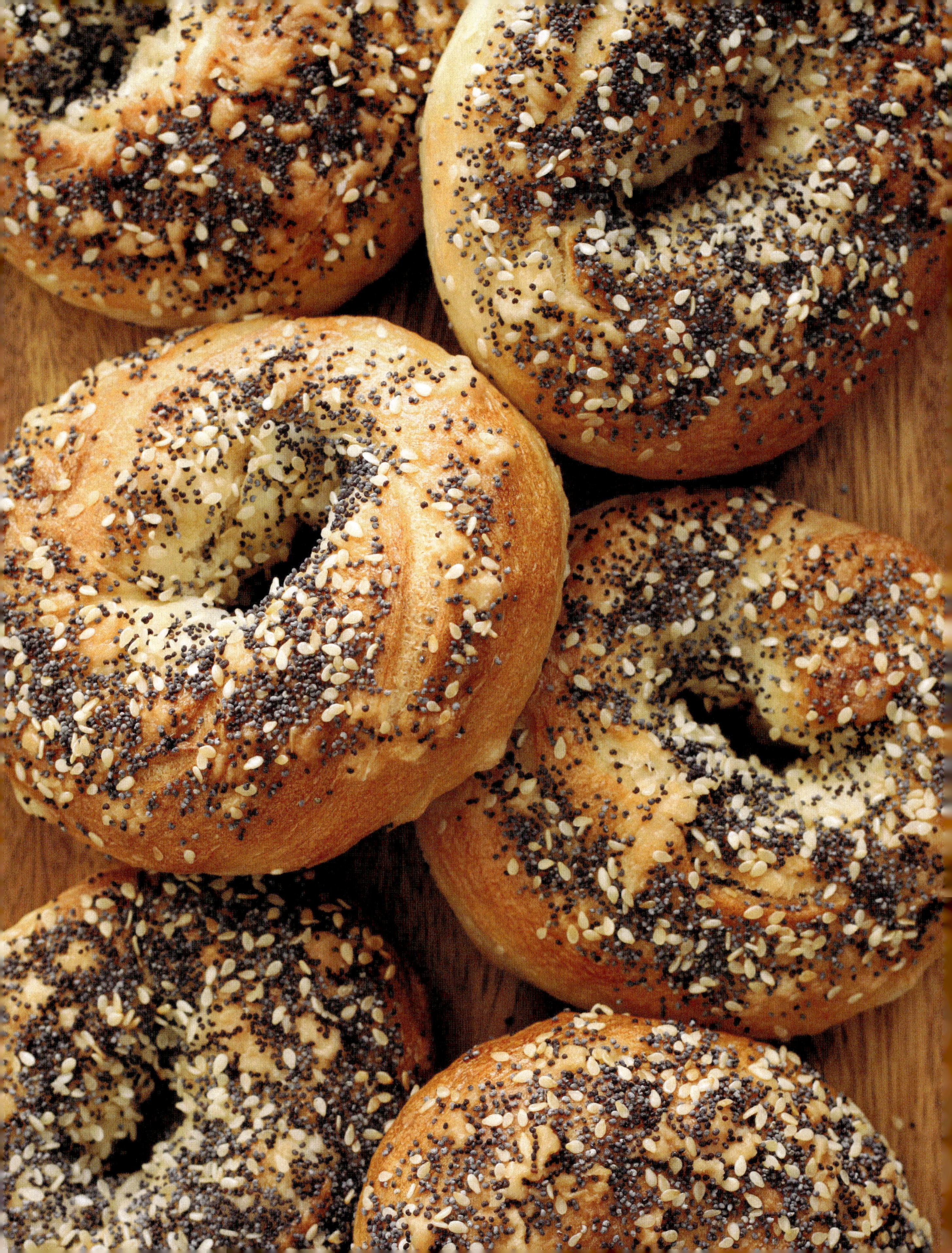

sunday BRUNCH

When it comes to brunch I tend to like the sweet things (eggs are great, but sometimes I just prefer them in a muffin). And, I think everyone enjoys a little sweetness at brunch, but not too sweet, right? That's what this chapter is about! I've included my favourite bagel recipe and my go-to apple snack cake that you can whip up in minutes. There are a few granola recipes, granola bars, muffins and then plenty of sweet loaves including 5 variations on banana bread! Don't forget the most effortless no knead cinnamon rolls that are ready to bake fresh on a Sunday morning!

New York style bagels

makes 10-11 bagels

Sponge:
2 cups (284g) all-purpose flour
1 ⅔ cups (415ml) warm water
1 tsp (3.5g) instant dried yeast

Dough:
1 tsp (3.5g) instant dried yeast
2 tbsp (30ml) honey
2 ½ cups (355g) all-purpose flour
1 ¾ tsp (10g) salt

Assembly:
2 tbsp (30ml) honey
¼ cup sesame seeds
¼ cup poppy seeds

Switch Up! For a pretzel-style flavour, add 1 teaspoon of baking soda to the boiling liquid. It will create a darker crust on the bagels and that signature pretzel taste. When you pull them out of the water, top with coarse salt just before baking.

1. For the sponge, combine flour, water and yeast in the bowl of a stand mixer fitted with the dough hook and stir to combine well. Let stand for 20 minutes.

2. For the dough, add the yeast, honey, flour and salt (in that order) to the sponge mixture in the mixer bowl and mix on a low speed for 10 minutes until the dough comes together and is elastic. Knead the dough by hand on a clean work surface for several minutes until it is smooth, elastic and extensible. When you gently pull the dough apart between your fingers, it should stretch out very thinly and be almost transparent (called the window test) rather than tear or shred – that's how you know the gluten is well developed.

3. Place the dough back into the mixer bowl and rub the surface with just ½ teaspoon of oil to prevent it from drying out. Cover the bowl with plastic wrap and a kitchen towel, place it in a warm place and leave to rise for 1 ½ to 2 hours or until it doubles in volume. You can also place it in the oven (turned off) with the light on or use the proof setting if your oven has one.

4. Once the dough has risen, gently push the air out of it with your hands then scrape it out onto a clean work surface. Use a bench scraper or a knife to divide it into 10 or 11 portions (100 to 110g each). To shape the bagels, roll each portion into a rope and then wrap it around your hand so that the seam where the two ends meet are under your palm, then roll your palm against the work surface back and forth to seal the ends together. Stretch it out to ensure the hole is at least 1 ½ to 2 inches wide since it will close up slightly as the dough proofs again. Place them onto parchment-lined baking trays with a bit of cornmeal to prevent sticking and then leave to rise for 30-40 minutes until a bit puffy. When you poke one with your finger, the indent should fill back out slowly.

5. Preheat oven to 450°F. Place a wide pot with about 2.5L of water over a high heat. Add honey and bring to a boil. Combine sesame and poppy seeds in a bowl and set aside.

6. Using a slotted spoon, gently drop the bagels into the water two at a time, taking care not to overcrowd the water. Boil the bagels for 30 seconds to 1 minute per side (the longer the boil, the chewier the crust – I prefer 1 minute per side). Remove with the slotted spoon and place back on the baking trays. Immediately sprinkle them generously with seeds or you can dip them directly into the seeds for a heavy coating. Bake for 10 minutes until they develop a nice dark crust. Lower oven temperature to 400°F and bake for another 10 minutes until evenly browned on top and bottom. Transfer bagels to a cooling rack to cool slightly before eating warm or toasted.

RIGHT: For hardcore sesame seed purists, skip the poppy seeds and double up on the sesame seeds with a sprinkle of sea salt.

LEFT: Lightly toasted with a big schmear of cream cheese or nut butter and honey is the perfect way to brunch!

The baking time will depend on the type of pan or dish you use – metal conducts heat faster than glass or ceramic. So, if you are baking in a metal pan, check at 25 minutes. Ceramics can take closer to 35 minutes.

overnight no knead cinnamon rolls
makes 10 rolls

Dough:
½ cup (120ml) whole milk

½ cup (120ml) boiling water

2 ½ cups (355g) all-purpose flour

¼ cup (50g) granulated sugar

2 tsp (7g) instant dry yeast

1 large egg, lightly beaten

¼ cup (56g) unsalted butter, melted

¾ tsp salt

Filling:
3 tbsp (42g) unsalted butter, melted

⅔ cup (145g) packed dark brown sugar

1 tbsp (9g) all-purpose flour

2 tsp ground cinnamon

Icing:
¾ cup (90g) icing sugar

¼ cup (60ml) thick full fat Greek yogurt

¼ tsp pure vanilla extract

1. Combine milk with boiling water (this warms up the milk to activate the yeast – you're aiming for 43°C/110°F).

2. Combine flour, sugar and yeast in a large bowl and whisk to blend well. Add milk mixture, beaten egg, melted butter and salt and mix it all together very well using a wooden spoon for 1 full minute until evenly blended and homogeneous. The dough will be wet and sticky. Scrape down the sides to pile it up in the centre of the bowl, cover with plastic wrap and a tea towel and let rise at room temperature for 2 hours until doubled in volume. Place it in the fridge overnight for at least 8 hours or up to 18 hours.

3. Generously flour a work surface and scrape the dough out of the bowl onto the flour. Liberally sprinkle more flour on top of the dough and pat it out flat. It will be very soft so use more flour as necessary to prevent it from sticking. Use a rolling pin to gently roll it out into a 16x11-inch rectangle. Brush it evenly with melted butter. Blend together the ingredients for the filling and sprinkle it evenly over the dough. Roll it up into a tight log from the long side and pinch it together at the seam. The dough will feel very soft and this is what makes these so tender.

4. Use a sharp serrated knife to slice the log at 1½-inch increments to make 10 rolls. Generously grease a 10 or 12-inch round baking dish or 13x9-inch baking dish with butter and arrange rolls with about ½-inch of space between them. Cover with a tea towel and let rest for 30-45 minutes in a warm place until puffed and the sides are touching. Meanwhile, preheat oven to 350°F.

5. Bake for 25-35 minutes until evenly golden and the centre roll is cooked – it should bounce back when pressed. Note that if you use a metal pan, the baking time will be slightly shorter. Transfer to a rack to cool for 20 minutes. For the glaze, whisk together icing sugar, yogurt and vanilla extract until smooth and drizzle it over the rolls while they are slightly warm.

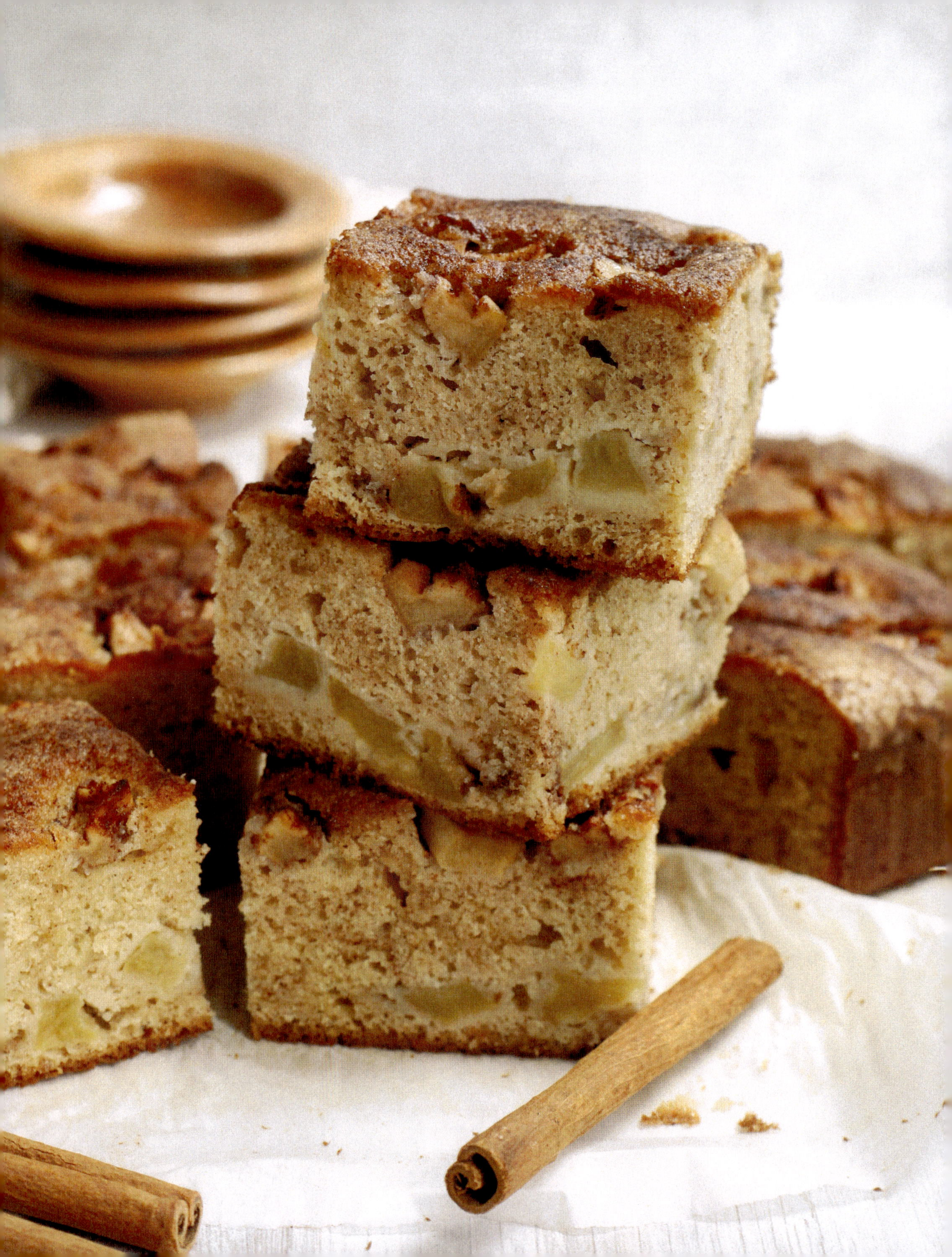

apple cinnamon sour cream snack cake

makes about 9 servings

Cake batter:

1 cup plus 2 tbsp (160g) all purpose flour

¾ tsp baking powder

¼ tsp baking soda

¼ tsp salt

4 tbsp (56g) unsalted butter, softened

⅔ cup (145g) packed light brown sugar

1 tsp (5ml) pure vanilla extract

2 large eggs, at room temperature

⅔ cup (160ml) full fat sour cream

2 cups (227g) chopped apple, cut into small ½-inch cubes from about 2 medium cored and peeled apples, divided

¾ tsp ground cinnamon

Topping:

1 tbsp (12g) granulated sugar

¼ tsp ground cinnamon

1. Preheat oven to 350°F. Line an 8x8-inch baking pan with parchment paper leaving a 2-inch overhang along each side.

2. Sift flour, baking powder, baking soda and salt into a medium bowl and whisk to blend evenly.

3. Combine butter, brown sugar and vanilla in a medium bowl and beat with an electric hand mixer for 2-3 minutes on medium-high speed until smooth, pale and fluffy. Beat in eggs one at a time, blending well after each addition and scraping down the sides and bottom of the bowl until it looks creamy. Add half of the flour mixture and mix on low to combine. Mix in sour cream. Gently beat in remaining flour mixture. Add 1 ½ cups (170g) of chopped apple to the bowl over the batter, sprinkle with cinnamon and then fold it in. This will create streaks of cinnamon throughout the cake for pops of spice flavour!

4. Spread the batter evenly into prepared pan. Scatter remaining ½ cup of chopped apple over top. For the topping, blend together sugar and cinnamon in a small bowl and sprinkle it over the top trying to cover the apples with the sugar. Bake for 30-35 minutes until a skewer inserted into the centre comes out clean. Transfer to a wire rack and let cool for at least 1 hour before serving.

> **Switch Up!** Make a Blueberry Sour Cream Snack Cake – Follow this recipe using either granulated sugar or brown sugar and substitute apples with ¾ cup (90g) of fresh or frozen blueberries. If using frozen berries, do not thaw and fold them in gently. Over-mixing will turn the batter blue. For the topping, combine sugar and cinnamon with 1 tsp cocoa powder. Bake as directed. If using frozen berries, bake for closer to 35 minutes.

honey olive oil muesli bars

makes 10-12 bars

1 ½ cups (150g) large flake rolled oats

⅓ cup (45g) raw cashews, coarsely chopped

¼ cup (35g) raw almonds, coarsely chopped

¼ cup (30g) dried cherries or cranberries

¼ cup (30g) chopped pitted dates

2 tbsp (18g) sunflower seeds

¼ cup (60ml) honey

2 tbsp (30g) packed light brown sugar

2 tbsp (30ml) olive oil

¼ tsp salt

¾ tsp ground cinnamon

1 tbsp (15ml) flaxseed meal (ground flaxseeds)

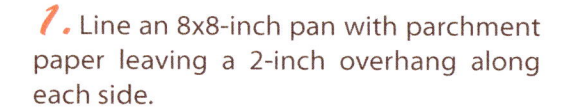

1. Line an 8x8-inch pan with parchment paper leaving a 2-inch overhang along each side.

2. Spread oats and chopped nuts out onto a baking tray and place in the oven. Turn oven on to 325°F and let it preheat. By the time it is ready, the oats and nuts should be gently toasted. Transfer them to a large bowl. Add dried cherries or cranberries, dates and sunflower seeds and set aside.

3. Combine honey, brown sugar and olive oil in a small saucepan over medium heat and stir until it just comes to a simmer. Stir in salt, cinnamon and flaxseed meal. Immediately pour it over the oat mixture in the bowl and stir until everything is evenly coated.

4. Scrape the sticky mixture into the prepared pan and press it down firmly in an even layer (this will help create less crumbly bars). Use the bottom of a measuring cup to make an even compact slab, running it firmly back and forth over the mixture. Bake for 15-18 minutes until lightly golden brown around the edges and the surface is slightly puffed. The muesli shouldn't be too hard, but rather slightly soft when gently pressed. Do not over-bake or it will be too hard once cooled and difficult to slice.

5. Transfer pan to a wire rack and immediately pack the granola down again while still hot using the bottom of a measuring cup. This will ensure that it holds together when sliced. Let it cool completely in the pan before slicing. Store bars in an airtight container at room temperature for up to 2 weeks.

double dark chocolate oat & almond bars

gluten free & vegan option

makes about 10 bars

- 1 cup (100g) large flake rolled oats
- 1 cup (100g) blanched almond flour
- ¼ tsp baking soda
- ¼ tsp salt
- 3 tbsp (45g) packed dark brown sugar
- 4 oz (113g) bittersweet chocolate, chopped into small pieces
- ¼ cup (60ml) peanut butter or almond butter
- ¼ cup (60ml) honey (or maple syrup for a vegan option)
- 2 tbsp (28g) coconut oil
- 1 tsp (5ml) pure vanilla extract
- 2 oz (56g) dark chocolate for drizzling

1. Preheat oven to 350°F. Line an 8x8-inch baking pan with parchment paper leaving a 2-inch overhang along each side.

2. Pulverize oats in a food processor until very fine. Add ground oats, almond flour, baking soda, salt and brown sugar to a large bowl. Mix well to remove any lumps of brown sugar and stir in chopped chocolate.

3. Combine peanut or almond butter, honey or maple syrup, coconut oil and vanilla in a saucepan over medium heat and stir until completely melted and bubbling hot (or heat it in the microwave). Pour this hot mixture into the bowl with the dry ingredients and mix well. The residual heat will melt some of the chocolate and help it all come together.

4. Spread it out into the prepared pan and press it down in an even layer with a spatula or using the bottom of a measuring cup. Bake for about 15 minutes until puffed and slightly darkened around the edges yet still quite soft in the center. Transfer to a rack and cool completely in the pan before slicing.

5. Melt the final 2 oz of dark chocolate gently in a heatproof bowl set over a saucepan of simmering water or in the microwave at 50% power with short bursts and frequent stirring. Drizzle melted chocolate over the bars and let set before serving.

ginger cardamom crumb cake

makes about 9 servings

Crumbs:
- 1 cup (142g) all-purpose flour
- ¼ cup (50g) granulated sugar
- ¼ cup (55g) packed dark brown sugar
- ½ tsp ground cinnamon
- ½ tsp ground ginger
- ⅛ tsp salt
- 7 tbsp (100g) unsalted butter, melted
- 2 tsp (10ml) water

Cake:
- ¼ cup (56g) unsalted butter, melted
- ½ cup (100g) granulated sugar
- 1 tsp (5ml) pure vanilla extract
- ½ tsp ground cardamom
- 1 large egg, at room temperature
- ¼ cup (60ml) sour cream
- 1 cup (142g) all-purpose flour
- 1 tsp baking powder
- ¼ tsp salt
- ¼ cup (60ml) whole milk

1. Preheat oven to 350°F. Line an 8x8-inch baking pan with parchment paper leaving a 2-inch overhang at each side.

2. For the crumb, combine flour, both sugars, cinnamon, ginger and salt in a medium bowl and whisk to blend evenly so that there are no lumps of brown sugar. Stir water into melted butter and pour it into the dry ingredients. Stir with a spoon until evenly combined, then toss with your fingertips to form large crumbs. Cover with a tea towel and set aside.

3. For the cake, combine melted butter, sugar, vanilla and cardamom in a medium bowl and beat on medium speed for 2 minutes until pale and fluffy. Beat in egg until very light and creamy. Mix in sour cream. Sift flour, baking powder and salt into a small bowl and whisk to blend evenly. Add it to the wet mixture and begin mixing on low speed until mostly combined, and then beat in milk just until batter is smooth.

4. Spread batter evenly into prepared pan and scatter clumps of crumb topping evenly on top to cover it. Bake for 30-35 minutes until the crumbs are lightly golden and a toothpick inserted into the centre comes out clean. Transfer to a wire rack, cover loosely with foil and let cool. Dust generously with icing sugar before serving.

blueberry buttermilk muffins

makes 12 muffins

2 cups (284g) all-purpose flour
1 ½ tsp baking powder
½ tsp baking soda
½ tsp ground cinnamon
½ tsp ground ginger
¼ tsp ground allspice
⅛ tsp ground nutmeg
½ tsp salt

½ cup (100g) granulated sugar
2 large eggs, at room temperature
⅓ cup (70g) packed dark brown sugar
¾ cup (180ml) buttermilk
⅓ cup (80ml) sunflower oil
1 tsp (5ml) pure vanilla extract
1 ½ cups (180g) fresh or frozen blueberries

1. Preheat oven to 350°F. Line a standard 12-cup muffin pan with paper liners.

2. Sift flour, baking powder, baking soda, spices and salt into a large bowl. Add granulated sugar and whisk to blend evenly.

3. Whisk together eggs, brown sugar, buttermilk, oil and vanilla in a medium bowl. Make a well in the centre of the dry ingredients and add the buttermilk mixture. Stir gently until just combined with some streaks of flour left. Add blueberries and fold them in gently. Do not over-mix. A few small lumps are OK.

4. Divide batter evenly among prepared muffin cups, filling them to the rim. Bake for 20-25 minutes until golden brown and firm to the touch. Transfer pan to a wire rack and let muffins cool for 5 minutes before transferring individually to the rack to finish cooling.

5. For the glaze, whisk ½ cup (60g) icing sugar with 2-3 tsp (10-15ml) lemon juice until smooth and drizzle it generously over the muffins.

gluten free & vegan option

sweet & salty chocolate peanut butter granola

makes about 4 cups

2 ½ cups (250g) large flake rolled oats
1 cup (130g) raw cashews
¼ cup (35g) sunflower seeds
3 tbsp (18g) cocoa powder
2 tbsp (12g) flaxseed meal (optional)
2 tbsp (30g) packed light brown sugar
¼ tsp salt
⅓ cup (80ml) honey
3 tbsp (45ml) smooth peanut butter
2 tbsp (30ml) coconut oil or olive oil
½ tsp pure vanilla extract
⅓ cup (56g) mini chocolate chips

1. Preheat oven to 300°F.

2. Combine oats, cashews, sunflower seeds, cocoa powder, flaxseed meal (if you're using it), brown sugar and salt in a large bowl and blend well.

3. Combine honey with peanut butter, coconut oil or olive oil and vanilla extract in a small saucepan over low heat. Stir until the peanut butter is just melted and the mixture is smooth.

4. Remove from heat and pour it into the bowl with the oats. Stir until all of the dry ingredients are evenly coated.

5. Spread granola evenly onto a large baking sheet and bake for 30-35 minutes tossing frequently (every 5-10 minutes) until it feels dry. It will still feel soft when ready and will crisp up as it cools. Keep an eye on it and do not let it darken since cocoa burns easily. Rotate your pan frequently if your oven has hot spots. Transfer pan to a wire rack and cool for 10 minutes, then sprinkle chocolate chips over top and let cool completely.

Switch Up! For a chunky big cluster granola, replace 1 cup (100g) of rolled oats with quick-cooking or minute oats. Stir in any dried fruits such as cranberries, cherries, raisins or chopped dates once it cools.

gluten free & vegan

vanilla chai coconut granola

makes about 4 cups

2 ½ cups (250g) large flake rolled oats

½ cup (45g) medium unsweetened shredded coconut

½ cup (70g) coarsely chopped mixed nuts (pistachios, cashews, walnuts and/or pecans)

¼ cup (35g) chopped raw almonds

¼ cup (35g) sunflower seeds or pepitas

½ cup (120ml) maple syrup

3 tbsp (45ml) melted coconut oil

½ tsp <u>each</u> ground cardamom, ginger and cinnamon

¼ tsp <u>each</u> ground nutmeg and black pepper

1 tsp (5ml) pure vanilla extract

¼ tsp salt

1. Preheat oven to 325°F.

2. Combine oats, coconut, mixed nuts, almonds and sunflower seeds or pepitas in a large bowl and toss to blend evenly.

3. Stir together maple syrup, melted coconut oil, spices, vanilla and salt in a medium bowl. Add it to the large bowl and toss with the oat mixture until evenly coated.

4. Spread it out in an even layer onto a large baking sheet and bake for 25-30 minutes until it feels dry and turns evenly golden brown. Stop to stir after 10 minutes so that it browns evenly. Transfer baking sheet to a wire rack and let cool completely (it will crisp up as it cools). Store in an airtight container for up to 3 weeks.

Switch Up! To make a chunky Maple Pecan Peanut Butter Granola, replace coconut oil with ¼ cup (60ml) smooth peanut butter and melt it together with the maple syrup in the microwave until drippy before mixing with the dry ingredients. Use mostly pecans for the nuts and just cinnamon for the spice!

banana bakes

BEST classic banana bread

makes 8-10 servings

1 ½ cups (215g) all-purpose flour*

1 ½ tsp baking powder

½ tsp baking soda

½ tsp salt

1 ½ cups (355ml) mashed ripe banana (from about 3 large bananas)

¾ cup (165g) packed light brown sugar

2 large eggs, at room temperature

¼ cup (56g) unsalted butter, melted

1 tsp (5ml) pure vanilla extract

½ cup (85g) milk or dark chocolate chips

*For a healthier, hearty version you can substitute up to half of the white all-purpose flour (up to ¾ cup or 105g) with whole wheat flour.

1. Preheat oven to 350°F. Line a 9x5-inch loaf pan with parchment paper letting it hang about an inch above the sides.

2. Whisk together flour, baking powder, baking soda and salt in medium bowl.

3. Place mashed banana in a large bowl (or you can mash the bananas right in the bowl with a fork – you will need 360g of banana flesh which is about 3 medium bananas). Add sugar and whisk until glossy and syrupy. Whisk in eggs, melted butter and vanilla until blended. Add dry ingredients with chocolate chips and fold them in until just combined.

4. Scrape batter into prepared pan and smooth it out. Bake for 45-55 minutes until the top is evenly browned and a skewer inserted into the centre comes out clean. Let cool for 10 minutes, then turn out onto a wire rack to cool completely.

Six different ways to make a classic!

peanut butter & oat chocolate swirl banana bread

makes 8-10 servings

1 ¼ cups (180g) all-purpose flour

1 ½ tsp baking powder

½ tsp baking soda

½ tsp ground cinnamon

½ tsp salt

½ cup (50g) large flake rolled oats

1 cup (240ml) mashed ripe banana (from about 2 large bananas)

¾ cup (150g) granulated sugar

½ cup (120ml) sour cream or plain yogurt

¼ cup (60ml) sunflower oil

¼ cup (60ml) smooth or chunky peanut butter

2 large eggs, at room temperature

3 oz (85g) dark chocolate, chopped

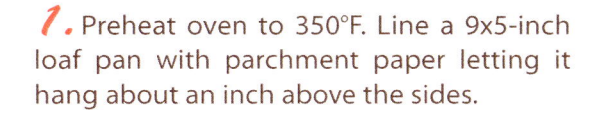

1. Preheat oven to 350°F. Line a 9x5-inch loaf pan with parchment paper letting it hang about an inch above the sides.

2. Combine flour, baking powder, baking soda, cinnamon, salt and oats in a medium bowl and whisk to blend evenly.

3. Place mashed bananas in a large mixing bowl (or you can mash the bananas right in the bowl with a fork – you will need 240g of banana flesh from about 2 large bananas). Stir in sugar. Add sour cream or yogurt and oil and whisk until combined. Mix in peanut butter. Whisk in eggs one at a time until smooth. Add dry ingredients all at once and fold together gently with a spatula until just blended. Do not over-mix. A few small lumps are fine.

4. Melt the dark chocolate gently in the microwave on medium power with short bursts and frequent stirring. Combine melted chocolate with 1 cup of batter in a separate bowl and stir to blend evenly. Dollop the original base batter alternately with the chocolate batter into the prepared pan and swirl together with a knife. Bake for 45-50 minutes until golden brown and slightly firm to the touch. Transfer pan to a wire rack to cool for 15 minutes, then turn the loaf out of the pan to finish cooling.

Switch Up! Try making Chocolate Chip Peanut Butter Banana Oat Muffins! Grease a standard 12-cup muffin pan or line it with paper liners. Follow this banana bread recipe, except replace granulated sugar with light brown sugar, omit the melted chocolate swirl and instead fold ⅔ cup (113g) chocolate chips into the batter. Divide it evenly among muffin cups. Sprinkle extra oats and chocolate chips on top. Bake for 18-20 minutes at 375°F until golden brown.

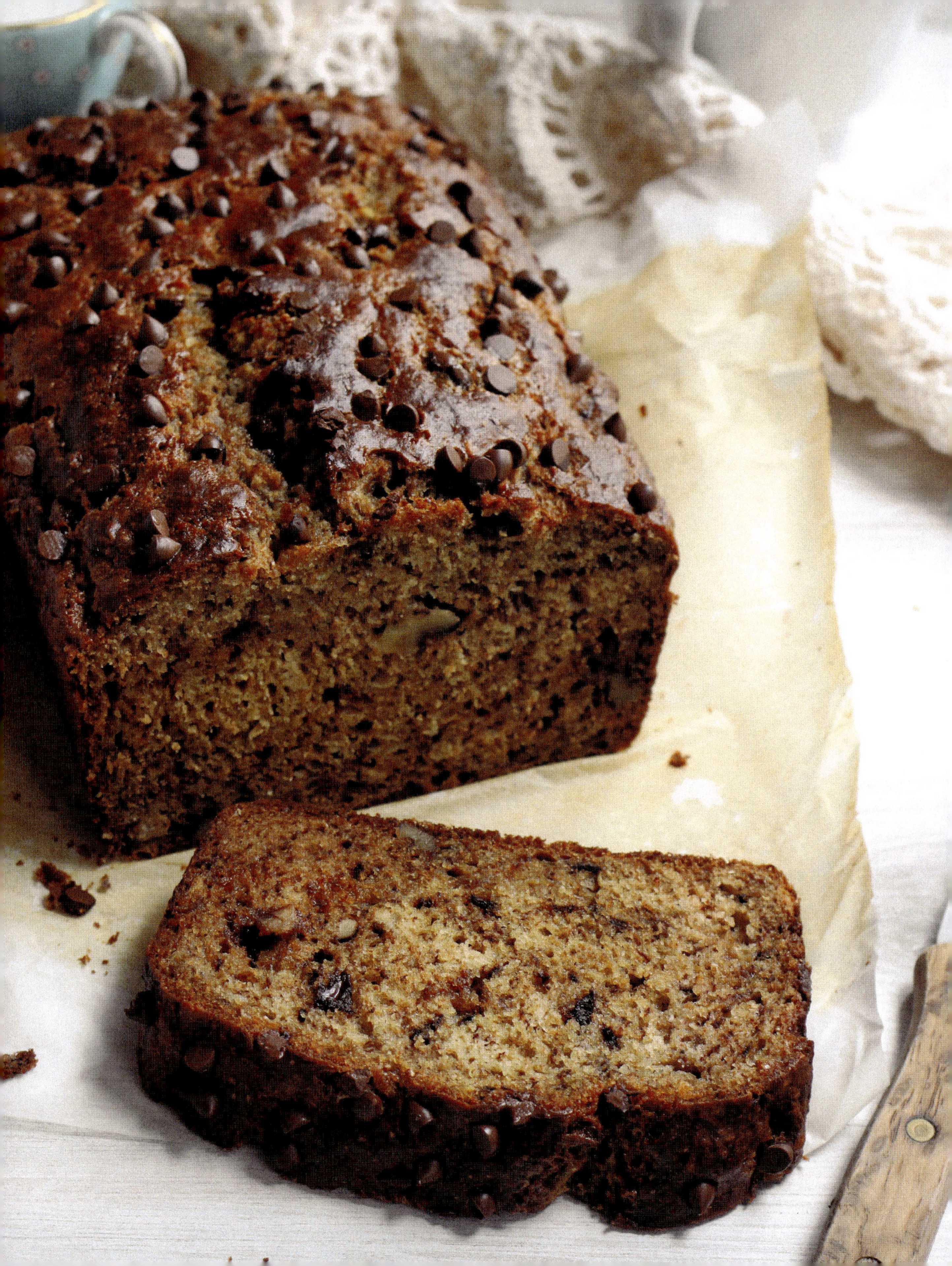

healthy whole wheat banana bread

makes 8-10 servings

1 ½ cups (355ml) mashed ripe banana (from about 3 large bananas)

¼ cup (55g) packed light brown sugar

¼ cup (60ml) pure maple syrup

2 large eggs, at room temperature

½ cup (120ml) thick Greek yogurt

¼ cup (60ml) sunflower or olive oil

1 tsp (5ml) pure vanilla extract

1 tsp baking soda

½ tsp baking powder

¼ tsp salt

1 ¾ cups (224g) whole wheat flour

½ cup (60g) chopped walnuts

½ cup (85g) dark or milk chocolate chips plus extra for topping

1. Preheat oven to 350°F. Line a 9x5-inch loaf pan with parchment paper letting it hang about an inch above the sides. Grease exposed sides.

2. Whisk together mashed banana, brown sugar and maple syrup in a large bowl. Let stand for a minute or two until sugar dissolves. Whisk in eggs one at a time, then whisk in yogurt, oil and vanilla. Add baking soda, baking powder and salt and whisk to blend evenly. Add the flour and fold it in gently with the chopped walnuts and chocolate chips just until combined. Do not over-mix.

3. Spread batter into prepared pan and sprinkle extra chocolate chips on top. Bake for 45-55 minutes until evenly browned and a skewer inserted into the centre comes out clean.

4. Transfer pan to a wire rack and let cool for 15 minutes. Lift the loaf from the pan using the parchment overhang and let cool completely on the rack before slicing.

cinnamon swirl banana bread

makes 8-10 servings

1. Follow the recipe for BEST Classic Banana Bread on page 132, except do not add chocolate chips to the batter. Transfer about 1 cup (240ml) of batter to a bowl and stir in 2 tsp of ground cinnamon.

2. Spread the base banana batter into prepared pan and then dollop spoonfuls of the cinnamon batter on top. Swirl it in with a skewer or a knife, pushing the cinnamon batter down through the base batter.

3. Place dark chocolate chunks all over the surface and bake as directed.

double chocolate banana bread

makes 8-10 servings

1. Follow the recipe for BEST Classic Banana Bread on page 132 and replace ¼ cup (35g) of the all-purpose flour with ½ cup (42g) of cocoa powder (either natural or Dutch process cocoa will work).

2. Add ½ cup (85g) of dark chocolate chips to the batter and fold them in. Sprinkle extra chocolate chips over top and then bake as directed.

honey walnut banana bread

makes 8-10 servings

1. Follow the recipe for Whole Wheat Maple Pecan Banana Bread on page 29, except replace all of the maple syrup with just ⅓ cup (80ml) honey and add 2 tbsp (30ml) of plain yogurt or milk in with the wet ingredients.

2. Add ⅛ tsp ground nutmeg in with the dry ingredients, and replace pecans with walnuts.

3. Spread the batter into a lined a 9x5-inch loaf pan, scatter some dark chocolate chunks on top and bake as directed.

chocolate fudge swirl banana muffins

makes 12 muffins

Muffin batter:

1 ½ cups (215g) all-purpose flour

1 ½ tsp baking powder

½ tsp baking soda

½ tsp salt

1 ½ cups (355ml) mashed ripe banana (from about 3 large bananas)

½ cup (100g) granulated sugar

¼ cup (55g) packed dark brown sugar

2 large eggs, at room temperature

¼ cup (56g) unsalted butter, melted

1 tsp (5ml) pure vanilla extract

Fudge Swirl:

3 oz (85g) dark chocolate

3 tbsp (45ml) 35% whipping cream

1. Preheat oven to 350°F. Line a standard 12-cup muffin pan with paper liners.

2. Combine flour, baking powder, baking soda and salt in medium bowl and whisk to blend evenly.

3. Place mashed bananas in a large bowl (or if you want to mash the bananas right in the bowl with a fork, weight out 360g of banana flesh so that you have the right amount). Add both sugars and whisk until glossy and syrupy. Whisk in eggs, melted butter and vanilla until well blended. Add dry ingredients all at once and fold them in until just combined.

4. For the fudge swirl, finely chop the chocolate and place it in a small saucepan with the cream. Stir over low heat until completely melted, smooth and glossy (you can also heat it in the microwave on medium power for about 1 minute until chocolate is melted). Add ¼ cup of banana batter and stir vigorously until it is smooth and thick. It might look oily and separated at first but continue to stir until it tightens up.

5. Divide banana batter evenly among muffin cups. Spoon about 1 teaspoon of the fudge mixture into the centre of each one and then swirl it through with a skewer or a knife. Tuck a few large chunks of chocolate on top if desired and bake for 18-20 minutes until golden brown and muffins feel firm to the touch. Transfer pan to a wire rack to cool for 5 minutes, then transfer muffins individually to the rack to finish cooling. They are incredibly delicious while warm!

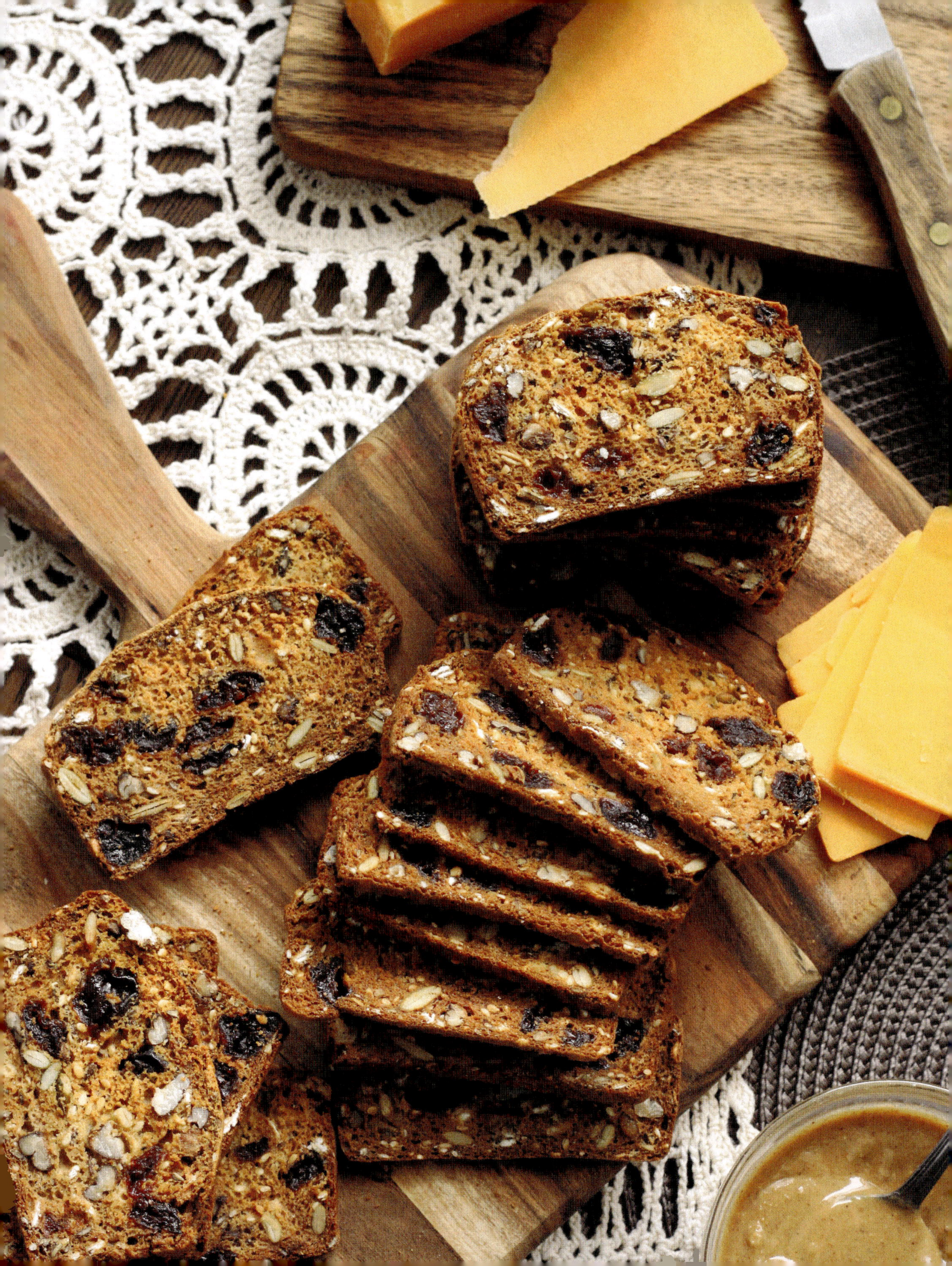

light SUMMER LUNCH

This chapter holds some incredible sweet & savoury crackers to make an impressive cheeseboard and many light and bright bakes to end a breezy Summer lunch. They're fresh-feeling and not too heavy because chances are you might be headed back to the beach or out to the pool soon after.

all about caramel

Caramel is extraordinary in that it can glamorize any dessert, yet it is made by one of the most ordinary and simplest ingredients: table sugar. Heat causes sucrose to break down into its component sugar molecules (monosaccharides): glucose and fructose. Eventually, these molecules break down into other compounds that undergo a series of reactions to make hundreds of new flavourful end products and brown colours. The final result is caramelized sugar. There are two methods for making caramel – wet caramel vs. dry caramel. Wet caramel involves dissolving sugar in water before caramelizing with no stirring. This slows the process so that you can control how dark you want the sauce to be. Dry caramel is cooked in a dry saucepan with no water added and frequent stirring until it melts and caramelizes. In this method the reaction is faster and always produces a very dark caramel.

DRY VS. WET CARAMEL

1) dry caramel, where sugar is melted directly over dry heat until it liquefies and caramelizes, and

2) wet caramel, where sugar is dissolved in water before caramelizing.

The dry method involves heating sugar in a dry pan until it liquefies and browns. Sucrose (table sugar) contains some inherent moisture that is tightly bound to its molecules due to its hygroscopic (water-loving) nature, so applying enough heat will melt it and the crystals liquefy when heated. This requires constant attention as the sugar tends to brown quickly and less evenly due to hot spots in the pan or the heat source. To use this method, sprinkle a thin even layer of sugar into a large heavy-bottomed skillet or saucepan over medium-high heat and cook until the sugar completely melts and begins to brown. When you see spots of sugar turning amber, slowly push it away with a wooden spoon and move the white sugar towards the centre to caramelize. Continue moving the sugar like this until completely liquefied and evenly browned. Use immediately for decorating or making hard caramel candy shards.

The wet method involves dissolving sugar first in water before cooking it until the water has evaporated enough that the sugar can caramelize. To use this method, combine sugar and water in a heavy saucepan. You can stir to moisten the sugar evenly at this point, but do not stir after it begins to boil. I choose not to stir and place the saucepan over medium heat and let the sugar dissolve slowly. Once dissolved, increase the temperature and let the liquid syrup boil. Gently swirl the pan as the syrup cooks for even browning. As drops of syrup sputter onto the sides of the pan, moisture will evaporate quickly and the sugar can re-crystallize. To prevent this, place a lid over the saucepan so the trapped steam will condense and drip down the sides to wash away the crystals. Otherwise, you can brush down the sides of the saucepan with a wet pastry brush. Some recipes can include an acid ingredient (lemon juice or vinegar) or corn syrup to prevent crystallization. Acid helps to cleave the bonds between glucose and fructose molecules that make up sucrose, whereas corn syrup introduces longer, bulky carbohydrate chains (oligosaccharides) that interfere with glucose molecules re-joining to crystallize. Since the water needs to boil off before the sugar completely caramelizes, the wet method prolongs the total time that the sugar is heated, making it easier to control the final colour. The biggest drawback to the wet method is that the sugar tends to recrystallize more easily. When the sugar and water boil, sugar syrup may splash onto the wall of the pot where it evaporates quickly and forms back into sugar crystals. If even one of these crystals falls back into the syrup, it can seed a chain reaction, turning the clear syrup opaque and grainy. Should this happen, you can remove it from the heat, add a few tablespoons of water, return it to the heat, and stir until the crystals dissolve before continuing on.

FLAVOUR REACTIONS

Making caramel sauce involves two delicious browning reactions: Caramelization and Maillard Browning. Caramelization happens first when plain sugar is heated. Then Maillard Browning occurs as sugar reacts with proteins from cream or milk and trace amounts in butter. These reactions produce delicious nutty aromas and golden brown colour compounds.

CRYSTALLIZATION

Crystallization occurs when sugar molecules (sucrose) come together and build upon themselves to make larger molecules that feel coarse. If this happens to caramel sauce, it will have a grainy or gritty texture and look more like wet sandy sludge than a smooth silky sauce. Ingredients that prevent crystallization are invert sugar (corn syrup, honey, glucose) and acid (vinegar or lemon juice).

ANTI-CRYSTALLIZATION

Invert sugar is liquid syrup that contains simple individual sugar molecules (glucose, fructose). With lots of these simple sugars floating around it's harder for sucrose molecules to connect and crystallize. Corn syrup contains larger molecules (oligosaccharides) that physically interfere and prevent sucrose from clumping. Acids break bonds within sucrose molecules and ensure that they stay apart.

TIPS for perfect caramel

1 Ingredient prep – making caramel requires almost constant attention so it is best to have all of your ingredients measured out and at the right temperature before turning on the heat. Prepare the butter, cream, flavourings and salt as required before starting to cook.

2 Use a heavy stainless steel saucepan as it conducts heat more evenly. The light-coloured steel will enable you to see the caramel change colour, hence avoid dark pans.

3 Avoid stirring a 'wet' caramel as it can trigger recrystallization. Place water in the pan first, then add sugar on top of the water. By respecting this order the sugar dissolves more readily and evenly. Set the pan over medium heat and let it come to a boil slowly. Do not stir once the syrup is boiling.

4 Be vigilant and attentive – do not walk away from the pan. First the sugar will turn to a translucent syrup. Once it starts to change colour, the process moves fast. When it turns light amber, lower the heat and stay by the pan to monitor the progression to deep amber. Swirl the pan to promote even cooking as you see golden-coloured syrup forming in spots in the pan and around the edges.

5 Be careful when adding liquids to make a caramel sauce. Adding butter or cream will cause the hot syrup to bubble up vigorously. Add liquids off the heat and stand back or wear an oven-safe glove if it is your first time.

6 Avoid adding cold liquids to caramel – it is best to heat the cream first since adding cold ingredients to very hot caramel will cause the mixture to sputter and steam will arise quickly. If the two ingredients are closer in temperature, the reaction will be less violent. Also, adding cold cream to caramel may cause the sugar to seize or clump up. If you find hard pieces of sugar in your caramel, just place it back over medium-low heat and cook it gently while stirring until it is melted and smooth.

7 Don't skimp on the salt – you'll need at least ½ teaspoon for every 1 cup of sugar.

avocado mojito cheesecake bars

makes 12-16 squares

Base:

¾ cup (105g) all-purpose flour

¼ cup (55g) packed light brown sugar

⅛ tsp salt

¼ cup (56g) unsalted butter, melted and cooled

*You'll need about 1 small avocado or half of a large avocado to get ⅓ cup for this recipe.

Filling:

1 block (250g) cream cheese, softened

⅓ cup (65g) granulated sugar

1 tsp finely grated lime zest

⅓ cup (80ml) mashed ripe avocado*

1 tsp (5ml) lime juice

1 large egg, at room temperature

¼ cup (60ml) thick Greek yogurt

1 tbsp finely chopped fresh mint leaves

1. Preheat oven to 350°F. Line an 8x8-inch baking pan with parchment paper leaving a 2-inch overhang along each side.

2. For the base, combine flour, brown sugar and salt in a medium bowl and mix together to blend well and break up any lumps of brown sugar. Add cooled melted butter and begin to stir together, then blend with your fingertips until evenly combined. Tip the crumbly mixture into your prepared pan and pat it down into the base to make an even layer. Run the back of a spoon over the surface to smooth it out. Bake for 10-12 minutes until evenly golden brown. Transfer pan to a wire rack to cool. Reduce oven temperature to 300°F.

3. For the filling, place cream cheese in the bowl of a food processor and blend until creamy. Add sugar and lime zest and process until very smooth and glossy. Blend in mashed avocado and lime juice. Add egg, yogurt and mint and process until well combined.

4. Spread the filling evenly over the pre-baked crust. Bake for 22-26 minutes until just set. It should be slightly puffed around the edges with the slightest wobble in the centre. Transfer to a wire rack to cool completely and then refrigerate for at least 2 hours before slicing.

egg free

ultimate cheeseboard crisps

makes about 36 crackers

1 cup (142g) all-purpose flour
1 tsp baking soda
½ tsp salt
¼ tsp ground black pepper
1 tsp caraway seeds or fennel seeds
½ cup (120ml) plain low fat yogurt
½ cup (120ml) whole milk
2 tbsp (30g) light brown sugar
2 tbsp (30ml) honey

2 tsp (10ml) olive oil
¼ cup (35g) roasted pumpkin seeds
¼ cup (35g) sunflower seeds
2 tbsp (15g) rolled oats
½ cup (70g) chopped dried figs
½ cup (65g) whole roasted hazelnuts

Switch Up! Try replacing sunflower seeds with 2 tbsp (20g) flaxseeds and 2 tbsp (16g) sesame seeds, then replace dried figs and hazelnuts with equal amounts of dried cherries and pecans! (pictured on page 138)

1. Preheat oven to 350°F. Line an 8x4-inch loaf pan with parchment paper leaving a 1 inch overhang at each side.

2. Combine flour, baking soda, salt, black pepper and caraway/fennel seeds in a medium bowl. Whisk to blend evenly.

3. Combine yogurt, milk, brown sugar, honey and oil in a large bowl and whisk well. Add the flour mixture and stir a few strokes. Add pumpkin seeds, sunflower seeds, oats, chopped dried figs and hazelnuts and stir just until blended and evenly combined.

4. Spread batter evenly into prepared pan. Bake for 45-50 minutes until evenly browned and springy to the touch. It will get quite dark brown. Invert loaf onto a wire rack and let cool completely. A cold loaf will slice more easily, so I recommend to put it in the fridge overnight or in the freezer for 30 minutes. Slice the loaf as thin as you can and place the slices in a single layer on a baking sheet.

5. Preheat oven to 300°F and bake the slices for about 10 minutes, then flip them over and bake for another 10 minutes until crisp and golden.

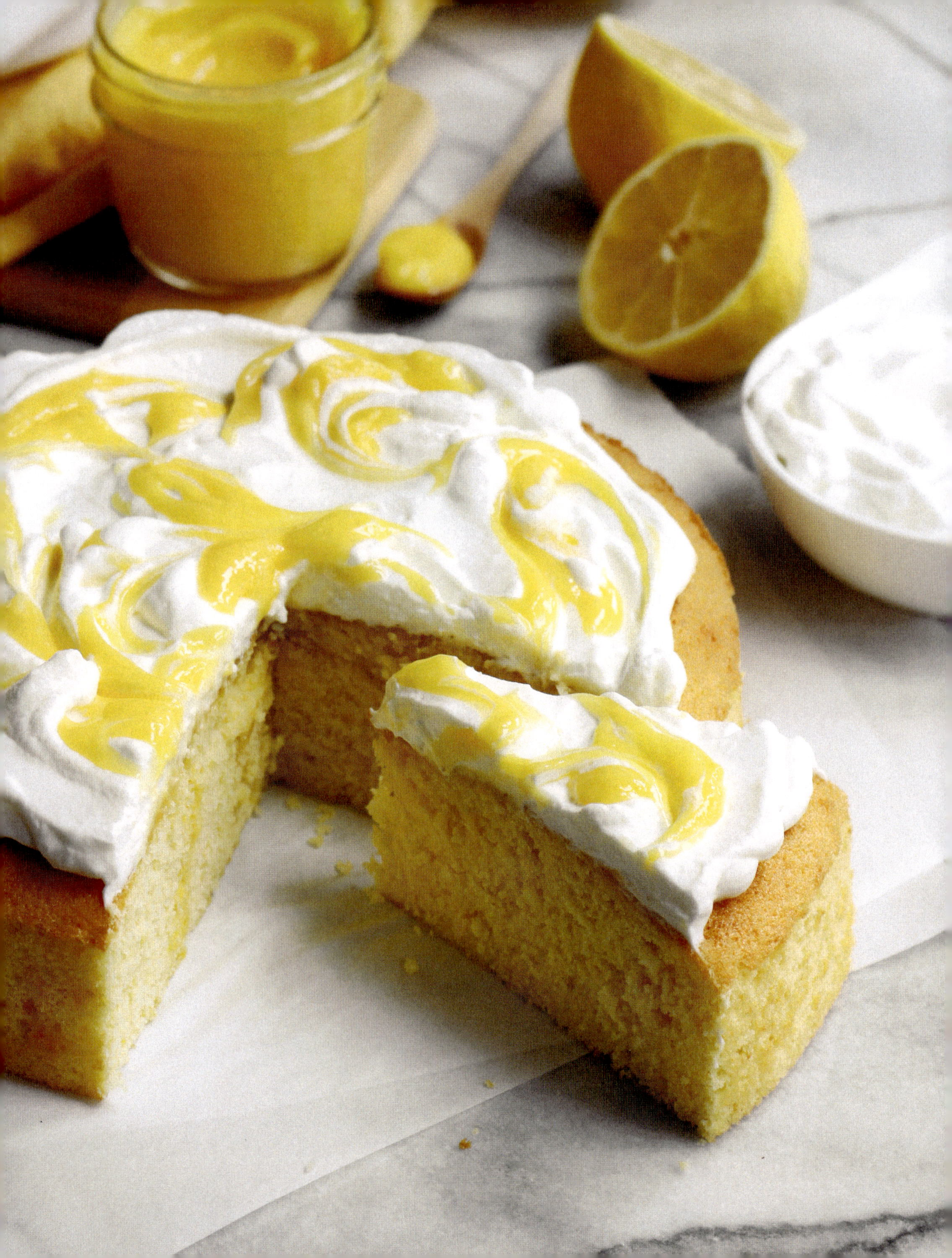

light & luscious lemon cake

makes 8-10 servings

Cake:

½ cup (120ml) whole milk

3 tbsp (42g) unsalted butter

1 tbsp finely grated lemon zest (from about 2 lemons)

¾ cup plus 2 tbsp (125g) all-purpose flour

2 tbsp (16g) corn starch

1 tsp baking powder

¼ tsp salt

2 large eggs, at room temperature

2 large egg yolks

¾ cup (150g) granulated sugar

1 tsp (5ml) pure vanilla extract

2 tbsp (30ml) fresh lemon juice

Lemon curd:

1 large egg

2 large egg yolks

¼ cup (50g) granulated sugar

¼ cup (60ml) fresh lemon juice

2 tbsp (28g) cold unsalted butter, cut into small pieces

Topping:

¾ cup (180ml) 35% whipping cream

This makes a small batch of lemon curd, but you can easily double the recipe to use it to fill tarts or between cake layers!

1. Preheat oven to 350°F. Line the base of an 8-inch round cake pan with parchment paper. Do not grease the sides.

2. Combine milk, butter and lemon zest in a small saucepan over medium heat and bring to a simmer. Remove from heat and let stand for 10 minutes to infuse.

3. Sift flour, corn starch and baking powder into a medium bowl. Add salt and whisk to blend evenly.

4. Combine whole eggs, yolks and sugar in the bowl of a stand mixer fitted with the whisk attachment and beat on medium-high speed for 2 minutes. Increase to high speed and beat for 4 minutes until pale, thick and tripled in volume. Mix in vanilla and lemon juice. With the mixer on medium speed, slowly pour in the warm milk mixture and mix just until incorporated. With mixer on low, gradually add flour mixture until combined and batter is smooth.

5. Pour batter into prepared pan and bake for 30-35 minutes until evenly golden and a toothpick inserted in the centre comes out clean. Transfer pan to a wire rack to cool for 20 minutes. Run a knife around the edges of the pan, invert to release the cake and allow to cool completely.

6. For the lemon curd, whisk together whole egg, yolks, sugar and lemon juice in a small saucepan until evenly blended. Add pieces of butter and place over low heat. Cook while whisking or stirring constantly for about 10 minutes until it thickens to the consistency of pudding. Press the curd through a sieve and into a clean bowl. Cover and refrigerate for at least 1 hour until set.

7. For the topping, whip cream to soft peaks using an electric mixer and spread over cooled cake. Dollop teaspoons of chilled lemon curd over the cream and swirl it through. Serve with extra curd on the side.

egg free

rosemary pecan press-in shortbread
makes 15 cookies

½ cup (55g) roasted pecan halves
1 cup (142g) all-purpose flour
¼ cup (55g) packed light brown sugar
¼ tsp salt
½ tsp finely chopped fresh rosemary
6 tbsp (84g) cold unsalted butter, cut into small pieces
4 oz (113g) dark chocolate, melted

1. Preheat oven to 350°F. Line an 8x8-inch pan with parchment paper leaving a 2-inch overhang along each side.

2. Place pecans in the bowl of a food processor and pulse until ground into coarse crumbs, but don't over-process or it can turn into pecan butter! Add flour, brown sugar, salt and rosemary to the bowl and process until finely ground and uniform.

3. Add cold butter to the processor bowl and pulse until the mixture forms crumbs that hold together when squeezed in your hand. Tip the mixture into prepared pan and press it into an even layer, packing it down firmly with the bottom of a measuring cup or the back of a spoon. Score it with a sharp knife 5 ways in one direction and 3 ways in the opposite direction to create 15 rectangles.

4. Bake for 16-18 minutes until golden and firm to the touch. Transfer pan to a wire rack and let cool for 30 minutes. Lift the cookie slab from the pan and transfer it to a cutting board. Slice along the score lines with a sharp knife. Dip each cookie into melted dark chocolate and then place them onto a piece of parchment or waxed paper to set before serving.

pumpkin seed & black pepper crispbreads

makes about 20 crispbreads

egg free

½ cup (75g) pumpkin seeds

⅓ cup (35g) large flake rolled oats

3 tbsp (30g) flaxseeds

4 tbsp (30g) white sesame seeds

1 tsp black sesame seeds

½ cup (64g) whole wheat flour

¾ tsp salt

¼ tsp cracked black pepper

⅛ tsp baking powder

2 tbsp (30ml) olive oil

1 tsp (5ml) honey

4 tbsp (60ml) cold water

1. Preheat oven to 350°F. Have ready a large 16x12-inch baking sheet.

2. Combine pumpkin seeds, oats, flax seeds, white and black sesame seeds, flour, salt, black pepper and baking powder in a large bowl and mix to blend evenly. Add olive oil, honey and water and stir well until everything is nicely combined and it forms a soft and slightly sticky (but not wet) dough.

3. Lay a large piece of parchment paper the size of your baking sheet onto a work surface. Place the dough onto the sheet, lay another piece of parchment on top and roll it out between the paper as thinly as possible. Transfer the parchment with the rolled-out dough to the baking sheet and peel off the top piece of parchment. Score the dough by slicing through it with a sharp knife or a pizza cutter to mark the size of the crispbreads. I score it into 2x3-inch rectangles. Alternatively, you can bake the rolled-out dough without scoring and then break it up into random shapes after baking – this creates a nice rustic look.

4. Bake for 13-16 minutes until evenly golden brown and dry. Transfer baking sheet to a wire rack and let cool before breaking into pieces along the score marks. Store in an airtight container.

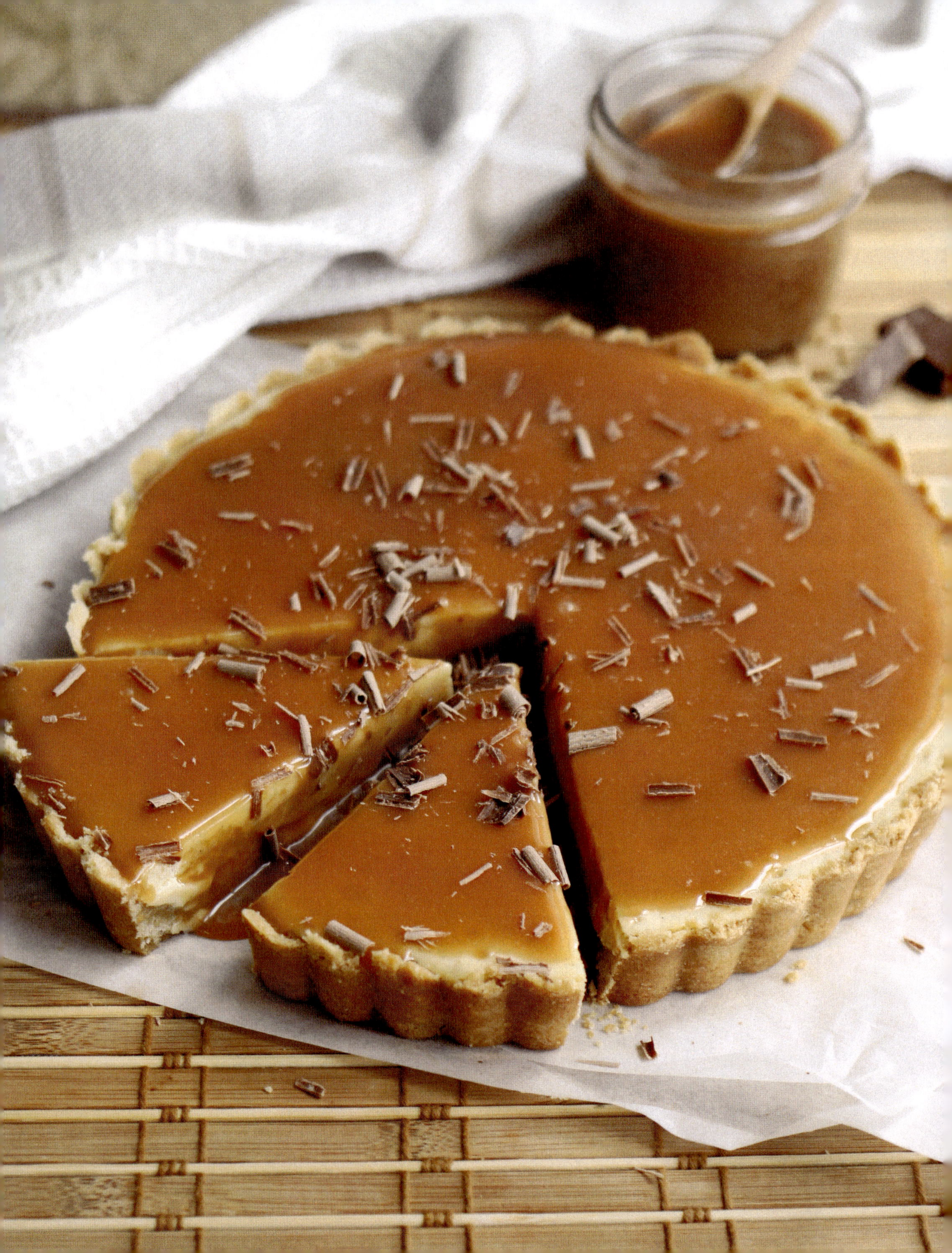

silk cream cheese custard tart
with creamy caramel sauce

makes about 8 servings

Crust:
1 cup (142g) all-purpose flour

⅓ cup (70g) packed light brown sugar

⅛ tsp salt

⅛ tsp ground cinnamon

⅓ cup (75g) unsalted butter, softened

> *Dulce de Leche ("milk candy") is a type of milky caramel with origins in South America, particularly Argentina. It is made by slowly cooking milk with sugar and a bit of baking soda (to promote browning) over several hours until it reduces to a thick caramel consistency. Sometimes it is made with goat milk, and it is delicious on this tart!

Filling:
1 block (250g) cream cheese, softened

⅓ cup (70g) packed light brown sugar

1 large egg, at room temperature

¼ cup (60ml) sour cream

1 tsp (5ml) pure vanilla extract

¾ cup (180ml) Extra Creamy Caramel Sauce (page 156) or prepared Dulce de Leche spread*

1. Preheat oven to 350°F.

2. For the crust, combine flour, brown sugar, salt and cinnamon in a medium bowl and mix together to blend well and break up any lumps of sugar. Add butter in small pieces and rub it in with your fingertips until evenly blended. Tip the crumbly mixture into an 8-inch round tart pan with a removable bottom and press it evenly into the base and up the sides. Bake for 12-17 minutes until golden and fragrant. Transfer pan to a wire rack to cool.

3. For the filling, beat cream cheese in a medium bowl with an electric hand mixer until creamy. Mix in sugar until very smooth and glossy. Beat in egg until well combined. Add sour cream and vanilla and blend well. Pour this mixture into the cooled pre-baked crust and bake for 12 minutes. Turn the oven off and leave the tart in the oven for another 8-10 minutes until the surface looks matte and set but with a slight wobble in the centre.

4. Transfer tart to a wire rack to cool completely and then refrigerate for at least 2 hours. Spread caramel sauce or dulce de leche over the tart and garnish with some milk chocolate shavings before serving.

To make a chocolate filling, place ⅓ cup (80ml) whipping cream in a small saucepan over medium-low heat until it just comes to a simmer. Remove from heat and add 3 oz (85g) finely chopped dark chocolate. Let stand for 1 minute then whisk until smooth and glossy. Let cool for 15 minutes. Place ¾ cup (180ml) whipping cream in another clean bowl and beat until it holds firm peaks. Add chocolate mixture and fold it in evenly.

chocolate vanilla swiss roll

makes about 10 servings

Sponge cake:

4 large eggs, at room temperature

½ cup (100g) granulated sugar

½ tsp pure vanilla extract

¼ tsp salt

3 tbsp (45ml) sunflower oil

½ cup (71g) all-purpose flour

¼ cup (21g) Dutch process cocoa powder, plus more for dusting

½ tsp baking powder

Vanilla filling:

4 tbsp (60g) cream cheese, softened

2 tbsp (25g) granulated sugar

1 cup (240ml) 35% whipping cream

1 tsp (5ml) pure vanilla extract

Switch Up! See the note on the recipe image to the left for instructions on how to make a rich chocolate filling to create a Double Chocolate Swiss Roll!

1. Preheat oven to 350°F. Lightly grease the bottom and sides of a 16x12-inch or 10x15-inch rimmed baking sheet with cooking spray or melted butter. Line it with parchment paper.

2. For the sponge cake, beat eggs for 3 minutes on medium-high speed until frothy and pale in the bowl of an electric stand mixer fitted with the whisk attachment or in a large mixing bowl if using an electric hand mixer. Gradually add sugar and beat for 4-5 minutes longer until it nearly triples in volume and is very thick, pale and fluffy (like shaving cream). When you lift the mixture up with the beater and it slides back down into the base mixture, it should fall back onto itself in folds or ribbons rather than sink down into it. Mix in vanilla and salt, then mix in oil just until it is evenly blended.

3. Sift flour, cocoa and baking powder into a medium bowl and whisk to blend evenly. Sift it again over the bowl with the egg mixture and use a large rubber spatula to carefully fold the dry ingredients into the whipped egg mixture just until combined without over-mixing.

4. Spread batter evenly into prepared pan in a thin layer. Bake for 9-11 minutes until it springs back when pressed gently. Transfer pan to a wire rack and let cool for 3 minutes so it is easier to handle. Dust top of cake evenly with cocoa powder. Run a knife along the edges of the pan to release the cake, then invert it onto a clean kitchen towel or another large piece of parchment paper. Gently peel off the top layer of parchment. While the cake is still warm, gently roll it into a log starting from the short side and incorporating the kitchen towel or parchment as you are rolling. Let the cake cool completely in this rolled shape.

5. For the vanilla filling, combine soft cream cheese with sugar and half of the cream in a medium bowl and beat on medium speed with an electric hand mixer to smooth out the cream cheese. Add the remaining cream and beat until it forms stiff peaks. Beat in vanilla extract. Gently unroll the sponge cake and spread the filling evenly over it leaving a ½-inch border all around. Re-roll the cake to enclose the filling starting at a short end. Transfer the cake roll to a serving plate, cover loosely and refrigerate for at least 1 hour before slicing. Dust with extra cocoa powder, slice and serve.

white chocolate & cranberry peanut butter oatmeal cookies

makes 20-22 cookies

6 tbsp (84g) unsalted butter, softened
½ cup (110g) packed light brown sugar
⅓ cup (65g) granulated sugar
⅓ cup (80ml) smooth natural peanut butter
1 large egg, at room temperature
½ tsp pure vanilla extract
1 ¼ cups (125g) large flake rolled oats

¾ cup (105g) all-purpose flour
½ tsp baking soda
¼ tsp baking powder
½ tsp salt
½ tsp ground cinnamon
½ cup (70g) white chocolate chunks
⅔ cup (70g) dried cranberries

1. Preheat oven to 350°F. Line 2 large baking sheets with parchment paper.

2. Beat butter with both sugars in a large bowl using a wide spatula or hand mixer for 1-2 minutes until smooth and a bit fluffy – it will look like damp sand. Mix in peanut butter. Add egg and vanilla and mix until well incorporated. Stir in rolled oats and set aside.

3. Combine flour, baking soda, baking powder, salt and cinnamon in a medium bowl and whisk to blend evenly. Add it to the butter mixture and stir it in until mostly combined. Then, add white chocolate chunks and dried cranberries and fold them through until evenly distributed and the dough is uniform.

4. Roll heaped tablespoons of dough into balls and place them onto prepared baking sheets spacing them at least 2 inches apart. Flatten each dough ball with the palm of your hand or bottom of a measuring cup and bake for 10-12 minutes until lightly golden around the edges yet still soft in the centre. Let cookies cool for 3 minutes on the baking sheets, then transfer individually to a wire rack to finish cooling.

salted peanut caramel crumb bars

(egg free)

makes 16 squares

Crumb:
- 1 cup (142g) all-purpose flour
- ½ cup (110g) packed light brown sugar
- ¼ tsp baking powder
- ¼ tsp salt
- ½ cup (50g) large flake rolled oats
- ¼ cup (22g) quick-cooking or minute oats
- 7 tbsp (100g) cool (but pliable) unsalted butter, cut into small pieces*
- ⅓ cup (50g) dry roasted & salted peanuts, finely chopped

Filling:
- ¾ cup (180ml) Rich Salted Caramel Sauce recipe (page 196)
- 1 tbsp (9g) all-purpose flour

*This recipe works best when the butter is cool, but not hard (i.e. not straight from the fridge).

1. Preheat oven to 350°F. Line an 8x8-inch baking pan with parchment paper leaving 1-inch overhang along the sides.

2. For the crumb, mix together flour, brown sugar, baking powder, salt and both oats in a medium bowl. Add butter and blend it in with your fingertips (or use a stand mixer with the paddle attachment on low speed for 3-4 minutes) until evenly distributed and forms clumps when you squeeze it in your hand. It will be crumbly but should hold together when pinched. Reserve about 1 cup and press remaining crumbs firmly into the base of prepared pan. Use the bottom of a measuring cup to pack it down in an even layer. Bake for about 12 minutes until lightly golden. Mix peanuts into reserved crumb mixture and refrigerate until ready to use.

3. For the filling, stir prepared Rich Salted Caramel Sauce with flour until smooth. Spread it evenly over the pre-baked base. Sprinkle reserved crumb mixture over top. Bake for 16-20 minutes until caramel is bubbling and crumbs are golden. Cool completely in the pan and then refrigerate for 1 hour before cutting into squares.

crostata marmellata (Italian jam tart)

makes 8-10 servings

Pastry:

1 ½ cups (215g) all-purpose flour

⅓ cup (65g) granulated sugar

heaped ¼ tsp salt

¼ tsp baking powder

½ cup (113g) soft unsalted butter

zest of one orange

1 large egg

1 large egg yolk

1 tsp (5ml) pure vanilla extract

Filling:

¾ to 1 cup (180-240ml) jam of choice (such as strawberry, raspberry or apricot)

2-3 tsp (10-15ml) water

1. For the pastry, combine flour, sugar, salt and baking powder in a large bowl and blend well. Add soft butter in pieces and mash it in with a fork, then use your fingertips to break it down further until it resembles coarse crumbs. Beat and blend the egg, yolk and vanilla in a small bowl with a fork. Make a well in the centre of the flour mixture and add the egg mixture. Use a fork to toss it all together until moistened and then bring it together with your hands, squeezing and pressing it together until it forms a smooth dough. Fold it over itself a few times if necessary. Divide the dough in two so that one half is slightly larger than the other. The larger one will be for the base. Flatten each portion into a round disk, wrap each one well and refrigerate for 2 hours.

2. Preheat oven to 350°F.

3. Lightly flour a work surface and roll out the larger disk of dough to just over ⅛-inch thickness. Fit it into the base and up the sides of a 9-inch round tart pan with removable bottom. Fold the excess pastry in over the sides to make a thicker edge crust. Stir together jam and water and spread it over the base. Roll out the other portion of pastry into a circle with about ⅛-inch thickness and then slice it into 1-inch wide strips. Lay the strips diagonally over the jam and press the ends onto the edge crust to seal them.

4. Bake for about 40 minutes until pastry is golden and the filling starts to bubble. Transfer to a wire rack to cool completely.

sour cherry pistachio butter cookies
makes 26-30 cookies

⅔ cup (150g) unsalted butter, softened

¼ cup (50g) granulated sugar

¼ cup (55g) packed light brown sugar

1 tsp lemon zest

½ tsp pure vanilla extract

heaped ¼ tsp salt

1 large egg, at room temperature

1 ⅓ cups plus 1 tbsp (200g) all-purpose flour

½ cup (60g) roasted pistachios, ground

½ cup (70g) dried sour cherries, coarsely chopped

¼ cup (30g) cacao nibs or mini dark chocolate chips

raw or coarse sugar for coating

1. Combine butter, both sugars, lemon zest, vanilla and salt in the bowl of a stand mixer (or in a large bowl if using a hand mixer) and beat on medium for 2-3 minutes until light and fluffy, scraping down the bowl as needed. Beat in egg until well combined and fluffy. Scrape down the mixer bowl as needed. Add flour and mix on low speed. Once the flour starts to blend in, mix in the ground pistachios. Add the chopped dried cherries and cacao nibs or mini chocolate chips and mix them in by hand just until the ingredients are evenly incorporated. The dough will be soft and a bit sticky.

2. Scrape the dough out onto a sheet of parchment or waxed paper or plastic wrap and form it into a log about 11 inches long. Sprinkle raw sugar generously over all sides of the log and onto the paper beneath it, rolling it so the sugar adheres. Refrigerate for at least 2 hours until totally firm.

3. Preheat oven to 350°F. Line two large baking sheets with parchment paper. Use a sharp knife to slice the log into ¼ to ½-inch-thick rounds. You're going to hit some cherry chunks, so slice with purpose and squeeze the dough together as needed. Place slices 1 inch apart onto prepared baking sheets and bake for 14-16 minutes until edges are evenly browned. Let cool for 2 minutes before transferring cookies to a wire rack.

gluten free *egg free*

extra creamy caramel sauce

makes about 1¼ cups

¾ cup (180ml) 35% whipping cream

¼ cup (60ml) water

1 tbsp (15ml) light corn syrup or honey

a squeeze of lemon juice*

1 cup (200g) granulated sugar

2 tbsp (28g) unsalted butter

½ tsp pure vanilla extract

½ tsp salt

Switch Up! For Sour Cream Salted Caramel, change the amount of whipping cream to just ⅔ cup (160ml), then whisk in 2 tbsp (30ml) of full fat sour cream before placing it back over the heat to simmer. It makes a luscious and pleasantly tangy caramel sauce!

1. Place cream in a small saucepan over medium-low heat and keep warm or warm it in the microwave.

2. Pour water into a 1 or 2-quart heavy-bottomed saucepan with high sides. Add corn syrup and lemon juice, then pour in sugar. Place the pan over medium heat. Do not stir. Let it cook until it begins to bubble, the sugar is dissolved and it turns to a translucent white syrup. Increase heat slightly and continue to cook until it turns a rich amber colour. Once you see that it starts to turn golden, you can swirl the pan gently to help it colour evenly. The whole cooking process will take 10-12 minutes. Continue to swirl the pan as needed to promote even colouring.

3. Once the syrup is crystal clear and amber-coloured (almost like copper), remove the pan from over the heat and carefully add the hot cream in a slow stream while whisking constantly. The mixture will bubble up, so be cautious. Continue stirring to make sure there are no lumps and the caramel is well dissolved. Return the pan to medium heat and bring the sauce back to a simmer. Cook for 2 minutes until thickened. It will look very fluid at first but it will thicken as it cools. Remove from heat and stir in butter, vanilla and salt. Transfer caramel sauce to a clean bowl or jar to cool completely. Cover and refrigerate for up to 3 weeks.

*The acid from a squeeze of lemon juice (about ½ teaspoon) helps to prevent re-crystallization of sugar crystals that would otherwise lead to a grainy texture, thus keeping this caramel sauce extra smooth and creamy.

creamy lemon squares

makes 16 bars

Base:

1 cup (142g) all-purpose flour

¼ cup (30g) icing sugar

¼ tsp salt

⅛ tsp baking powder

7 tbsp (100g) unsalted butter, softened but cool and cut into small cubes

> *For lining the pan, aluminum foil adheres closely to the crust so that it doesn't shrink and pull away from the sides on cooling which would leave a gap where the lemon filling can leak to the bottom and make a soggy crust.

Filling:

¾ cup (150g) granulated sugar

2 tsp lemon zest

2 large eggs

1 large egg yolk

⅓ cup (80ml) freshly squeezed lemon juice (from 2-3 lemons)

¼ cup (60ml) 35% whipping cream

1 tbsp (9g) all-purpose flour

> **Switch Up!** For an extra tangy version, replace whipping cream with an equal amount of full fat sour cream! For a colourful and fruity flare, sprinkle with freeze dried raspberry powder.

1. Preheat oven to 325°F. Line an 8x8-inch pan with aluminum foil* and grease lightly.

2. Whisk together flour, icing sugar, salt and baking powder in a medium bowl (or in the bowl of a stand mixer). Add butter and blend it in with your fingertips until well dispersed and it resembles coarse crumbs (or mix on low speed for 3-4 minutes with the paddle attachment). Press the crumb mixture evenly into the prepared pan using your hands, building it up about ½-inch along the sides to create a thin edge to keep the filling in. Use the back of a spoon to smooth over the surface. Bake for 20-25 minutes until edges are browned and surface is lightly golden.

3. Combine sugar and lemon zest in a medium bowl and rub it together so the sugar is fragrant. Whisk in eggs and yolk until well blended. Do not beat to avoid air incorporation. Whisk in lemon juice, then mix in cream and flour until smooth.

4. Slowly pour the filling over the hot crust and bake for 16-20 minutes until it is just set in the centre. Do not over-bake or the filling can become too firm. Transfer pan to a wire rack to cool completely, then cover and refrigerate for 2 hours before slicing.

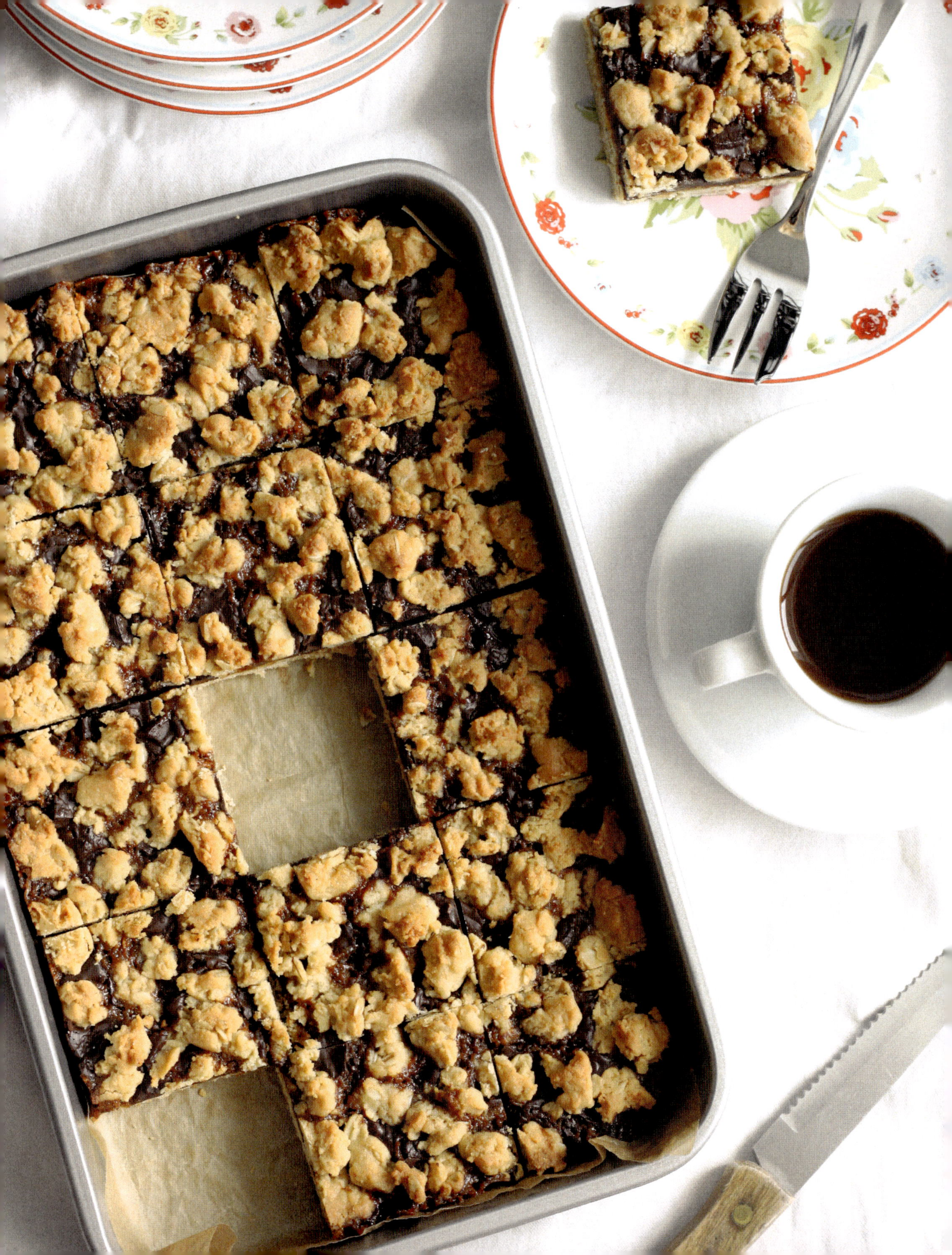

tea TIME

Tea time is time for something sweet and indulgent! I'm talking about afternoon tea – that 3 or 4pm mark when your energy starts to slump and the tummy rumbles but it's too early for dinner and another cup of coffee or tea is in order. Most of these treats are simple one-pan bakes that slice up nicely to share with friends and satisfy any mood from a light custard-filled sponge cake and delicate amaretti almond cookies to buttery shortbread and decadent chocolate truffles. What mood are you in?

pastry cream

Pastry cream is something that pastry chefs could not live without. It is as delicious as it is versatile and forms the bases of many fillings for a multitude of pastries, cakes and layered desserts.

Making pastry cream turns eggs into the most luscious creamy filling. It's made from milk, eggs, sugar, starch and sometimes cream. It is classically flavored with vanilla, but really it is a canvas for anything that you can imagine from chocolate to chai tea — check out all of the variations below!

Eggs function as a thickening agent and stabilizer while also creating a smooth and luscious mouthfeel thanks to creamy egg yolks. To make pastry cream, you generally start by warming milk and then gradually adding it to a mixture of eggs, sugar and starch (typically corn starch or flour) and then this mixture is cooked with constant stirring until it comes to a boil and thickens into luscious cream. Starch helps stabilize eggs and interferes with curdling, making pastry cream a bit more forgiving than other egg-thickened custards and sauces. However, it can scorch easily so it is important to stir constantly.

What Does It Mean to Temper Eggs?

Tempering is a simple yet important technique when making pastry cream to avoid curdling the heat-sensitive egg proteins. This is more crucial when making custards from whole eggs, but when making pastry cream from only the yolks, you can get away with a one-pot method and skip the tempering process all together! Check out my master recipe for Pastry Cream on page 163.

To temper eggs, warm the milk by itself first, then take the pan off the heat and slowly drizzle the warm milk into the eggs a little at a time while whisking. This helps to slowly bring up the temperature of the eggs without scrambling them. Once the milk and eggs are combined, it's safe to put everything back on the stovetop directly and continue cooking the pastry cream. Egg whites are more sensitive because they are essentially just protein and water – there's nothing there to protect those proteins from cooking. Egg albumin is very tight and doesn't disperse easily, so it is best to whisk it up with sugar to loosen it first before adding milk or cream. Egg yolk, on the other hand, contains a substantial amount of fat which serves to protect the proteins and interfere with coagulation.

CHOCOLATE
Pour hot custard over 3 oz (85g) of chopped milk or dark chocolate. Stir until melted & smooth.

PEANUT BUTTER
Stir ¼ cup (60ml) of smooth peanut butter into the warm custard.

COFFEE
Add 1 tsp of instant espresso powder or replace ¼ cup (60ml) of milk with strong espresso.

TAHINI WHITE CHOCOLATE
Pour hot custard over 3 oz (85g) of chopped white chocolate and stir in 2 tbsp of tahini.

EARL GREY
Steep 2 bags of earl grey tea in the hot milk for 10 minutes before continuing with the recipe.

PECAN PRALINE
Make praline paste: combine ⅔ cup (70g) pecan halves with ⅓ cup (40g) icing sugar in a saucepan and cook over medium-high heat stirring constantly until the sugar liquifies to an amber syrup and caramelizes over the pecans. Sprinkle sea salt on top and spread over a piece of parchment to cool completely. Pulverize in a blender or food processor until smooth then stir into pastry cream.

CHAI TEA
Heat the milk with 2 bags of black tea, 1 cinnamon stick, 2 slices of fresh ginger, 4 cardamom pods and 5 cloves. Cover and let it infuse for 10 minutes, then strain and continue with the recipe.

egg free

cream cheese caramelitas

makes 16 bars

Caramel & Topping:

¾ cup (150g) granulated sugar

2 tbsp (28g) unsalted butter

½ cup (120ml) 35% whipping cream

½ tsp salt

½ tsp pure vanilla extract

1 tbsp (9g) all-purpose flour

¾ cup (130g) dark chocolate chips

Base:

7 tbsp (100g) unsalted butter, softened

⅓ cup (70g) packed dark brown sugar

⅓ cup (65g) granulated sugar

7 tbsp (100g) cream cheese, softened

½ tsp pure vanilla extract

1 ¼ cups (180g) all-purpose flour

1 cup (100g) large flake rolled oats

¼ tsp salt

⅛ tsp baking soda

1. For the caramel, pour sugar in an even layer in a wide stainless steel saucepan over medium-high heat. As sugar crystals around the edge of the pan melt and liquefy, use a wooden spoon to push sugar from the edges to the centre and then push the unmelted sugar from the centre out to the sides to help it melt evenly. Continue to move the sugar like this until it begins to turn golden and liquefy. It will clump up and look dry before it liquefies, but trust that it will. Once it melts completely and transforms into a clear amber syrup, remove from heat and carefully whisk in butter. The mixture will bubble up. Carefully whisk in cream until smooth. Whisk in salt, vanilla and flour. Pour it into a bowl and let cool and thicken for 30 minutes.

2. Preheat oven to 350°F. Line a 9x9-inch baking pan with parchment paper.

3. For the base, beat butter with both sugars in a large bowl until smooth and a bit fluffy. Mix in cream cheese and vanilla. Combine flour, oats, salt and baking soda in another bowl and then mix it in. Transfer two-thirds of the dough to the prepared pan and press it evenly into the base using lightly floured hands. Bake for 15-20 minutes until golden, then cool for 5 minutes.

4. Spread cooled caramel evenly over the pre-baked base. Scatter chocolate chips evenly over the caramel. Crumble pieces of remaining base dough on top. Bake for 15-20 minutes until the crumble is lightly golden and caramel is bubbling. Transfer pan to a wire rack and let cool completely. Refrigerate for 1 hour before slicing.

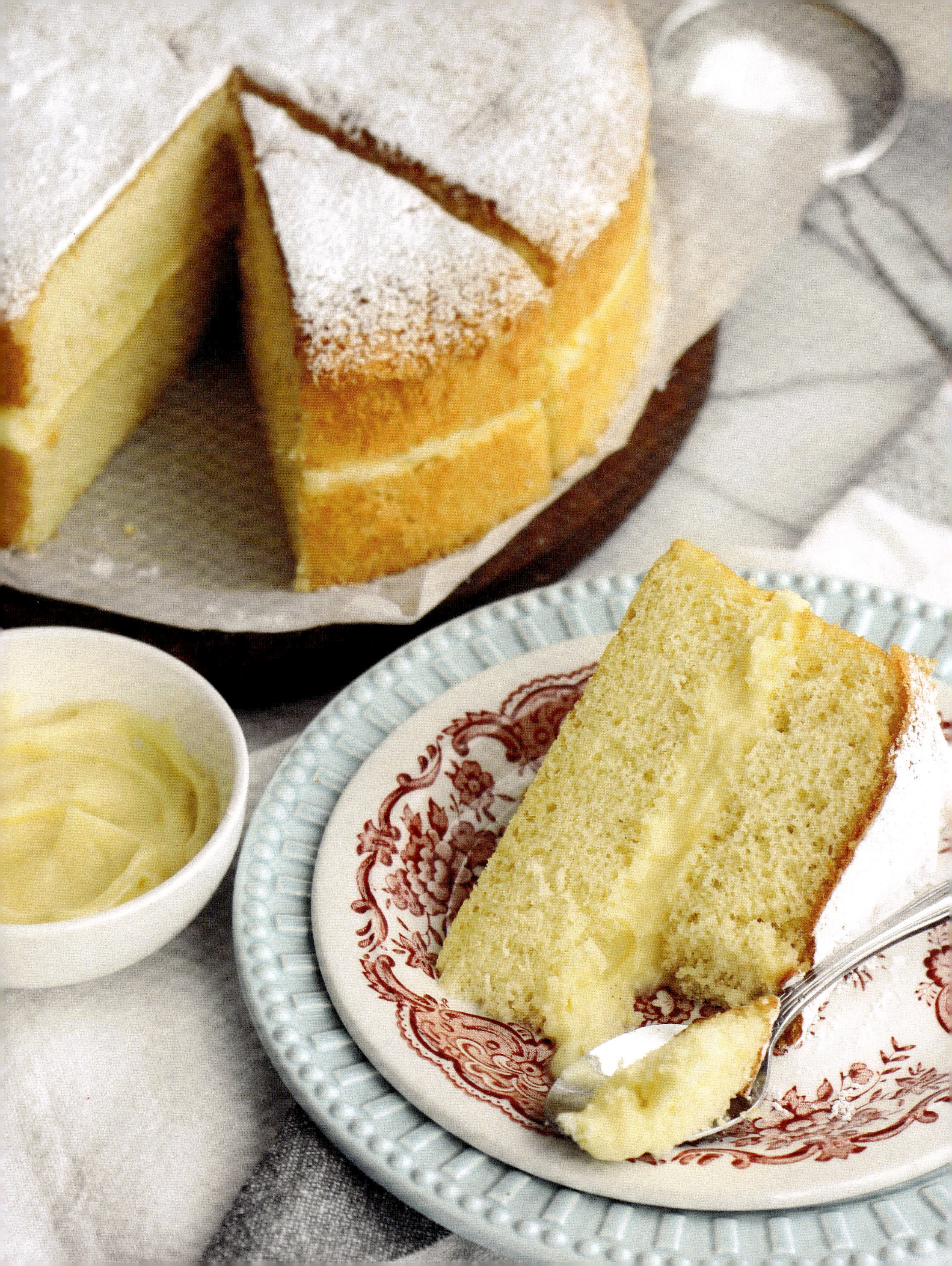

vanilla custard sponge cake

makes 8-10 servings

Pastry Cream filling:

¼ cup (50g) granulated sugar

2 ½ tbsp (20g) cornstarch

1 cup (240ml) whole milk

¼ cup (60ml) 35% whipping cream

3 large egg yolks

1 ½ tbsp (20g) unsalted butter

½ tsp pure vanilla extract

pinch of salt

Sponge cake:

1 cup (142g) all-purpose flour

¾ tsp baking powder

4 large eggs, at room temperature

¾ cup (150g) granulated sugar

¼ tsp salt

3 tbsp (45ml) whole milk

3 tbsp (45ml) sunflower oil

1 tsp (5ml) freshly squeezed lemon juice

1 tsp (5ml) pure vanilla extract

1. For the filling, whisk together sugar and cornstarch in a medium saucepan until evenly blended. Slowly whisk in milk and cream. Whisk in egg yolks. Add butter and cook over medium heat for 5-7 minutes while whisking constantly until it thickens to the consistency of pudding and starts to bubble. Let it bubble for 30 seconds. Remove from heat and stir in vanilla and salt. Strain the pastry cream into a clean bowl through a fine sieve. Cover with plastic wrap directly on the surface and refrigerate for at least 2 hours until thoroughly chilled.

2. Preheat oven to 350°F. Line the base of a high-sided 8x3-inch round cake pan or springform pan with parchment paper. Do not grease the sides.

3. For the sponge, sift flour and baking powder into a medium bowl. Whisk to blend well and set aside.

4. Beat eggs in the bowl of a stand mixer fitted with the whisk attachment on high speed for 2 minutes until very frothy and lightened in color (beat for 4 minutes if using a hand mixer). Add sugar one tablespoon at a time and beat for 5-6 minutes on medium-high speed until pale, thick and tripled in volume. The mixture should be billowy and reach the "ribbon stage" where it will fall back onto itself in folds like a ribbon when lifted with the beaters. Mix in salt.

5. Combine milk, oil, lemon juice and vanilla in a small bowl and slowly pour it into the egg mixture while mixing on medium-low speed until it is blended. Gradually add the sifted dry ingredients while mixing on low just until incorporated, then finish folding the batter by hand, scraping along the bottom of the bowl to evenly combine the ingredients. Try not to knock too much air out. Do not add the dry ingredients all at once since its weight will cause it to sink to the bottom of the bowl and create lumps in the batter.

6. Pour batter into prepared pan and bake for 30-35 minutes until evenly browned and the cake springs back when pressed gently. (You can also divide the batter between two 8x3-inch round cake pans and bake for about 20 minutes). Let cool for 5 minutes, then invert pan and let cool completely upside down on a wire rack. Once cooled, slice it in half horizontally. Beat the chilled pastry cream with a whisk to smooth it out, then spread it between the layers. Dust with icing sugar before serving.

egg free

maple sesame snickerdoodles
makes 20-22 cookies

1 ¼ cups (180g) all-purpose flour
½ tsp baking powder
¼ tsp salt
¼ tsp ground cinnamon
½ cup (113g) unsalted butter, softened
½ cup (100g) granulated sugar
2 tbsp (30ml) pure maple syrup
½ tsp pure vanilla extract
¼ cup (60ml) tahini*, well stirred

For rolling:
⅓ cup (40g) icing sugar
1 tsp ground cinnamon
22 pecan halves for topping

*The consistency of tahini (sesame seed paste) can vary by brand. If yours is very silky smooth and runny, the cookies may spread more whereas if it is more thick and grainy then the cookies will be slightly taller. Either way, they'll be delicious!

1. Preheat oven to 350°F. Line two large baking sheets with parchment paper.

2. Combine flour, baking powder, salt and cinnamon in a medium bowl and whisk to blend evenly.

3. Combine butter with sugar in a medium bowl and beat using an electric hand mixer on medium-high speed for 2 minutes until pale and creamy. Beat in maple syrup and vanilla, then mix in tahini until evenly blended. Add flour mixture and fold it in gently using a spatula until evenly incorporated. Do not over-mix.

4. Roll about 1 tablespoon portions of dough into smooth balls. Stir together icing sugar and cinnamon in a small bowl and then roll dough balls around in this sugar mixture so they are evenly coated. Place onto prepared baking sheets with about 2 inches of space between them.

5. Press a pecan gently into the centre of each dough ball. Bake for 10-12 minutes until they look crackled and lightly browned around the edges. Transfer pans to a wire rack to cool for 5 minutes before transferring cookies individually to the rack to finish cooling.

chocolate chip breton shortbread

makes 8 wedges

2 large egg yolks (plus 1 extra for brushing)

½ tsp pure vanilla extract

⅛ tsp salt*

⅓ cup (65g) granulated sugar

6 tbsp (84g) salted butter, very soft and cut into small pieces

¼ tsp baking powder

¾ cup (105g) all-purpose flour

2 oz (56g) dark chocolate, finely chopped

> *Traditional French "Breton" shortbread is based on high quality salted butter and rich in egg yolks. If you are using unsalted butter, increase the salt in the recipe to ¼ teaspoon.

1. Lightly grease an 8-inch round fluted tart pan with a removable bottom or a springform pan.

2. Add egg yolks, vanilla and salt to a medium bowl and whisk to break them up. Gradually add sugar while whisking and continue to whisk vigorously until pale, thick and fluffy. It will be stiff. Whisk in pieces of soft butter bit by bit until well incorporated, smooth, pale and thick. The mixture will look whipped like buttercream. Mix in baking powder. Sprinkle in flour, add chopped chocolate and fold it in with a spatula until well combined. Scrape mixture into prepared pan and spread it out in an even layer with an offset spatula. Refrigerate for 20 minutes.

3. Preheat oven to 350°F.

4. Beat the extra egg yolk in a small bowl with a fork and then brush it generously over the chilled dough. Make a crisscross design over top using a fork. Bake for 25-30 minutes until very golden brown. Transfer to a wire rack to cool completely and then slice into wedges.

Italian amaretti cookies

makes 20-24 cookies

gluten free

2 large egg whites

⅛ tsp salt

½ tsp pure almond extract

⅔ cup (135g) granulated sugar

1 ¾ cups (175g) fine almond flour or finely ground blanched almonds

icing sugar for dusting

> **Switch Up!** This recipe makes cookies that are crisp on the outside but soft and chewy in the middle. If you prefer them more golden and crisp through-and-through, beat the egg whites further until they form stiff peaks and use just 1 ½ cups (150g) almond flour for a looser mixture. Also, bake the cookies at a lower temperature for a longer time – 325°F for about 25 minutes.

1. Preheat oven to 375°F. Line two large baking sheets with parchment paper.

2. Combine egg whites with salt in a medium bowl and whisk vigorously (or beat with an electric hand mixer) until very frothy, tripled in volume, and they form soft peaks. Add almond extract and then gradually stir in sugar. After adding the sugar, the mixture will become thicker. Add almond flour/ground almonds and fold them in with a spatula. The mixture will resemble a thick sticky paste.

3. Wet your hands slightly to prevent sticking and then roll about 2 teaspoons of the mixture into small balls. If it feels too soft, cover the bowl and refrigerate for about 20 minutes. Place the balls onto prepared baking sheets spacing them 2 inches apart. Flatten them just slightly and dust the tops generously with icing sugar using a fine sieve.

4. Bake for 12-15 minutes until lightly golden and cracked on top, and evenly browned on the bottom. Transfer baking sheets to a wire rack to cool completely then store in an airtight container. They will be crisp on the outside and soft and chewy inside.

chewy coconut macaroons

makes 18-20 macaroons

gluten free

- 2 large egg whites
- 1 large egg
- ½ cup (100g) granulated sugar
- ⅛ tsp salt
- 1 tsp (5ml) honey
- 1 ¾ cups (160g) unsweetened desiccated coconut (or fine shredded coconut)
- ¼ cup (25g) blanched almond flour or ground blanched almonds
- ½ tsp pure vanilla extract
- 4 oz (113g) dark chocolate, finely chopped for dipping & drizzling

1. Combine egg whites, whole egg, sugar, salt, honey, coconut and almond flour in a medium heavy-bottomed saucepan and mix together until well blended. Place pan over medium-low heat on the stovetop and stir constantly for 2-3 minutes until the mixture dries out slightly and feels very thick. Be sure to scrape the bottom as you stir. It will start to ball up and form a film at the bottom of the pan when it is ready. Remove from heat and stir in vanilla extract. Set aside to cool slightly.

2. Preheat oven to 350°F. Line a large baking sheet with parchment paper.

3. Use an ice-cream scoop or two spoons to drop heaped tablespoons in mounds onto the prepared baking sheet spacing them an inch apart. Wet your fingers lightly and tap down any pointed tips or jagged edges. Bake for 14-16 minutes until evenly golden. Transfer pan to a wire rack to cool.

4. Melt the chopped chocolate gently over a double boiler or in short bursts in the microwave. Dip the bottoms of each macaroon in the melted chocolate and then place back onto the baking sheet to set. Use a spoon to drizzle remaining chocolate on top.

tiramisu brownies

makes 16 brownies

Brownie batter:

4 oz (113g) dark chocolate (60-70% cocoa), coarsely chopped

⅓ cup (75g) unsalted butter

1 large egg, at room temperature

1 large egg white (reserve the yolk)

¾ cup (150g) granulated sugar

1 ½ tsp instant espresso powder dissolved in 1 tbsp (15ml) water

1 tsp (5ml) pure vanilla extract

¼ tsp salt

2 tbsp (12g) cocoa powder

½ cup (71g) all-purpose flour

Mascarpone swirl:

⅔ cup (160ml) mascarpone

2 tbsp (25g) granulated sugar

1 large egg yolk

1 tbsp (15ml) brandy or vermouth

1 tbsp (9g) all-purpose flour

1. Preheat oven to 325°F. Line an 8x8-inch baking pan with parchment paper leaving a 2-inch overhang along each side.

2. For the brownie batter, combine chocolate and butter in a medium heatproof bowl set over a saucepan containing ½-inch of simmering water and stir until melted and smooth (or melt in the microwave with short bursts and frequent stirring).

3. Whisk together egg, egg white and sugar in a medium bowl until pale and thickened. Whisk in dissolved espresso, vanilla and salt. Stir in melted chocolate mixture. Sift cocoa and flour over the batter and fold it in gently. Reserve about ½ cup (120ml) of batter and spread the rest into the prepared pan.

4. For the swirl, beat mascarpone with sugar in a medium bowl with a wooden spoon until smooth. Stir in egg yolk, brandy and flour until thick and creamy. Spread it evenly over the brownie batter in the pan. Dollop small spoonfuls of reserved brownie batter randomly over the mascarpone layer and swirl it in using a knife.

5. Bake for 27-30 minutes until puffed and a toothpick inserted into the centre comes out with just a few moist crumbs attached. Let brownies cool completely in the pan and refrigerate for 1 hour before slicing with a hot dry knife. Dust with extra cocoa powder and grated chocolate before serving.

fennel orange & almond biscotti

makes about 24 cookies

1 ⅔ cups (235g) all-purpose flour

½ cup (70g) roasted almonds, finely ground

1 tbsp fennel seeds, lightly crushed

1 tsp baking powder

¼ tsp salt

½ cup (85g) mini dark chocolate chips

2 large eggs, at room temperature

⅔ cup (135g) granulated sugar

3 tbsp (45ml) olive oil

2 tsp finely grated orange zest

1 tsp (5ml) pure vanilla extract

½ tsp pure almond extract

2 tbsp (30ml) cream for brushing

1. Preheat oven to 350°F. Line a large baking sheet with parchment paper.

2. Combine flour, ground almonds, fennel seeds, baking powder, salt and chocolate chips in a medium bowl. Whisk to blend.

3. In the bowl of a stand mixer fitted with the paddle attachment, beat eggs on medium speed until blended. Gradually add sugar and continue to beat for 2-3 minutes on high until pale and thick. Add olive oil, orange zest, vanilla and almond extracts and mix until well combined. Add the flour mixture all at once and mix on low speed just until blended. The dough will be sticky. Cover the bowl and let the dough rest for 5 minutes.

4. Turn dough out onto a lightly floured work surface and bring it together to form a smooth mass, folding it over itself a couple of times. Add a tablespoon or so more flour if necessary to prevent sticking. It will be soft. Divide it in half and roll each half into a 10-inch log and transfer to prepared baking sheet. Flatten logs so they are 2 inches wide. Brush the tops and sides with cream and sprinkle with sugar. Bake for 23-25 minutes until golden brown and puffed.

5. Transfer baking sheet to a wire rack and let biscotti logs cool for 20 minutes. Reduce oven temperature to 300°F. Use a serrated knife to slice diagonally at ½-inch increments. Place cookies back upright onto the baking sheet and bake for 10-15 minutes until dry and crisp.

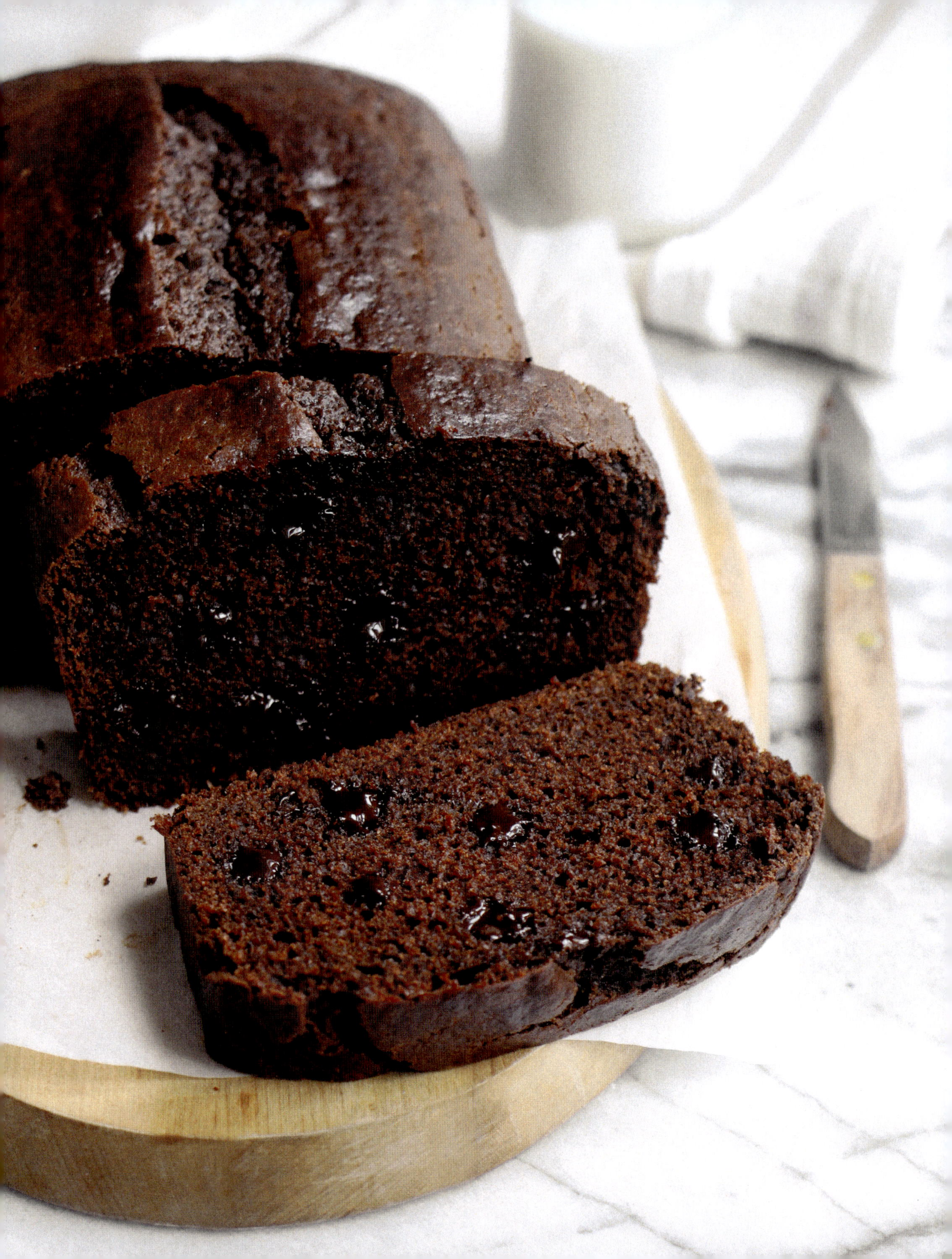

decadent double chocolate loaf cake

makes 8-10 servings

⅔ cup (160ml) sour cream

2 large eggs, at room temperature

1 tsp (5ml) pure vanilla extract

1 tsp espresso powder

½ cup (110g) packed dark brown sugar

½ cup (120ml) sunflower oil*

1 ⅔ cups (235g) all-purpose flour

½ cup plus 1 tbsp (48g) cocoa powder*

2 tsp baking powder

½ tsp baking soda

½ cup (100g) granulated sugar

½ tsp salt

¾ cup (130g) dark chocolate chips

½ cup (120ml) whole milk

1. Preheat oven to 350°F. Line a 9x5-inch loaf pan with parchment paper leaving a 2-inch overhang along the long sides. Grease the exposed short sides with butter.

2. Whisk together sour cream, eggs, vanilla, espresso powder and brown sugar in a medium bowl until sugar is mostly dissolved and there are no lumps. Whisk in oil.

3. Sift flour, cocoa powder, baking powder and baking soda into a large bowl. Add granulated sugar, salt and chocolate chips and whisk to blend evenly.

4. Make a well in the centre of the dry ingredients and pour in sour cream mixture. Gently stir until it starts to blend, but a few streaks remain. Add milk and continue mixing until batter is evenly combined. Pour batter into prepared pan and smooth it out. Bake for 45-55 minutes until a skewer inserted into the centre comes out clean despite any remnants of melted chocolate chips.

5. Transfer pan to a wire rack and let cool for 10 minutes. Run a knife along the short sides to release the loaf, lift it out of the pan and transfer it onto the rack to cool completely before slicing.

*Sunflower oil is best for for its clean flavour, however this recipe will work with any neutral-tasting vegetable oil. Always use fresh oil and store it in a cool dark place away from direct sunlight to prevent it from turning rancid. Try using olive oil for an extra special flavour – it complements the natural fruitiness of cocoa!

I prefer natural cocoa in this recipe for its fruity character and acidity, but the addition of baking powder means that this recipe will also work with alkalized Dutched cocoa too!

single acting *vs* double acting

You use the exact same amount of double-acting baking powder in a recipe as you would single-acting baking powder. The difference lies in their chemical compositions and the rate at which they react and release carbon dioxide gas. They both contain sodium bicarbonate (baking soda), but double-acting baking powder contains two types of acids – fast-acting and slow-acting – and reacts in two stages to express its leavening power. A fast-acting acid reacts immediately in the presence of moisture as it dissolves in liquid batters to form gas bubbles as soon as the ingredients are mixed. A slow-acting acid reacts later during baking since it requires heat to dissolve completely. Double-acting baking powder is the one found most commonly in supermarkets. Single-acting baking powders are mainly used in commercial applications so that leavening power isn't wasted when batters are prepared in advance.

egg free

salted cinnamon butterscotch walnut bars

makes 18 bars

Base:

6 tbsp (84g) unsalted butter, softened
¼ cup (55g) packed light brown sugar
1 tsp (5ml) pure vanilla extract
1 cup (142g) all-purpose flour
¼ tsp ground cinnamon
¼ tsp salt

Butterscotch topping:

½ cup (110g) packed light brown sugar
⅓ cup (80ml) 35% whipping cream
3 tbsp (42g) unsalted butter, cut into pieces
2 tbsp (30ml) honey
½ tsp pure vanilla extract
¼ tsp salt
1 cup (120g) roughly chopped walnuts

1. Preheat oven to 350°F. Line an 8x8-inch pan with aluminum foil, letting it extend over the edges of the pan. Lightly butter the foil.

2. For the base, beat butter with brown sugar and vanilla in a medium bowl using a spatula until pale and fluffy. Add flour, cinnamon and salt and stir it in until combined. The mixture will feel a bit dry and crumbly – use your fingertips to blend the ingredients. Tip the mixture into your prepared pan and then pat and press it in an even layer, pushing it up the sides slightly to form an edge crust. Run the back of a spoon back and forth over the surface to smooth it out. Bake for 14-16 minutes until evenly golden and slightly firm to the touch. Transfer to a wire rack to cool and reduce oven temperature to 325°F.

3. For the topping, combine brown sugar, cream, butter and honey in a medium saucepan over medium heat and stir constantly until butter is completely melted and the mixture starts bubbling. Bring it to a full boil for 3 minutes. Remove from heat. Stir in vanilla, salt and chopped walnuts.

4. Pour mixture over cooled crust and spread it out so the nuts are evenly distributed. Bake for 15 minutes until bubbling and the edges are a deep caramel colour. The centre will sill look runny when you pull it from the oven but it will set as it cools. If it over-cooks it can actually set into hard candy around the edges and be very difficult to slice, so err on the side of under-baking. Transfer pan to a wire rack and let cool completely, then refrigerate for 2 hours before slicing.

This topping recipe makes delicious butterscotch sauce. Follow step 3, except do not add the nuts. Pour it into a heatproof jar, seal and let cool at room temperature before storing in the fridge.

chunky brown butter chocolate chip cookies

makes 18-20 cookies

½ cup (113g) unsalted butter
½ cup (110g) packed dark brown sugar
¼ cup (50g) granulated sugar
1 tbsp (15ml) whole milk
1 tsp (5ml) pure vanilla extract
1 large egg

½ tsp baking soda
½ tsp salt
1 ¼ cups (180g) all-purpose flour
1 cup (142g) dark chocolate chunks

For extra thick cookies, refrigerate the dough for 40 minutes before baking.

1. Preheat oven to 350°F. Line two large baking sheets with parchment paper.

2. Place butter in a saucepan over medium heat until melted and then continue to cook while stirring occasionally until butter begins to bubble and crackle as the moisture boils off. Keep cooking with frequent stirring until it turns a deep golden color. A dense foam will form at the surface when it is nearly ready and brown flecks will come up through the foam as you stir. Pour it into a large mixing bowl, then place in the freezer for 15-20 minutes until cool and set to a firm yet pliable consistency (not hard).

3. Preheat oven to 350°F. Line two large baking sheets with parchment paper.

4. Add both sugars, milk and vanilla to the soft brown butter and beat with a spatula (or use a hand mixer) for 1-2 minutes until a bit fluffy. Beat in egg until incorporated and creamy smooth. Mix in baking soda and salt. Add flour and fold it in until mostly incorporated. Add chocolate chunks and fold them in evenly.

5. Roll heaped tablespoons of dough into balls and place onto prepared baking trays spacing them 2 inches apart. Flatten dough balls slightly and bake for 8-10 minutes until golden brown and soft in the centre. Transfer cookies to a wire rack to cool.

gluten free

toasted coconut truffle tartlets

makes 24 tartlets

1 x Chewy Coconut Macaroons (page 167)

6 oz (170g) dark chocolate, chopped

½ cup (120ml) 35% whipping cream

1. Make the macaroon mixture and press about 1 tablespoon into well-greased cups of a 24-cup mini muffin pan using wetted fingers to push it up the sides. Bake for 10-15 minutes at 325°F until evenly browned. Let cool. Slide a sharp knife around each cup to loosen and then pop them out carefully with a spoon.

2. For the filling, heat cream in a saucepan until it simmers and pour it over chocolate in a bowl. Stir until glossy and smooth. Spoon it into tart shells and let set. Top with coconut.

florentine lace cookies

egg free

makes about 24 cookies

1. To make traditional lace cookies, follow the recipe for Florentine Medallions on page 62 and chop all of the sliced almonds so they distribute better throughout the batter.

2. Spoon 2 level teaspoons of batter onto parchment or silicone-lined baking sheets leaving at least 4 inches of space between them. They will spread a lot. Bake for 10-14 minutes until evenly browned and bubbling around the edges. Transfer pans to a wire rack to cool completely – they will harden as they cool.

3. Spread chocolate lightly over the back side of each lace cookie. Transfer to a baking sheet lined with waxed paper until chocolate sets and hardens.

brown butter pecan cookies

makes 28-30 cookies

⅔ cup (150g) unsalted butter, browned (that's 125g brown butter)

½ cup (110g) packed dark brown sugar

¼ cup (50g) granulated sugar

1 large egg, at room temperature

1 tsp (5ml) pure vanilla extract

1 ¼ cups (180g) all-purpose flour

½ tsp baking soda

½ tsp salt

1 cup (120g) coarsely chopped pecans

3 oz (100g) white chocolate for drizzling (optional)

HOW TO MAKE BROWN BUTTER

Place butter in a small saucepan over medium heat and stir until completely melted. Allow butter to come to a boil and then continue to cook while stirring occasionally while it bubbles and crackles as the moisture boils off. Keep cooking with frequent stirring until it reaches a deep golden colour. It will progress from golden yellow to tan and finally, brown. The crackling noises will fade, the bubbles will subside and a dense foam will form at the surface as the last bit of water squeezes out. Stir constantly until you see brown flecks come up through the foam. The whole process takes around 8-10 minutes. Immediately pour it into a large mixing bowl, then place it in the freezer for about 10 minutes until cool and thick. It should be cool enough that it is opaque and firm, but not hard. If you freeze it for too long, just leave it at room temperature for 10-20 minutes until it softens up.

1. Beat cooled brown butter in a large bowl with an electric hand mixer on high speed until smooth, pale and creamy. It may take a few minutes if the butter has hardened too much (i.e. if you forgot about it in the freezer!). Add both sugars and beat for about 2 minutes until pale and fluffy. Beat in egg and vanilla until well incorporated. Combine flour, baking soda and salt in a medium bowl and whisk to blend evenly. Add it to the butter mixture. Mix on low until incorporated and then fold in chopped pecans. The dough will be soft. Place it onto a large piece of plastic wrap or parchment paper and roll it into a 12-inch log. Wrap well and refrigerate for about 1 hour or until firm.

2. Preheat oven to 350°F. Line two large baking sheets with parchment paper.

3. Use a sharp knife to slice the chilled cookie dough log into rounds with just under ½-inch thickness and place them onto prepared baking sheets spacing them about 2 inches apart. If the dough is too hard, let it rest at room temperature for 10 minutes before slicing. Bake for 8-10 minutes until golden brown. Transfer baking sheets to a wire rack to cool completely, then drizzle with melted white chocolate if desired. Let chocolate set before storing in an airtight container.

toasted coconut & dark chocolate chunk brown butter blondies

makes 16 squares

½ cup (45g) medium unsweetened shredded coconut

½ cup (113g) unsalted butter

⅔ cup (145g) packed light brown sugar

¼ cup (50g) granulated sugar

1 tbsp (15ml) whole milk

1 tsp (5ml) pure vanilla extract

1 large egg, at room temperature

½ tsp salt

½ tsp baking powder

1 cup (142g) all-purpose flour

3 oz (85g) bittersweet chocolate, coarsely chopped (or ½ cup of dark chocolate chips)

1. Preheat oven to 350°F. Line an 8x8-inch pan with parchment paper leaving a 2-inch overhang at each side. Spread coconut in an even layer on a baking sheet and place it in the oven while it preheats. Check after about 7 minutes and remove it once it turns golden and smells nutty. Transfer coconut to a bowl.

2. To brown the butter, place it in a small saucepan over medium-low heat and stir until completely melted. Increase heat slightly and let it come to a boil, stirring constantly. It will bubble and crackle as water evaporates. Continue to cook while stirring frequently until the crackling noises begin to fade and the bubbles subside. A dense golden foam will form at the surface as the last bit of water squeezes out and the colour will progress from golden yellow to brown. This takes around 8-10 minutes. Once you smell that nutty aroma and begin to see little brown bits as you stir, take the pan off the heat and immediately pour the brown butter into a large heatproof bowl.

3. Add both sugars to the brown butter and whisk vigorously until combined. Mix in milk and vanilla until creamy. Beat in egg until blended and the mixture is smooth and glossy. Mix in salt and baking powder. Add flour and stir it in until mostly combined before folding in the chocolate chunks and toasted coconut. The batter will be thick.

4. Spread the mixture evenly into the prepared pan. and bake for 22-25 minutes until the top is golden, puffed and shiny. It should still feel slightly soft in the middle. Transfer pan to a wire rack to cool completely before cutting into squares.

silky dark chocolate truffles

gluten free · egg free

makes about 36 truffles

⅔ cup (160ml) 35% whipping cream

½ tsp espresso powder (optional)

8 oz (227g) semi-sweet or dark chocolate (50-60% cocoa), finely chopped

1. Heat cream with espresso powder (if using it) in a small saucepan over medium heat until it just comes to a simmer. Remove from the heat, add chopped chocolate, cover and let stand undisturbed for 2 minutes. Then, stir gently until silky, smooth and glossy.

2. Pour it into a bowl and let it cool for 1 hour then cover and refrigerate until firm. Scoop up teaspoonfuls, roll into smooth balls and then roll in cocoa powder to coat evenly.

orange sables (butter cookies)

makes 20-25 cookies

1. Preheat oven to 350°F. Line 2 large baking sheets with parchment paper.

2. Follow the pastry recipe for Crostata Marmellata on page 154, except instead of using 1 whole egg plus 1 egg yolk, use 2 egg yolks mixed with 1 tbsp (15ml) milk. Blend the yolks, milk and vanilla in a small bowl before adding to the dry ingredients. Mix and shape the dough as directed. Wrap well and refrigerate for 2 hours.

3. Roll the chilled dough out to ⅛-inch thickness. Cut out shapes with 1 to 2-inch diameter and place onto prepared trays. Brush with cream and sprinkle with sugar. Bake for 14-18 minutes (depending on size), until golden brown. Once cool, spread caramel or jam between two cookies.

sticky salted caramel date cakes

makes about 18 cakes

Cakes:

1 ½ cups (200g) chopped pitted dates

1 ¼ cups (300ml) water

7 tbsp (100g) unsalted butter

⅔ cup (145g) packed light brown sugar

2 tbsp (30ml) honey

1 tsp (5ml) pure vanilla extract

2 large eggs, at room temperature

1 ½ cups (215g) all-purpose flour

1 tsp baking powder

½ tsp baking soda

½ tsp salt

½ tsp ground cinnamon

¼ tsp ground ginger

⅛ tsp ground nutmeg

Caramel sauce:

⅓ cup (80ml) 35% whipping cream

¾ cup (150g) granulated sugar

2 tbsp (28g) unsalted butter

½ tsp pure vanilla extract

¼ tsp salt

Switch Up! You can divide this batter between two 8x4-inch loaf pans and bake for 30-35 minutes to make two mini loaves. You can also make the caramel sauce up to 2 weeks in advance and reheat it gently before glazing the cakes.

1. For the cakes, combine chopped dates and water in a medium saucepan over medium-high heat and bring to a boil. Once boiling, reduce heat, cover and simmer for 10 minutes until very soft. Mash until dates absorb the liquid and it resembles applesauce. It should measure out to about 1 ½ (355ml) cups. Set it aside to cool slightly for at least 10 minutes so that it is still warm but not hot.

2. Preheat oven to 350°F. Line 18 cups of two standard 12-cup muffin pans with paper liners or grease the pan well with butter if not using liners.

3. Beat butter with brown sugar, honey and vanilla in the bowl of a stand mixer fitted with the paddle attachment for 2-3 minutes on medium-high speed until pale and fluffy (or in a large bowl if using an electric hand mixer). Add eggs one at a time and beat well after each addition until each egg is well incorporated. Beat on high to smooth out the mixture so it starts to look creamy and pale. It may look slightly curdled in spots but that's ok because it will come together once the dry ingredients are added.

4. Whisk together flour, baking powder, baking soda, salt and spices in a medium bowl, then gradually add it to the wet ingredients while mixing on low speed until just combined. Fold in warm date mixture using a spatula until evenly incorporated and smooth.

5. Spoon batter into prepared pan, dividing it evenly among paper cups and filling them about three-quarters full. Bake for 15-18 minutes until a skewer inserted into the centre comes out clean and the cakes spring back when pressed gently. Transfer pan to a wire rack and let cakes cool slightly while you make the sauce. If not using paper liners, run a knife around the sides of the cakes to release them from the muffin pan.

6. For the caramel, first heat the cream in the microwave or in a saucepan over medium heat until it is hot, but do not let it boil.

7. Add sugar in an even layer in the base of a 1 or 2-quart heavy-bottomed stainless steel saucepan over medium-high heat. Make sure there are no lumps. Let the sugar melt. As you see the crystals around the edge of the pan melt and liquefy, use a wooden spoon to push sugar from the edges to the centre and then push the unmelted sugar from the centre out to the sides to help it melt evenly. Continue to move the sugar like this until it begins to turn golden and liquefy. It will clump up and look dry before it liquefies, but trust that it will. Continue to cook until it all melts into a liquid and turns into a clear amber syrup. Remove from heat and whisk in butter. Gradually add hot cream while whisking until smooth, being careful as it will bubble up vigorously. Stir in vanilla and salt to create a smooth sauce.

8. Poke holes liberally into each cake using a skewer and then spoon warm caramel sauce over each cake. Serve with extra sauce.

homemade ladyfinger biscuits

makes about 32 cookies

3 large eggs

½ cup plus 2 tbsp (125g) granulated sugar

⅛ tsp salt

1 tsp (5ml) pure vanilla extract

1 cup (142g) all-purpose flour, sifted

raw or coarse sugar for sprinkling

icing sugar for dusting

1. Preheat oven to 375°F. Line two large baking sheets with parchment paper.

2. Whisk together eggs, sugar and salt in a heatproof bowl or the bowl of a stand mixer and set it over a saucepan of simmering water. Continue whisking constantly for 2-3 minutes until the mixture thickens, feels very warm to the touch and the sugar feels dissolved when you rub it between your fingers. If you are measuring, it should reach 150°F on an instant-read thermometer.

3. Transfer mixture to the bowl of a stand mixer fitted with the whisk attachment and beat on medium-high speed for 4-5 minutes until pale, thick, creamy and nearly tripled in volume. If using a hand mixer, you will need to beat for closer to 7 minutes. Mix in vanilla.

4. Sift flour over the egg mixture and fold it in gently until evenly combined.

5. Fit a piping bag with a large open plain (round) tip and fill it with batter. Pipe rows of batter roughly 4 inches long, 1 inch wide and ½-inch high. Leave plenty of space between each one.

6. Sprinkle piped batter with coarse sugar and then sift icing sugar over top. Bake for 9-12 minutes until cookies are golden, puffed and dry to the touch.

7. Transfer baking sheets to a wire rack and let cookies cool completely on the trays before removing carefully. Transfer to an airtight container and use them to make Classic Tiramisu (page 203) or store for up to 2 weeks.

maple pecan millionaire's shortbread

makes 12-16 bars

Base:

½ cup (113g) unsalted butter, softened

¼ cup (55g) packed light brown sugar

⅛ tsp salt

1 tsp (5ml) pure vanilla extract

1 cup (142g) all-purpose flour

¼ cup (22g) desiccated coconut

Filling:

1 ¼ cups (1 x 300ml can) sweetened condensed milk

2 tbsp (30ml) maple syrup

1 tbsp (14g) unsalted butter

1 tsp (5ml) fancy (light) molasses

½ tsp pure vanilla extract

¼ tsp salt

⅓ cup (40g) chopped roasted pecans

Topping:

4 oz (113g) dark chocolate, chopped

1 tsp (5ml) olive oil

1. Preheat oven to 350°F. Line an 8x8-inch baking pan with parchment paper.

2. For the base, beat butter, brown sugar and salt in a large bowl using a wooden spoon until pale and fluffy. Mix in vanilla. Sprinkle in flour and coconut and fold it through until a soft dough forms. Use floured hands to pat and press it down evenly into prepared pan. Run the back of a spoon over the surface to smooth it out. Bake for 16-18 minutes until evenly golden on top.

3. Meanwhile, make the filling. Combine condensed milk, maple syrup and butter in a small saucepan over medium heat. Cook while stirring constantly for 8-12 minutes until golden and thickened like pudding or molten fudge. Do not walk away – the condensed milk burns easily and you will feel it catch to the bottom of the pan as you stir, so don't stop! Stir in molasses, vanilla, salt and pecans. Pour it over the warm crust and bake again for 10-12 minutes until the caramel starts to bubble and turns golden. Transfer to a wire rack to cool completely, then refrigerate for 3-4 hours until set.

4. For the topping, melt chocolate gently in a heatproof bowl set over a saucepan with ½-inch of simmering water (or melt gently in the microwave). Stir in olive oil until smooth and glossy. Pour it over the chilled bars and tilt the pan around so it spreads out evenly. Sprinkle with toasted coconut if desired and refrigerate until set. Slice into bars using a hot dry knife.

raspberry swirl cheesecake brownies, page 184

date NIGHT

So… this chapter is mostly chocolate! I mean, what better way to show how much you love someone than showering them with chocolate? The recipes that follow are rich, creamy, silky and smooth. Most of the desserts look fancy, but they're simple to execute which is what makes them so impressive! Read right to the end to learn the simplest technique for tempering chocolate, and the "Cheat's" Opera Cake is a must-make!

raspberry swirl cheesecake brownies

makes 16 brownies

Brownie batter:

4 oz (113g) bittersweet chocolate (70% cocoa), coarsely chopped

⅓ cup (75g) unsalted butter

2 large eggs, at room temperature

¾ cup (150g) granulated sugar

½ tsp pure vanilla extract

¼ tsp salt

⅓ cup (50g) all-purpose flour

Cheesecake:

1 block (250g) cream cheese, softened

¼ cup (50g) granulated sugar

1 tsp (5ml) pure vanilla extract

1 large egg, at room temperature

Rasberry swirl:

1 cup (120g) fresh or frozen raspberries (slightly thawed)

1 tbsp (12g) granulated sugar

1 tsp (3g) corn starch

1 oz (28g) dark chocolate, coarsely chopped for topping

> **Switch Up!** Use blueberries, blackberries or diced strawberries in place of raspberries for making the swirl to make the most of whichever fruit is in season! If you're in a pinch, you can also use ⅓ cup (80ml) of your favourite jam and stir in 1 teaspoon of corn starch before swirling it into the batter.

1. Preheat oven to 350°F. Line an 8x8 or 9x9-inch baking pan with parchment paper leaving a 2-inch overhang along each side.

2. For the brownie batter, combine chocolate and butter in a saucepan over very low heat and stir constantly until melted and smooth, or melt in the microwave at medium power in short 30 second bursts with frequent stirring.

3. Combine eggs, sugar, vanilla and salt in a large bowl and whisk or beat with an electric hand mixer until pale and thick. Beat in warm melted chocolate mixture. Sprinkle flour over the surface and fold it in. Reserve about ¼ cup (60ml) of brownie batter and then spread the rest evenly into prepared pan.

4. For the cheesecake, beat cream cheese in a medium bowl with an electric hand mixer or spatula until smooth. Add sugar and vanilla and beat until glossy. Beat in egg until well incorporated. Spread it evenly over the brownie batter in the pan, then spoon teaspoons of reserved brownie batter randomly over top.

5. For the raspberry swirl, combine raspberries, sugar and corn starch in a small bowl and mash it roughly with a fork leaving it a bit chunky. Spoon teaspoons of raspberry mixture over the batter in the pan and then use a skewer to swirl all of the flavours together.

6. Sprinkle chopped dark chocolate pieces over top and bake for 30-35 minutes until puffed and the cheesecake is set in the middle with lightly golden edges. Transfer pan to a wire rack and let cool completely in the pan. Refrigerate for at least 1 hour before slicing with a hot dry knife.

gluten free · *no bake*

frozen chocolate custard cake

makes 9 servings

Base:
- 1 cup (100g) rolled oats
- ⅓ cup (45g) roasted cashews
- 2 tbsp (30g) packed dark brown sugar
- 2 tbsp (28g) salted butter, melted
- 2 tbsp (30ml) natural nut butter (any variety)

> For the chocolate sauce, combine ¼ cup (60ml) 35% whipping cream, 1 tbsp (15g) brown sugar and 1 ½ oz (42g) chopped dark chocolate in a small saucepan. Whisk over low heat until smooth and glossy.

Mousse:
- 3 large egg yolks
- ⅓ cup (65g) granulated sugar
- ½ cup (120ml) whole milk
- 2 ½ oz (70g) bittersweet chocolate (70% cocoa), chopped
- 2 oz (56g) milk chocolate, chopped
- 1 cup (237ml) 35% whipping cream

1. For the base, spread oats in a dry frying pan over medium heat and toast until very lightly golden and smells nutty, about 6-8 minutes. Shake the pan frequently to prevent burning. Transfer to the bowl of a food processor and pulse until finely ground. Add cashews and brown sugar and process until fine. Add melted butter and nut butter and pulse until it clumps together. Press it evenly into a thin layer in an 8x8-inch pan lined with aluminum foil.

2. For the mousse, beat egg yolks with sugar in a medium bowl using a hand mixer (or a whisk) for 2-3 minutes until pale and very thick. Heat milk in a small saucepan over medium heat until it just simmers and then gradually whisk it into the egg yolk mixture. Pour the mixture back into the saucepan and cook gently over low heat for 3-5 minutes until thickened, stirring constantly. It should coat the back of a spoon like thick cream. Remove from heat. Place both types of chocolate into a medium bowl and pour the warm custard over it. Stir gently until chocolate is melted and the mixture is smooth. Set aside to cool for about 10 minutes.

3. Whip cream to soft peaks and gently fold it into the cooled chocolate custard. Spoon it over the oat base in the pan and spread it out evenly. Freeze for about 4 hours until set and then let soften for 10 minutes before serving.

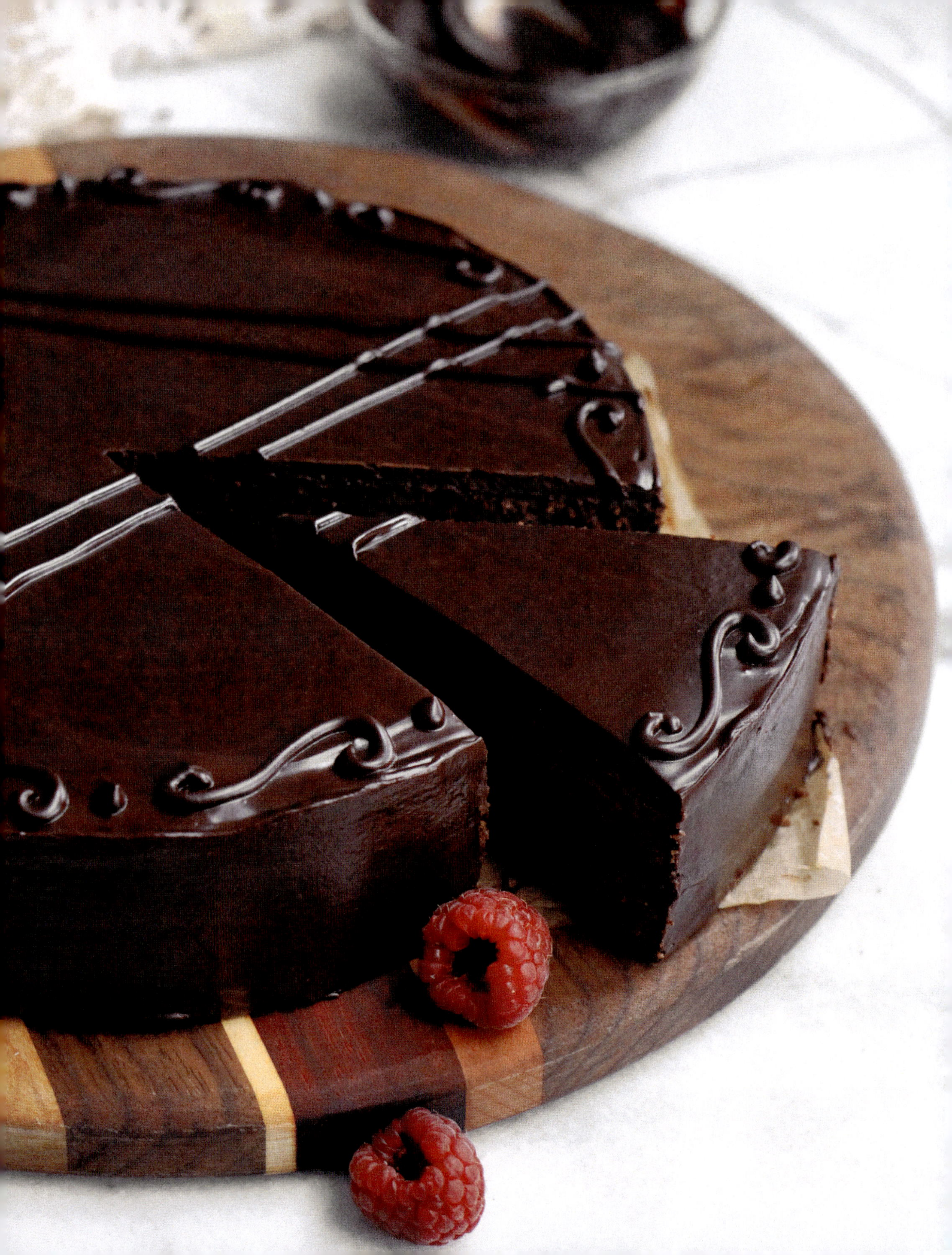

raspberry sachertorte

makes 8-10 servings

Cake:

4 oz (113g) dark chocolate (60-65% cocoa), coarsely chopped

½ cup (71g) all-purpose flour

½ cup (50g) blanched almond flour

¼ tsp salt

4 large eggs, separated

⅔ cup plus 3 tbsp (175g) granulated sugar, divided

½ cup (113g) unsalted butter, softened

1 tsp (5ml) pure vanilla extract

Icing & Filling:

⅓ cup (80ml) water

2 tbsp (28g) unsalted butter

1 tbsp (15ml) honey

6 oz (170g) dark chocolate (60% cocoa), finely chopped

½ cup (120ml) raspberry jam

1. Preheat oven to 350°F. Lightly butter a deep 8-inch round cake pan or springform pan. Line the base with parchment paper.

2. For the cake, gently melt chocolate in a heatproof bowl set over a saucepan with ½-inch of simmering water. Let cool.

3. Sift flour into a medium bowl. Whisk in almond flour and salt until evenly blended.

4. Beat egg whites until very frothy on high speed in the bowl of a stand mixer fitted with the whisk attachment (or in a large bowl using an electric hand mixer). Gradually beat in remaining 3 tablespoons (40g) of sugar one tablespoon at a time and continue to whip until soft peaks form, then set aside.

5. Beat butter with vanilla in a large bowl using a spatula or the mixer until very soft and creamy. Gradually beat in ⅔ cup (135g) sugar until pale and fluffy. Beat in egg yolks one at a time. Mix in melted chocolate, then fold in the flour mixture. It will be quite thick at this point. Add about one-third of the whipped meringue and mix it in vigorously to combine evenly and loosen the mixture. Gently fold in remaining meringue in two parts until evenly incorporated with no streaks remaining. Spread batter into prepared pan and smooth out the surface.

6. Bake for 35-40 minutes until puffed and slightly cracked at the surface. It will feel firm to the touch. Transfer pan to a wire rack and let cool for 10 minutes, then invert onto the rack to finish cooling. It will deflate a bit so you will have a nice even layer.

7. For the icing, bring water, butter and honey to a boil in a small saucepan over medium heat. Remove from heat and add chocolate. Let stand for 2 minutes and then whisk until smooth. Refrigerate until thick, but still pourable, stirring every few minutes.

8. Slice the cooled cake in half horizontally. Spread raspberry jam over the bottom half and replace the top half. Spoon a couple tablespoons of icing into a small piping bag for decorating later. Pour half of the remaining icing onto the centre of the cake. Spread it out quickly over the top and down the sides. Pour the rest of the icing over top, spreading it out to the edges to drape the sides. Working quickly will ensure that it stays smooth and shiny. Let the icing set for about 30 minutes, then snip off the tip of the filled icing bag and pipe 'Sacher' across the top. This cake is best stored and served at room temperature for up to 4 days.

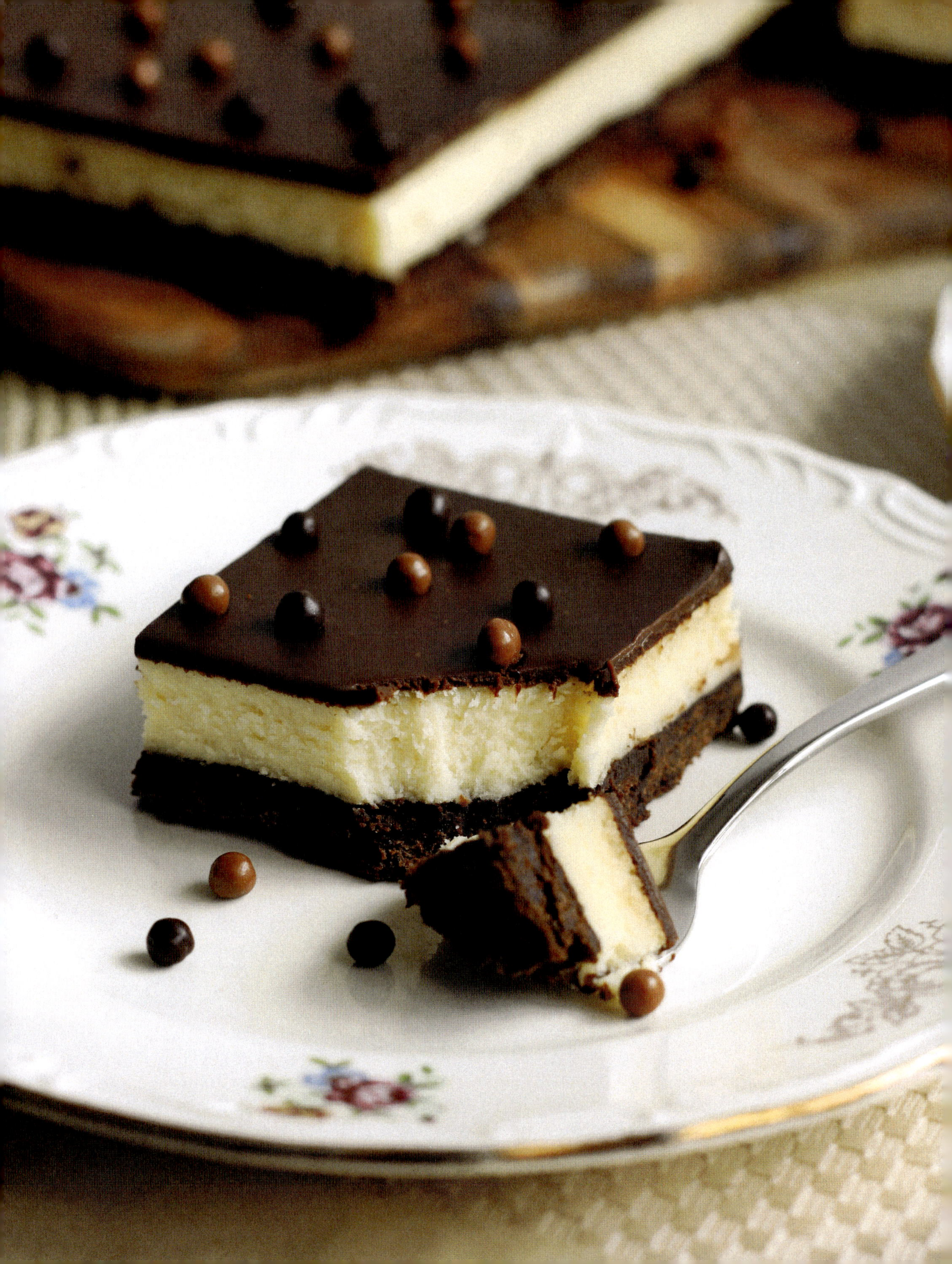

tuxedo cheesecake bars

makes 12-16 squares

Base:
⅔ cup (95g) all-purpose flour

¼ cup (21g) cocoa powder

⅓ cup (70g) packed light brown sugar

¼ tsp salt

¼ cup (56g) unsalted butter, melted

Filling:
1 block (250g) cream cheese, softened

¼ cup (50g) granulated sugar

1 large egg, at room temperature

1 tsp (5ml) pure vanilla extract

¼ cup (60ml) sour cream

3 ½ oz (100g) pure white chocolate, melted

Glaze:
¼ cup (60ml) 35% whipping cream

2 tsp (10ml) honey

pinch of salt

3 oz (85g) bittersweet chocolate (70% cocoa), finely chopped

3 tsp (15ml) warm water

Switch Up! These are called "Tuxedo" for the obvious reason of the black and white contrast and also for how sophisticated the finished dessert looks! Try replacing white chocolate with milk or dark chocolate in the filling for the hardcore chocoholic in your life.

---

1. Preheat oven to 350°F. Line an 8x8-inch baking pan with parchment paper or aluminum foil leaving a 2-inch overhang along each side.

2. For the base, combine flour, cocoa powder, brown sugar and salt in a medium bowl and mix to blend evenly, pressing out any lumps of brown sugar. Add melted butter and stir to combine. Use your fingertips to evenly blend the mixture until it forms damp crumbs. Turn it out into prepared pan and press it down in an even layer using your hands. Run the back of a spoon back and forth over the surface to smooth it out. Bake for 10-14 minutes until slightly puffed and feels somewhat dry. Transfer to a wire rack to cool. Reduce oven temperature to 300°F.

3. For the filling, beat cream cheese in a medium bowl until smooth. Add sugar and beat until very silky and glossy. Beat in egg until well combined, then mix in vanilla and sour cream. Stir in melted white chocolate. Pour the cheesecake mixture over the pre-baked crust and bake for 25-30 minutes until set around the edges with just the slightest wobble in the centre. Transfer to a wire rack to cool completely and then refrigerate for at least 2 hours.

4. For the glaze, combine cream, honey and salt in a small saucepan over medium heat and bring to a simmer. Remove from heat and add chopped chocolate. Cover and let stand for a minute to let the cream gently melt the chocolate, then gently whisk until smooth and glossy. Stir in warm water one teaspoon at a time. Pour the glaze over chilled cheesecake and spread it out evenly. Refrigerate until set before decorating with chocolate pearls or sprinkles. Slice with a hot dry knife.

These truffles are an absolute dream! Although using a thermometer is the most accurate way to judge the caramel consistency, I almost always make these without it and use the old-fashioned "cold water test" to judge. Firm Ball Stage refers to the point when the caramel can be formed into a pliable yet firm ball once cooled in cold water. It should not be sticky, but also not hard. The right stage of cooking means that the finished candy will set up with a firm yet chewy consistency!

dark chocolate sea salt caramels

makes about 36 pieces

gluten free · egg free

Caramel:

⅓ cup (80ml) 35% whipping cream

3 tbsp (45ml) water

1 tsp (5ml) honey

1 cup (200g) granulated sugar

3 tbsp (42g) salted butter

¾ tsp salt

½ tsp pure vanilla extract

Ganache:

⅓ cup (80ml) 35% whipping cream

½ tsp espresso powder (optional)

4 ¼ oz (120g) dark chocolate (55-65% cocoa), finely chopped

Coating:

8 oz (227g) dark chocolate

sea salt flakes for sprinkling

1. Line a 9x5-inch loaf pan with parchment paper leaving a 2-inch overhang at each side and lightly butter the parchment.

2. First have a glass of ice cold water ready to do the "cold water" test to check the doneness of your caramel. Heat cream in the microwave or over the stove until hot, but not boiling, then set it aside until needed.

3. For the caramel, add water and honey to a high-sided 1 or 2-quart saucepan and pour sugar over the water in an even layer. Place over medium heat and bring to a boil without stirring. Increase heat slightly and let the syrup bubble away for about 10-12 minutes until it turns to a rich amber colour, swirling the pan occasionally to cook evenly. It will progress from a clear syrup to a golden/amber colour to copper. Remove pan from heat and very carefully whisk in cream. The mixture will bubble up vigorously so stand back. Whisk in butter one tablespoon at a time. Place the saucepan back over medium heat and bring to a boil. Continue to boil gently for 2 minutes while stirring constantly. Check for firm ball stage: working quickly, drop a small spoonful of syrup into a glass of ice cold water, wait a second and then roll it between your fingers – it should form a firm and stable yet pliable ball of caramel. If it is still too soft and doesn't form a ball, boil for another 30-60 seconds and check again. If using a candy thermometer, it should reach 246°F. Remove from heat and whisk in salt and vanilla. Pour caramel into prepared pan without scraping the bottom and let cool for 2 hours until firm.

4. For the ganache layer, heat cream with espresso powder (if you're using it) in a small saucepan over medium heat or in the microwave in a heatproof bowl or jug until it just comes to a boil. Remove from heat and add chopped chocolate. Cover and let stand for 2 minutes, then stir gently until smooth and glossy. Pour it over the caramel layer and spread it out evenly. Refrigerate for 1-2 hours until firm.

5. Lift the slab out of the pan and place it on a cutting board. Cut it into small squares or rectangles. I slice it widthwise into 9 strips and then cut each strip into 4 pieces. Place each caramel onto a parchment-lined tray and refrigerate while you melt or temper the chocolate for coating. If the ganache layer slips off of the caramels, just move it back in alignment. When ready to coat, dip each piece into tempered chocolate (see page 205 for tempering techniques), then transfer coated caramels back to the tray. Sprinkle sea salt flakes on top and let set completely.

sour cream & honey chocolate cake

makes 8-10 servings

⅓ cup (75g) unsalted butter

2 oz (56g) unsweetened chocolate, coarsely chopped

¼ cup (60ml) honey

1 cup (142g) all-purpose flour

⅓ cup (28g) cocoa powder

1 tsp baking soda

1 cup (200g) granulated sugar

½ tsp salt

2 large eggs, at room temperature

½ cup (120ml) sour cream

½ cup (120ml) whole milk

1 tsp (5ml) pure vanilla extract

Switch Up! Try baking in a bundt pan! The sturdy cake crumb will hold up to the intricate shape.

1. Preheat oven to 350°F. Lightly grease a high-sided 8-inch round cake pan or springform pan and line the base with parchment paper.

2. Combine butter, chocolate and honey in a small saucepan over low heat and stir constantly until smooth. Set aside.

3. Sift flour, cocoa and baking soda into a large bowl. Add sugar and salt and whisk to blend evenly. Add eggs, sour cream, milk and vanilla. Begin whisking to start blending with the dry ingredients – it will be a bit dry at first – then add the chocolate mixture and continue whisking until the batter is smooth. Do not over-mix.

4. Pour batter into prepared pan and spread it out evenly. Bake for 40-45 minutes until a skewer inserted into the centre comes out clean. It will sink slightly in the centre. Transfer pan to a wire rack to cool for 15 minutes, then run a knife around the sides and invert the cake onto the rack to continue cooling.

5. Serve warm or at room temperature with softly whipped cream and a generous dusting of cocoa powder.

butter cake vs sponge cake

Butter cakes, also known as shortened cakes, are typically made with butter as the primary fat. Their relatively high fat content compared to foam cakes 'shortens' the texture by weakening the gluten protein network. This gives them a soft, delicate melt-in-your mouth texture, fine crumb and rich flavour; however, they can be slightly dense. Most butter cakes depend on chemical leavening agents, such as baking powder and baking soda, for their height and lightness. Sponge cakes, including Génoise and Chiffon, have a high proportion of eggs compared to flour. The texture of these light and simple cakes is more open, spongy and dry compared to butter cakes since they are generally leaner, containing little or no fat. They depend almost entirely on the air beaten into whipped eggs for their sturdy structure and lightness. Some foam cakes use chemical leaveners for extra lift and always require gentle folding to combine the ingredients to help retain an airy texture.

white sugar vs brown sugar

White granulated sugar is refined cane or beet sugar that is mostly pure sucrose. It is made from extraction and evaporation of sugar cane or beet juice. The syrup is cooked to remove water and concentrate the sugar content. After crystallization and drying, this super concentrated substance transforms into free-flowing crystals. The refining process removes the last bit of molasses and impurities that coat these crystals (also known as "raw sugar") to produce white sugar. Brown sugar is technically partially refined cane sugar with some of the molasses content still remaining, and this results in larger crystals labeled as turbinado, demerara and muscavado sugar. Most commercial soft brown sugar used for baking is mainly produced by adding molasses back to refined granulated white sugar to create "light brown" (about 3% molasses) and "dark brown" (about 6%).

tart pastry vs pie pastry

Pie pastry is a thoughtful combination of wheat flour and solid fat (preferably butter, and sometimes with a fraction of lard) brought together by water to form a cohesive mass. It is both tender and flaky. Tart pastry gains richness from egg (whole or yolks only) and tenderness from sugar. It is generally more crumbly in texture and richer in flavour. In either case it is important to remember three things: keep everything cold (your hands, the fat and the liquid), work quickly but with restraint, rest the dough for at least 2 hours before rolling.

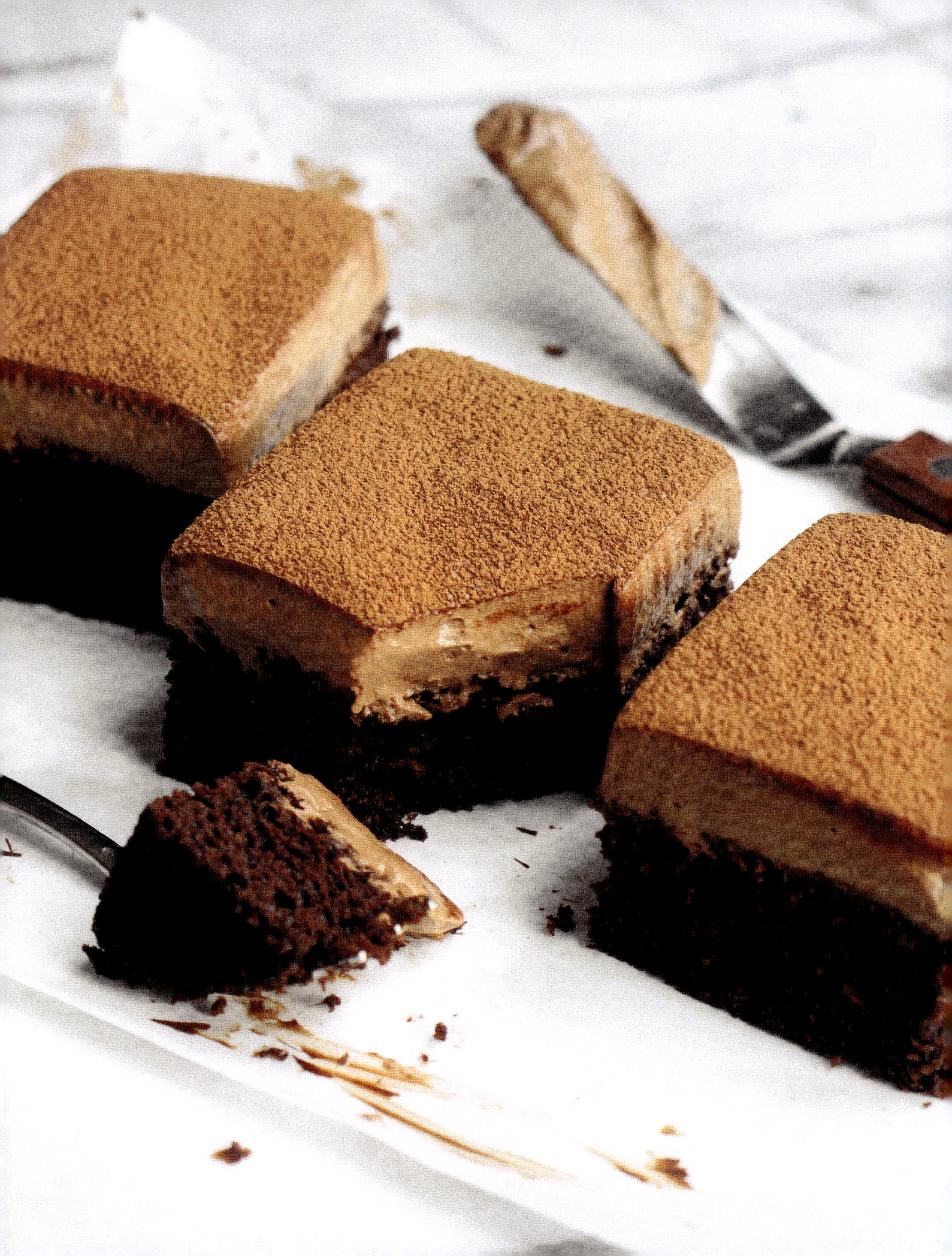

dark chocolate mousse cake
makes about 9 servings

Cake:
⅔ cup (95g) all-purpose flour

⅓ cup (28g) cocoa powder

½ tsp baking powder

¼ tsp baking soda

⅔ cup (135g) granulated sugar

¼ tsp salt

¼ cup (60ml) sunflower oil

1 large egg, well beaten

½ cup (120ml) buttermilk*

1 tsp (5ml) pure vanilla extract

Chocolate mousse:
4 oz (113g) dark chocolate (60-70% cocoa), coarsely chopped

⅓ cup (80ml) whole milk

1 tbsp (15ml) honey

¾ cup (180ml) 35% whipping cream

> *You can substitute the buttermilk with a blend of ¼ cup (60ml) sour cream and ¼ cup (60ml) milk. Just stir them together evenly before adding it to the batter.

1. Preheat oven to 350°F. Line an 8×8-inch pan with parchment paper leaving a 1-inch overhang at each side.

2. For the cake, sift flour, cocoa powder, baking powder and baking soda into a medium bowl. Add sugar and salt, then whisk to blend evenly. Add oil and the beaten egg and begin to whisk gently. It will be thick. Combine buttermilk with vanilla and slowly whisk it in until combined and the batter is smooth.

3. Spread batter evenly into prepared pan and bake for 20-25 minutes until a skewer inserted into the centre comes out clean. Transfer to a wire rack and let cool completely in the pan. Trim the top of the cake to level it out and make it flat if necessary.

4. For the mousse, combine chopped dark chocolate, milk and honey in a small saucepan over medium-low heat. Stir until melted and smooth. Pour it into a bowl and let it cool down to room temperature for 10-15 minutes so that it is no longer warm. Whip cream to firm peaks in a medium bowl using an electric hand mixer and gently fold it into the cooled chocolate mixture in two parts. Dollop the mousse over the cooled cake and gently spread it out evenly to cover the cake in the pan. Refrigerate for at least 2 hours, then sift extra cocoa powder over top just before slicing and serving.

butter *vs* oil

Butter is almost always better. *Almost.* When it comes to flavour, butter always wins hands down, but there are some recipes that benefit from a bit of oil from a textural point of view. Oil cannot contribute structure like butter does since it is a liquid and can't be creamed, whipped or aerated. It can, however, keep cakes and muffins soft for longer since it does not harden on cooling – it remains liquid at ambient and refrigerated temperatures so it contributes a softer mouthfeel and thus increases the perception of "moistness". Butter is solid at room temperature and very hard when refrigerated so it creates a firmer, crumbly texture and is slower to melt in the mouth.

rich salted caramel sauce

makes about ¾ cup

gluten free · **egg free**

¾ cup (150g) granulated sugar

3 tbsp (42g) unsalted butter

⅓ cup (80ml) 35% whipping cream

heaped ¼ tsp salt

> **Switch Up!** Stir ½ teaspoon of pure vanilla extract in with the salt; infuse the cream with espresso powder; add 2 tbsp (30ml) sour cream with the whipping cream; or, stir in 2 oz dark chocolate at the end to make a luscious thick chocolate caramel sauce!

1. Pour sugar in an even layer in a 1 or 2-quart heavy-bottomed stainless steel saucepan (preferably with a wide base). Place the pan over medium-high heat and let the sugar melt. As you see the crystals around the sides of the pan melt and liquefy, use a wooden spoon to push sugar from the edges to the centre and then push the unmelted sugar from the centre out to the sides to help it melt evenly. Continue to move the sugar like this until it begins to turn golden and liquefy. It will clump up and look dry before it liquefies, but trust that it will.

2. Continue to stir gently until it all melts and transforms into a clear amber syrup and use the wooden spoon to press out any large lumps of sugar. Reduce the heat slightly if necessary to control the cooking process and prevent the syrup from getting too dark before all of the sugar lumps melt completely.

3. Once it is copper-coloured and lump-free, remove from heat and carefully whisk in butter. The mixture will bubble up like lava, so be cautious. Slowly pour in the cream, then whisk until smooth. Mix in salt. If you still feel some hard bits of sugar along the base of the pan, return the pan to medium heat and cook while stirring just until melted. Pour the sauce into a heatproof jar and let cool at room temperature before storing in the fridge.

> *When is caramel ready? It depends on colour – undercooked (blonde) caramel just tastes sweet, while dark brown caramel is burnt and unusable. Instead of using a thermometer, learn to rely on visual cues. Perfectly caramelized sugar will have an even deep orange-brown or amber colour.*

gluten free
egg free

chocolate-covered chocolate caramels

makes about 36 pieces

1 x Rich Salted Caramel Sauce (page 196)

5 ½ oz (156g) bittersweet chocolate (70%)

10 oz (284g) dark chocolate for coating

1. Line a 9x5-inch loaf pan with parchment paper and lightly grease the paper.

2. Finely chop the bittersweet chocolate and place it into a heatproof bowl.

3. Prepare caramel sauce as per directions on page 196 with ½ teaspoon vanilla extract. Pour hot caramel over the chopped chocolate in the bowl, let stand for a minute then stir until melted and smooth. Pour it into prepared pan and spread it out evenly. Refrigerate until firm. Peel off the parchment and slice it into squares. Dip each square into melted tempered chocolate and transfer to a lined tray to set.

3-ingredient choc tahini fudge

makes 8-10 pieces

gluten free & vegan option

5 oz (142g) dark chocolate (60% cocoa)

6 tbsp (90ml) tahini, divided

2 oz (56g) pure white chocolate (omit the swirl for vegan option)

1. Chop the dark chocolate, place it in a heatproof bowl and melt it gently in the microwave. Stir until smooth and glossy. Stir in 5 tbsp (75ml) tahini. Pour it into an 8x4-inch loaf pan lined with parchment.

2. Melt white chocolate gently in another heatproof bowl and stir until smooth. Stir in 1 tbsp (15ml) tahini. Drizzle over dark chocolate mixture and swirl it in with a knife. Sprinkle sea salt flakes on top if desired and refrigerate for 2 hours until set. Slice and then store at room temperature.

Switch Up! For a softer texture, stir 1 tbsp (15ml) of honey into the dark chocolate mixture. Also, try replacing tahini with any natural drippy nut butter!

vegan dark chocolate coconut cream tart

makes 8-10 servings

gluten free vegan

Crust:

1 ⅓ cups (135g) blanched sliced or slivered almonds (or use almond flour)

2 tbsp (16g) corn starch or tapioca starch

2 tbsp (12g) cocoa powder

pinch of salt

2 tbsp (28g) coconut oil, melted

2 tbsp (30ml) pure maple syrup

Filling:

6 oz (170g) bittersweet chocolate (70% cocoa), finely chopped

⅔ cup (160ml) high quality coconut milk (at least 20% fat)

2 tbsp (30ml) pure maple syrup

cacao nibs for topping

sea salt flakes for topping

1. Preheat oven to 350°F.

2. For the crust, place sliced almonds, corn or tapioca starch, cocoa powder and salt in the bowl of a food processor and pulse until nuts are broken down to fine crumbs (or use almond flour and blend with other ingredients). Add melted coconut oil and maple syrup and pulse again until it comes together in a ball. It will feel like a paste but shouldn't be too sticky or oily. Turn the mixture out into an 8-inch round tart pan with removable bottom and press it out evenly over the base and up the sides – it may not be enough to go all the way up the sides, but that's ok. Bake for 15-18 minutes until it looks matte and feels dry and firm. Transfer pan to a wire rack to cool completely.

3. For the filling, place chopped chocolate into a medium bowl. Combine coconut milk and maple syrup in a small saucepan over medium heat and bring it to a simmer, then pour it over the chopped chocolate in the bowl. Cover and let stand for 2 minutes to let the chocolate melt gently, then stir from the centre until completely melted, smooth and glossy. Pour into cooled crust and tilt the pan around to let the filling spread out to the edges. Refrigerate until set. Sprinkle cacao nibs and sea salt on top before serving.

coconut lime margarita truffles

makes about 20 truffles

gluten free · **egg free**

Ganache:

5 oz (142g) dark chocolate (60% cocoa), finely chopped

3 tbsp (45ml) water

1 tbsp (15ml) freshly squeezed lime juice

1 tbsp (15ml) honey

2 tsp (10ml) Tequila

hefty pinch of salt

2 tbsp (28g) unsalted butter

Coating:

½ cup (45g) medium unsweetened shredded coconut

zest of one lime, finely grated

2 oz (56g) bittersweet chocolate, melted

1. For the ganache, combine chopped chocolate, water, lime juice and honey in a small saucepan over low heat and whisk constantly until smooth and glossy. Remove from heat and stir in tequila and salt. Whisk in butter one tablespoon at a time until melted and smooth. Let stand a room temperature for 30 minutes then refrigerate until firm.

2. Use a small spoon to scoop up teaspoon-sized portions of ganache and roll into smooth balls. Place them onto a parchment-lined baking tray and refrigerate for 10 minutes.

3. For the coating, combine coconut and lime zest in a small bowl and set aside. Have melted chocolate ready in a small bowl. Place truffles one by one into the melted chocolate and roll them around using a spoon to create a thin layer. Don't worry if the truffles don't get evenly coated – it's meant to be a rough thin coating. Immediately place them into the bowl with the coconut and roll around to cover them evenly. Place them back onto the baking tray to set. Store refrigerated and serve cold.

cheat's opera cake

makes 8-10 servings

Traditionally Opera cake is quite a labour-intensive project built of layers of delicate moist Joconde (almond-based) sponge cake, coffee flavoured buttercream and hyper glossy mirror glaze. In this version we'll still make the Joconde, but use a quick coffee cream and chocolate ganache glaze for a faster turnaround. I assure you it is just as delicious!

Sponge cake:

3 large egg whites, at room temperature

⅛ tsp salt

2 tbsp (25g) granulated sugar

⅔ cup (80g) icing sugar, sifted

¾ cup (70g) blanched almond flour

2 large eggs, at room temperature

2 tbsp (28g) unsalted butter, melted

2 tbsp (18g) all-purpose flour

Ganache:

6 oz (170g) dark chocolate (60% cocoa)

⅔ (160ml) 35% whipping cream

1 tbsp (15ml) corn syrup or honey

Coffee cream:

3 tbsp (45g) cream cheese, softened

1 tbsp (15g) packed light brown sugar

2 tsp espresso powder

¾ cup (180ml) 35% whipping cream

1. Preheat oven to 375°F. Line a 13x9-inch rimmed baking sheet with parchment paper and lightly grease the paper.

2. Whip egg whites with salt to soft peaks in the bowl of a stand mixer fitted with the whisk attachment on medium-high speed. Gradually add sugar and beat to firm peaks.

3. Combine icing sugar, almond flour and whole eggs in a large bowl. Whisk vigorously or beat with a mixer until pale, thick and creamy. Whisk in melted butter and flour. Gently fold in whipped egg whites.

4. Spread batter evenly into prepared pan and bake for 10-12 minutes until lightly golden and it springs back when pressed gently. Transfer pan to a rack to cool completely. Cover the cake with a sheet of parchment paper, flip the pan over onto the countertop to release the cake and carefully peel off the top layer of parchment. Slice the sponge widthwise into 3 equal rectangles.

5. For the ganache, finely chop the chocolate and place it in a heatproof bowl. Combine cream with corn syrup or honey in a small saucepan over medium heat until it simmers. Pour it over chopped chocolate and let stand for 2 minutes. Stir until completely melted, smooth and glossy. Let cool until slightly thickened but still pourable.

6. For the coffee cream, combine cream cheese, brown sugar and espresso powder in a medium bowl with ¼ cup (60ml) of whipping cream. Beat with an electric hand mixer on medium speed to smooth out and blend the cream cheese. Add remaining cream and beat until it holds stiff peaks.

7. Reserve one-quarter of the ganache and then divide the rest evenly over the sponge rectangles, spreading it out evenly. Refrigerate until set. Place one sponge onto a tray or serving platter and spread one-third of the cream over ganache. Place the other ganache-covered sponge on top and spread half of the remaining cream over top in an even layer. Place the third sponge on top and chill the whole cake for 15 minutes. Spread the rest of the cream over top and chill for 30 minutes. Pour remaining ganache over top and quickly spread it out to cover evenly. Refrigerate for 1 hour before serving.

date night 201

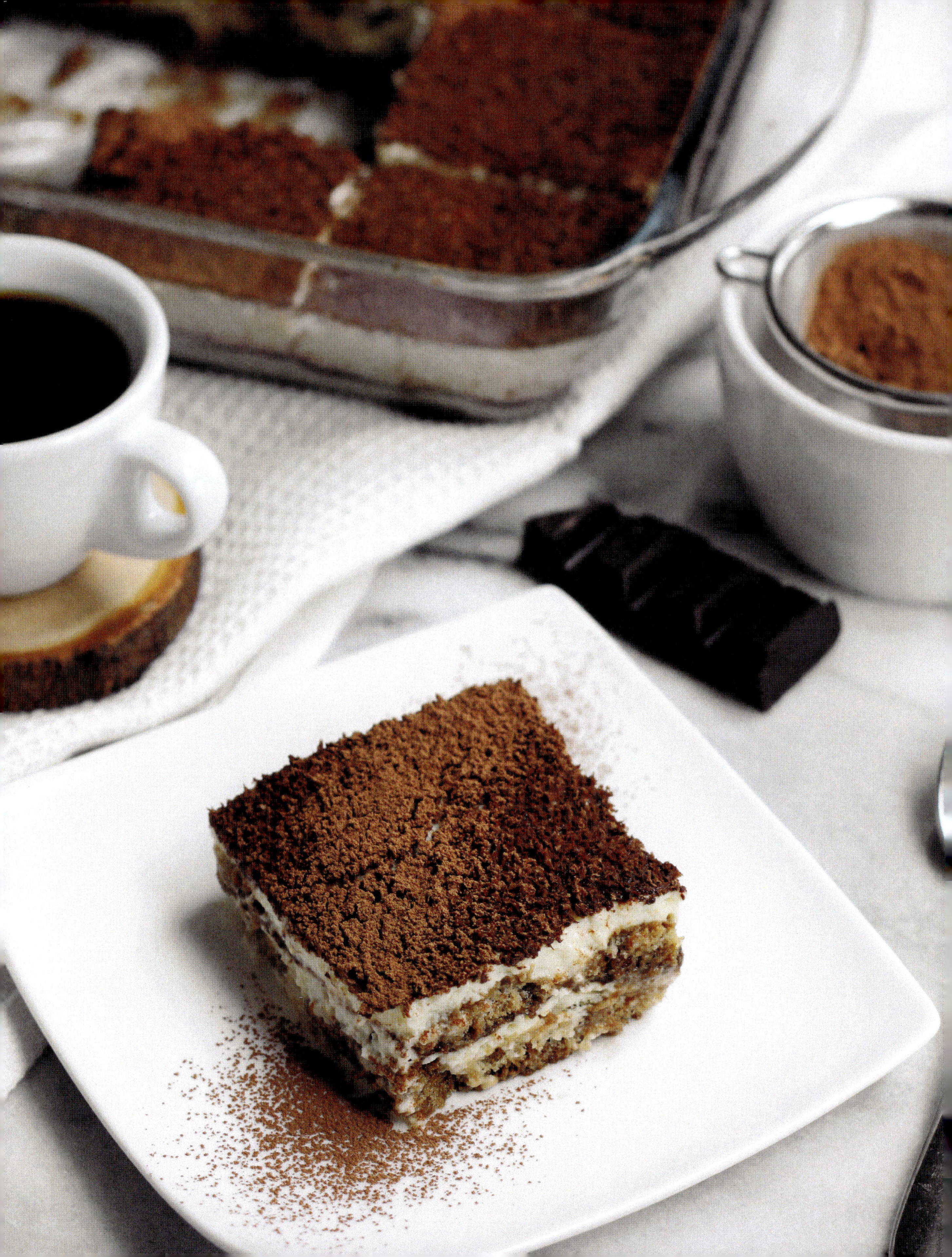

classic tiramisu

makes about 9 servings

3 large egg yolks

3 tbsp (45ml) dry Marsala wine*, divided

6 tbsp (75g) granulated sugar, divided

1 cup (240ml) mascarpone

3 large egg whites (or ¾ cup (180ml) 35% whipping cream)

24-28 Homemade Ladyfinger Biscuits (recipe on page 180)

1 cup (240ml) brewed strong coffee or espresso, cooled

1 oz (28g) bittersweet chocolate for grating

2 tbsp (12g) cocoa powder for dusting

> *Tiramisu is best made with fresh eggs, but if you prefer not to use raw egg whites, you can replace them with whipped cream. It will make a richer dessert, and it is equally delicious!*

1. Combine egg yolks with 2 tablespoons (30ml) of Marsala wine and 3 tablespoons (40g) of sugar in a heatproof bowl. Set the bowl over a saucepan with 1-inch of simmering water and whisk vigorously for 6-8 minutes until pale, thick and tripled in volume. To make this step easier, use an electric hand mixer on medium speed. Remove the bowl from over the heat and gently whisk in mascarpone until just combined.

2. For the lighter (more traditional) version, combine egg whites with remaining 3 tbsp of sugar in a heatproof bowl. Set the bowl over a saucepan with 1-inch of simmering water and beat with an electric hand mixer until it holds firm peaks. Whipping over a pan of simmering water will slightly cook and stabilize the egg whites. Gently fold half of the beaten egg whites into the mascarpone mixture to loosen it, then fold in the rest while trying to keep the air in. If not using egg whites, then whip the cream in a medium bowl using an electric mixer until it holds firm peaks. Fold the cream gently into the mascarpone mixture.

3. Combine coffee or espresso with remaining 1 tbsp (15ml) of Marsala in a small bowl. Dip half of the ladyfingers very quickly into this coffee mixture and line the bottom of an 8x8-inch baking dish. You might find that you need to break a few into pieces to fit them in snuggly to cover the base of the dish. Spread half of the mascarpone filling evenly over the lady fingers. Grate half of the chocolate over top. Dip the remaining ladyfingers quickly into the coffee and arrange a second layer over the filling. Spoon the rest of the mascarpone mixture over the ladyfingers. Grate more chocolate on top and then dust with cocoa powder. Cover with plastic wrap and refrigerate for at least 6 hours.

4. Dust the surface with extra cocoa powder just before you are ready to serve it. This Tiramisu can be refrigerated for up to 2 days before serving, but any longer and it will become too soggy.

*Marsala is a fortified wine that is traditionally used in Tiramisu, but you can also try substituting with dark rum, brandy or any other liqueur. Since Marsala is less potent than some of these other spirits and liqueurs, I suggest using about half the amount. For a non-alcoholic version, leave it out all together and use ½ teaspoon of rum extract or vanilla extract.

icy chocolate squares

makes 25 truffles

gluten free **egg free**

Ganache:

8 oz (227g) dark chocolate (60-65% cocoa), very finely chopped

¾ cup (180ml) 35% whipping cream

1 tbsp (14g) unsalted butter or coconut oil

½ tsp pure flavour extract of choice (optional)

pinch of salt

Coating:

¾ cup (65g) cocoa powder

1. Line a 7x7 or 8x8-inch baking pan with parchment paper leaving a 1-inch overhang along each side.

2. Place finely chopped chocolate in a medium bowl and set aside.

3. Combine cream with any optional flavours for infusing (*see note*) in a small saucepan and place over medium heat until it just comes to a simmer. You should see fine bubbles forming around the sides of the pan. Remove from heat and immediately pour it over chopped chocolate in the bowl (strain it if infusing with whole spices or coffee beans). Swirl the bowl gently to submerge all of the chocolate, cover and let stand without stirring for 2 minutes. This will allow the cream to gently melt the chocolate.

4. Use a wire whisk to stir in one direction (i.e. clockwise) starting in the centre and working your way out toward the sides until the mixture is glossy and smooth. While still warm, add butter or coconut oil, salt and optional flavour extract of choice and gently whisk it in. Pour it into prepared pan and spread it out evenly. Let cool at room temperature for 1 hour, then refrigerate for at least 2 hours until firm.

5. Lift chilled ganache out of the pan and slice it lengthwise into 5 strips, then cut each strip into 5 squares. Toss each square in cocoa powder to coat all sides or dip them in tempered dark chocolate (pg. 205) and store in an airtight container in the fridge.

> **Switch Up!** These taste just like one of my favourite childhood confections – can you guess by the name? Make them your own by infusing the cream with any of the following flavours and then pour it through a strainer over the chocolate: crushed coffee beans, tea leaves, citrus peel, chai spice (cinnamon bark, star anise, cardamom pods, black pepper, cloves), or gingerbread (fresh sliced ginger, cinnamon bark, cloves, nutmeg).

HOW TO TEMPER CHOCOLATE THE FAST WAY

Tempering refers to the process of melting chocolate in a way that promises that when it sets back up again, it sets to a firm, glossy, snappy texture with a smooth mouthfeel. It's the cocoa butter in chocolate that has various unique properties and once melted, it can re-crystallize into one of many forms or structures which all have different melting points. "Form V" is the ideal structure that is most stable, but it will only set this way under controlled conditions which requires a series of precise heating and cooling phases using a thermometer. Chocolate from the supermarket has already been tempered by the manufacturer and when we melt it at home, cocoa butter loses its structure and the organized crystals separate into a mixture of different forms. The fastest and easiest way to temper it is to gently melt it without actually melting the stable Form V cocoa butter crystals, and for dark chocolate that means not heating it above 90°F (32°C). For milk and white chocolate, do not heat above 88°F (31°C) and 84°F (29°C), respectively. To do this, chop the chocolate as finely as possible and place it in a heatproof bowl. Set the bowl over a saucepan of just barely simmering water (very hot, not boiling water). Stir constantly without stopping until about three-quarters of the chocolate is melted. Take the bowl off of the heat and continue stirring until the residual heat melts the rest of the chocolate pieces. This helps to make sure you don't over-heat it. If you have a thermometer you can check the temperature. At 90°F there are still plenty of Form V crystals within the molten cocoa butter and they will encourage the rest of the melted fat to set back in this Form V shape again.

INDEX

A

all-purpose flour
    function & properties, 14
    measurement equivalents, 9

almond(s)
    Apricot & Almond Olive Oil Cake, 31
    Cheat's Opera Cake, 200
    Cherry Almond Crisp, 23
    Chewy Coconut Macaroons, 167
    Double Dark Chocolate Oat & Almond Bars, 127
    Fennel Orange & Almond Biscotti, 169
    Florentine Medallions, 62
    Florentine Lace Cookies, 174
    Flourless Peanut Butter Swirl Brownies, 107
    Honey Olive Oil Muesli Bars, 126
    Italian Amaretti Cookies, 166
    Raspberry Maple Crumble Cheesecake Bars, 34
    Raspberry Sachertorte, 187
    Strawberry Maple Almond Tart, 39
    Summer Stone Fruit Almond & Olive Oil Cake, 31
    Vanilla Chai Coconut Granola, 131
    Vegan Dark Chocolate Coconut Cream Tart, 198

almond flour
    Apricot & Almond Olive Oil Cake, 31
    Cheat's Opera Cake, 200
    Chewy Coconut Macaroons, 167
    Double Dark Chocolate Oat & Almond Bars, 127
    Italian Amaretti Cookies, 166
    Raspberry Sachertorte, 187
    Strawberry Maple Almond Tart, 39
    Summer Stone Fruit Almond & Olive Oil Cake, 31

Anzac Fudge Bars, 58

apple
    Brandied Brown Butter Apple Galette, 33
    Caramel Apple Crumble Bars, 24
    Cinnamon Sour Cream Snack Cake, 125
    Sticky Ginger Apple Loaf, 41

Apple Cinnamon Sour Cream Snack Cake, 125

apricot
    Apricot Almond & Olive Oil Cake, 31
    Crostata Marmellata, 154
    Pecan Seed Loaf, Date &, 25

Apricot Almond & Olive Oil Cake, 31

Avocado Mojito Cheesecake Bars, 142

B

bain marie, 95

banana
    BEST Classic Banana Bread, 132
    Chocolate Fudge Swirl Banana Muffins, 137
    Cinnamon Swirl Banana Bread, 135
    Double Chocolate Banana Bread, 136
    Healthy Whole Wheat Banana Bread, 135
    Honey Walnut Banana Bread, 136
    Peanut Butter & Oat Chocolate Swirl Banana Bread, 133
    Whole Wheat Maple Pecan Banana Bread, 29

BEST Classic Banana Bread, 132

Best Vanilla Birthday Cake, 85

biscotti
    Double Chocolate Hazelnut, 66
    Fennel Orange & Almond, 169
    Pistachio Cherry & Chocolate, 67

blueberry
    Buttermilk Muffins, 129
    Sour Cream Coffee Cake, 131
    Summer Stone Fruit Almond & Olive Oil Cake, 31

Blueberry Buttermilk Muffins, 129

Blueberry Sour Cream Coffee Cake, 131

Brandied Brown Butter Apple Galette, 33

brown butter
    Apple Galette, Brandied, 33
    Blondies, Toasted Cocont & Dark Chocolate Chunk, 176
    Brown Butter Chunky Chocolate Chip Cookies, 173
    how to make, 175
    Pecan Cookies, 175
    Pecan Pie, Maple Bourbon, 57

Brown Butter Pecan Cookies, 175

brownies
    Flourless Peanut Butter Swirl, 107
    Funfetti Fudge, 85
    Irish Cream Coffee, 55
    Raspberry Swirl Cheesecake, 184
    Shiny Top Fudge, 110

buttermilk
    Dark Chocolate Mousse Cake, 195
    Muffins, Blueberry, 129
    substitution for, 10
    Triple Chocolate Fudge Cupcakes, 106

C

cake
    4-Ingredient Chocolate, 95
    Apricot Almond & Olive Oil, 31
    Best Vanilla Birthday, 85
    Blueberry Sour Cream Coffee, 131
    Cheat's Opera, 200
    Chocolate Celebration, 97
    Chocolate Chai Yule Log, 69
    Chocolate Peanut Butter Mousse, 109
    Chocolate Vanilla Swiss Roll, 151
    Dark Chocolate Mousse, 193
    Decadent Double Chocolate Loaf, 171
    Double Dark Chocolate, 91
    Fluffy Golden Vanilla Cupcakes, 88
    Ginger Cardamom Crumb, 128
    Light & Luscious Lemon, 145
    Neapolitan Layer Cake, 99
    Raspberry Sachertorte, 187
    Soft Spicy Gingerbread, 63
    Sour Cream & Honey Chocolate, 192
    Sticky Salted Caramel Date Cakes, 178
    Strawberry Shortcake Swiss Roll, 45
    Summer Stone Fruit Almond & Olive Oil, 31
    Triple Chocolate Fudge Cupcakes, 106
    Ultra Moist Chocolate Fudge, 93
    Vanilla Custard Sponge, 163

caramel(s)
    Crumb Bars, Salted Peanut, 153
    Dark Chocolate Sea Salt, 191
    Date Cakes, Sticky Salted, 178
    how to make, 140-141
    Sauce, Extra Creamy Caramel, 156
    Sauce, Rich Salted Caramel, 196
    Silk Cream Cheese Custard Tart with Creamy Caramel, 149

Caramel Apple Crumble Bars, 24

caramelization, 141

cardamom
    Chocolate Chai Spice Cookies, 73
    Chocolate Chai Yule Log, 69
    Crumb Cake, Ginger, 128
    Date Apricot & Pecan Seed Loaf, 25
    Honey Rhubarb Melt Cake, 37
    Pfeffernusse German Spice Cookies, 79
    Soft & Chewy Molasses Spice Crinkle Cookies, 77
    Vanilla Chai Coconut Granola, 131

cashew(s)
    Cookie Bars, Soft & Gooey Cream Cheese Caramel, 103
    Honey Olive Oil Muesli Bars, 126
    Sweet & Salty Chocolate Peanut Butter Granola, 130
    Sweet & Salty Magic Bars, 94
    Vanilla Chai Coconut Granola, 131

Cheat's Opera Cake, 200

cheesecake
    Bars, Avocado Mojito, 142
    Bars, Pumpkin Chocolate, 59
    Bars, Raspberry Maple Crumble, 34
    Bars, Tuxedo, 189
    Brownies, Raspberry Swirl, 184
    Triple Chocolate, 47

cherry
    Almond Crisp, 23
    Biscotti, Pistachio & Chocolate, 67
    Florentine Lace Cookies, 174
    Florentine Medallions, 62
    Honey Olive Oil Muesli Bars, 126
    Pistachio Butter Cookies, Sour, 155
    Ultimate Cheeseboard Crisps, 143

Cherry Almond Crisp, 23

Chewy Coconut Macaroons, 167

Chewy Gooey Double Ginger Molasses Cookies, 65

chocolate
    Anzac Fudge Bars, 58
    Banana Bread, Double, 136
    Best Vanilla Birthday Cake, 85
    Biscotti, Pistachio Cherry, 67
    Cake, 4-Ingredient Chocolate, 95
    Cake, Double Dark, 91
    Cake, Sour Cream & Honey, 192
    Celebration Cake, 97
    Chai Spice Cookies, 73
    Chai Yule Log, 69
    Cheat's Opera Cake, 200
    Cheesecake, Triple, 47
    Cheesecake Bars, Pumpkin, 59
    Chewy Coconut Macaroons, 167
    Chip Breton Shortbread, 165
    Chunk Blondies, Toasted Coconut & Dark, 176
    Chunk Cookies, Chewy Gluten Free, Double, 101
    Chunk Peanut Butter Cookies, Thick & Chewy, 102

Chunky Brown Butter Cookies, Chip, 173
Classic Tiramisu, 203
Coconut Cream Tart, Vegan Dark, 198
Coconut Lime Margarita Truffles, 199
Cookies, Secret Sauce, Chip, 84
Covered Caramels, 197
Cranberry Peanut Butter Oatmeal Cookies, White, 152
Cream Pie, Salted, 117
Custard Cake, Frozen, 185
Fennel Orange & Almond Biscotti, 169
Florentine Medallions, 62
Flourless Peanut Butter Swirl Brownies, 107
Fluffy Golden Vanilla Cupcakes with Whipped Chocolate Ganache Frosting, 88
Fudge Cake, Ultra Moist, 93
Fudge Cupcakes, Triple, 106
Fudge Swirl Banana Muffins, 137
Funfetti Fudge Brownies, 85
Ganache, Whipped, 89
Gianduja Rocher Crescent Cookies, 72
Gingerbread Cookies, Double, 81
Hazelnut Biscotti, Double, 64
Icy Chocolate Squares, 204
Irish Cream Coffee Brownies, 55
Loaf Cake, Decadent Double, 171
Oat & Almond Bars, Double Dark, 127
Pecan Butter Balls & Batons, Chip, 74
Peanut Butter Banana Oat Muffins, Chip, 131
Maple Pecan Millionaire's Shortbread, 181
Mousse Cake, Dark, 195
Neapolitan Layer Cake,
Peanut Butter Granola, Sweet & Salty, 130
Peanut Butter Mousse Cake, 109
Peppermint-Dipped Graham Crackers, 81
Rasberry Sachertorte, 187
Raspberry Swirl Cheesecake Brownies, 184
Sandwich Cookies, Peanut Butter, 115
andwich Cookies, Peppermint Crème, 75
Sea Salt Caramels, Dark, 191
Sea Salt S'mores Cookies, 107
Shiny Top Fudge Brownies, 110
Silk Pie with Press-In Gingerbread Crust, 80
Snowflake Crinkle Cookies, 71
Sour Cherry Pistachio Butter Cookies, 155
Sweet & Salty Magic Bars, 94
Swirl Banana Bread, Peanut Butter & Oat, 133
Swirl Pumpkin Spice Muffins, Milk, 28
Tahini Fudge, 3-Ingredient, 197
tempering, 205
Tiramisu Brownies, 168
Toasted Coconut Truffle Tartlets, 174
Truffles, Silky Dark, 177
Truffle Sandwich Cookies, 70
Truffle Squares, Peanut Butter, 51
Tuxedo Cheesecake Bars, 189
Vanilla Swiss Roll, 151
Yolk Cookies, 50

Chocolate Celebration Cake, 97
Chocolate Chai Spice Cookies, 73
Chocolate Chai Yule Log, 69
Chocolate Chip Breton Shortbread, 165
Chocolate Chip Peanut Butter Banana Oat Muffins, 131
Chocolate Chip Pecan Butter Balls & Batons, 74
Chocolate Covered Chocolate Caramels, 197
Chocolate Fudge Swirl Banana Muffins, 137
Chocolate Peanut Butter Mousse Cake, 109
Chocolate Peppermint-Dipped Graham Crackers, 81
Chocolate Silk Pie with Press-In Gingerbread Crust, 80
Chocolate Snowflake Crinkle Cookies, 71
Chocolate Truffle Sandwich Cookies, 70
Chocolate Vanilla Swiss Roll, 151
Chocolate Yolk Cookies, 50
Chewy Coconut Macaroons, 167
Chewy Gluten Free Double Chocolate Chunk Cookies, 101
Chunky Brown Butter Chocolate Chip Cookies, 173
Cinnamon Swirl Banana Bread, 135
Classic Creamy Lemon Tart, 27
Classic Gingerbread Cookies, 61
Classic Tiramisu, 203
Coconut Lime Margarita Truffles, 199

coconut
 Anzac Fudge Bars, 58
 Cream Tart, Vegan Dark Chocolate, 198
 Dark Chocolate Chunk Brown Butter Blondies, Toasted, 78
 Granola, Vanilla Chai, 131
 Lime Margarita Truffles, 199
 Truffle Tartlets, Toasted, 174

coffee (see espresso)
 Cheat's Opera Cake, 200
 Chocolate Chai Yule Log, 69
 Classic Tiramisu, 203
 Tiramisu Brownies, 168
 Dark Chocolate Sea Salt Caramels, 191
 Decadent Double Chocolate Loaf Cake, 171
 Irish Cream Coffee Brownies, 55
 Mocha Berry Cheesecake, 22
 Shiny Top Fudge Brownies, 112
 Silky Dark Chocolate Truffles, 177
 Triple Chocolate Cheesecake, 47
 Ultra Moist Chocolate Fudge Cake, 93

cookies
 tips for baking,
 flavour reactions,
 Brown Butter Pecan, 175
 Chewy Coconut Macaroons, 167
 Chewy Gluten Free Double Chocolate Chunk, 101
 Chewy Gooey Double Ginger Molasses, 65
 Chocolate Chai Spice, 73
 Chocolate Chip Pecan Butter Balls, 74
 Chocolate Chip Breton Shortbread, 165
 Chocolate Peppermint-Dipped Graham Crackers, 81
 Chocolate Snowflake Crinkle, 71
 Chocolate Truffle Sandwich, 70
 Chocolate Yolk, 50
 Chunky Brown Butter Chocolate Chip, 173
 Classic Gingerbread, 61
 Double Chocolate Gingerbread, 81
 Double Chocolate Hazelnut Biscotti, 64
 Fennel Orange & Almond Biscotti, 169
 Florentine Lace, 174
 Florentine Medallions, 62
 Gianduja Rocher Crescent, 72
 Homemade Graham Crackers, 111
 Homemade Ladyfinger Biscuits, 180
 Italian Amaretti, 166
 PB & Jelly Sandwich, 115
 Peanut Butter & Chocolate Sandwich, 115
 Peppermint Crème Chocolate Sandwich, 75
 Pfefferneuse German Spice, 79
 Pistachio Cherry & Chocolate Biscotti, 67
 Rosemary Pecan Press-In Shortbread, 146
 Secret Sauce Chocolate Chip, 84
 Softy & Chewy Molasses Spice Crinkle Cookies, 77
 Soft & Gooey Cream Cheese Caramel Cashew Cookie Bars, 103
 Sour Cherry Pistachio Butter, 155
 Thick & Chewy Flourless Chocolate Chunk Peanut Butter, 102
 Vanilla Sugar, 66
 Vanilla Walnut Crescent, 78
 White Chocolate & Cranberry Peanut Butter Oatmeal Cookies, 152

condensed milk
 Maple Pecan Millionaire's Shortbread, 183
 Sweet & Salty Magic Bars, 94

crackers
 Chocolate Peppermint-Dipped Graham, 81
 Homemade Graham, 111
 Pumpkin Seed & Black Pepper Crispbreads, 147
 Ultimate Cheeseboard Crisps, 143

cranberries (dried)
 Double Chocolate Hazelnut Biscotti, 64
 White Chocolate Peanut Butter Oatmeal Cookies, 152

cream, heavy, whipping (35%)
 Caramel Apple Crumble Bars, 24
 Cheat's Opera Cake, 200
 Chocolate Chai Yule Log, 69
 Chocolate Covered Chocolate Caramels, 297
 Chocolate Fudge Swirl Banana Muffins, 137
 Chocolate Peanut Butter Mousse Cake, 109
 Chocolate Truffle Sandwich Cookies, 70
 Chocolate Vanilla Swiss Roll, 151
 Classic Creamy Lemon Tart, 27
 Coconut Lime Margarita Truffles, 199
 Creamy Lemon Squares, 157
 Extra Creamy Caramel Sauce, 156
 Icy Chocolate Squares, 204
 Peanut Butter Chocolate Truffle Cream Cheese Cookie Bars, 51
 Rich Salted Caramel Sauce, 196
 Salted Cinnamon Butterscotch Walnut Bars, 172
 Salted Peanut Caramel Crumb Bars, 153
 Silky Dark Chocolate Truffles, 177
 Soft & Chewy Molasses Spice Crinkle, 77
 Soft & Gooey Cream Cheese Caramel Cashew Bars, 103
 Strawberry Shortcake Swiss Roll, 45
 Vanilla Custard Sponge Cake, 163
 Whipped Chocolate Ganache, 89

cream cheese
 Avocado Mojito Cheesecake Bars, 142
 Caramelitas, 161
 Chocolate Vanilla Swiss Roll, 151
 Cookie Bars, Peanut Butter Chocolate Truffle, 51
 Filled Carrot Cakes, 49
 Funfetti Fudge Brownies, 85
 Irish Cream Coffee Brownies, 55

index 207

Mocha Berry Cheesecake, 22
Raspberry Maple Crumble Cheesecake Bars, 34
Pumpkin Chocolate Cheesecake Bars, 59
Raspberry Swirl Cheesecake Brownies, 184
Silk Cream Cheese Custard Tart with Creamy Caramel, 149
Soft & Gooey Cream Cheese Caramel Cashew Cookies Bars, 103
Triple Chocolate Cheesecake, 47
Tuxedo Cheesecake Bars, 189

Cream Cheese Caramelitas, 161
Cream Cheese-Filled Carrot Cakes, 49
creaming
    method for cakes, 16-17
Creamy Lemon Squares, 157
Crostata Marmellata, 154
cupcakes
    Fluffy Golden Vanilla, with Whipped Chocolate Ganache Frosting, 88
    Triple Chocolate Fudge, 106
custard
    pastry cream, 161
    Sponge Cake, Vanilla, 163
    Tart, Silk Cream Cheese, 149

D

Dark Chocolate Mousse Cake, 195
Dark Chocolate Sea Salt Caramels, 191
date(s)
    Cakes, Sticky Salted Caramel, 178
Date Apricot & Pecan Seed Loaf, 25
Decadent Double Chocolate Loaf Cake, 171
Double Chocolate Banana Bread, 136
Double Chocolate Gingerbread Cookies, 81
Double Chocolate Hazelnut Biscotti, 64
Double Dark Chocolate Cake, 91
Double Dark Chocolate Oat & Almond Bars, 127
Dutch-process
    vs. natural cocoa, 10

E

espresso (see coffee)
Extra Creamy Caramel Sauce, 156

F

Fennel Orange & Almond Biscotti, 169
flax seed(s)
    Honey Olive Oil Muesli Bars, 126
    Pumpkin Seed & Black Pepper Crispbreads, 147
    Sweet & Salty Chocolate Peanut Butter Granola, 130
    Ultimate Cheeseboard Crisps, 143
Florentine Lace Cookies, 64
Florentine Medallions, 62
Flourless Peanut Butter Swirl Brownies, 107
Fluffy Golden Vanilla Cupcakes with Whipped Chocolate Ganache Frosting, 88
Four-Ingredient Chocolate Cake, 95
Frozen Chocolate Custard Cake, 185

Funfetti Fudge Brownies, 85

G

Gianduja Rocher Crescent Cookies, 72
ginger
    Apple Pie, 54
    Cardamom Crumb Cake, 128
    Chocolate Chai Yule Log, 69
    Classic Gingerbread Cookies, 61
    Molasses Cookies, Chewy Gooey Double, 65
Ginger Apple Pie, 52
Ginger Cardamom Crumb Cake, 128
gluten-free
    3-Ingredient Choc Tahini Fudge, 197
    Chewy Gluten Free Double Chocolate Chunk Cookies, 101
    Coconut Lime Margarita Truffles 199
    Dark Chocolate Sea Salt Caramels, 191
    Double Dark Chocolate Oat & Almond Bars, 127
    Extra Creamy Caramel Sauce, 156
    Flourless Peanut Butter Swirl Brownies, 107
    Honey Olive Oil Muesli Bars, 126
    Icy Chocolate Squares, 204
    Rich Salted Caramel Sauce, 196
    Silky Dark Chocolate Truffles, 177
    Sweet & Salty Chocolate Peanut Butter Granola, 130
    Thick & Chewy Flourless Chocolate Chunk Peanut Butter Cookies, 102
    Toasted Coconut Truffle Tartlets, 174
    Vanilla Chai Coconut Granola, 131
    Vegan Dark Chocolate Coconut Cream Tart, 198
Gooey Butter Tarts, 114
granola
    Sweet & Salty Chocolate Peanut Butter, 130
    Vanilla Chai Coconut, 131

H

hazelnut(s)
    Biscotti, Double Chocolate, 64
    Chocolate Yolk Cookies, 50
    Gianduja Rocher Crescent Cookies, 72
    Milk Chocolate Swirl Pumpkin Spice Muffins, 28
    Ultimate Cheeseboard Crisps, 143
Healthy Whole Wheat Banana Bread, 135
Homemade Ladyfinger Biscuits, 180
Homemade Graham Crackers, 111
honey
    as anti-crystallization agent in caramel,
    Chocolate Cake, Sour Cream, 192
    Cheat's Opera Cake, 200
    Chewy Coconut Macaroons, 167
    Chocolate Chai Yule Log, 69
    Chocolate Peppermint-Dipped Graham Crackers, 81
    Chocolate Peanut Butter Mousse Cake, 109
    Chocolate Silk Pie with Press-In Gingerbread Crust, 80
    Chocolate Truffle Sandwich Cookies, 70
    Chewy Gluten-Free Double Chocolate Chunk Cookies, 101
    Coconut Lime Margarita Truffles, 199
    Cream Cheese-Filled Carrot Cakes, 49
    Dark Chocolate Mousse Cake, 195
    Dark Chocolate Sea Salt Caramels, 191
    Double Dark Chocolate Cake, 91
    Double Dark Chocolate Oat & Almond Bars, 127
    Extra Creamy Caramel Sauce, 156
    Florentine Lace Cookies, 174
    Florentine Medallions, 62
    Homemade Graham Crackers, 111
    New York Style Bagels, 120
    Olive Oil Muesli Bars, 126
    Peanut Butter & Chocolate Sandwich Cookies, 115
    Pfeffernusse German Spice Cookies, 79
    Pumpkin Seed & Black Pepper Crispbreads, 147
    Raspberry Sachertorte, 187
    Salted Chocolate Cream Pie, 117
    Salted Cinnamon Butterscotch Walnut Bars, 172
    Sea Salt S'mores Cookies, 107
    Soft Spicy Gingerbread Cake, 63
    Sticky Apple Ginger Loaf, 41
    Sticky Salted Caramel Date Cakes, 178
    Sweet & Salty Chocolate Peanut Butter Granola, 130
    Triple Chocolate Cheesecake, 47
    Tuxedo Cheesecake Bars, 189
    Ultimate Cheeseboard Crisps, 143
    Vanilla Chai Coconut Granola, 131
    Walnut Banana Bread, 136
    Whipped Chocolate Ganache, 89
Honey Olive Oil Muesli Bars, 126
Honey Rhubarb Melt Cake, 37
Honey Walnut Banana Bread, 136

I

Icy Chocolate Squares, 204
Irish Cream Coffee Brownies, 55
Italian Amaretti Cookies, 166

L

lemon
    Blueberry Buttermilk Muffins, 129
    Cake, Light & Luscious, 145
    Cream Cheese-Filled Carrot Cakes, 49
    Curd, 145
    Strawberry Shortcake Swiss Roll, 45
    Squares, Creamy, 157
    Tart, Classic Creamy, 27
    Vanilla Custard Sponge Cake, 163
Light & Luscious Lemon Cake, 145

M

maillard browning (reactions),
marshmallow
    Sea Salt S'mores Cookies, 107
mascarpone
    Classic Creamy Lemon Tart, 27
    Classic Tiramisu, 203
    Strawberry Shortcake Swiss Roll, 45
    Tiramisu Brownies, 168
maple (syrup)
    Almond Tart, Strawberry, 39
    Anzac Fudge Bars, 58
    Brown Butter Bourbon Pecan Pie, 57
    Crumble Cheesecake Bars, Raspberry, 34

Double Dark Chocolate Oat & Almond Bars, 127
Healthy Whole Wheat Banana Bread, 135
Pecan Banana Bread, Whole Wheat, 31
Pecan Millionaire's Shortbread, 181
Sesame Snickerdoodles, 164
Sweet & Salty Chocolate Peanut Butter Granola, 130
Raisin Butter Tarts, 115
Vanilla Chai Coconut Granola, 131
Vegan Dark Chocolate Coconut Cream Tart, 198

Maple Brown Butter Bourbon Pecan Pie, 57

Maple Raisin Butter Tarts, 115

Maple Pecan Millionaire's Shortbread, 181

Maple Sesame Snickerdoodles, 164

measuring
technique & conversions, 8-9

milk chocolate
Chocolate Peanut Butter Mousse Cake, 109
Creamy Chocolate Buttercream, 97
Healthy Whole Wheat Banana Bread, 135
Neapolitan Layer Cake, 99
Swirl Pumpkin Spice Muffins, 28
Triple Chocolate Fudge Cupcakes, 106

Milk Chocolate Swirl Pumpkin Spice Muffins, 28

Mocha Berry Cheesecake, 22

mint
Chocolate Peppermint-Dipped Graham Crackers, 81
Peppermint Crème Chocolate Sandwich Cookies, 75

molasses
in brown sugar, 193
Chocolate Chai Spice Cookies, 73
Chocolate Peppermint-Dipped Graham Crackers, 81
Classic Gingerbread Cookies, 61
Cookies, Chewy Gooey Double Ginger, 65
Double Chocolate Gingerbread Cookies, 81
Ginger Apple Pie, 52
Maple Pecan Millionaire's Shortbread, 181
Soft Spicy Gingerbread Cake, 63
Spice Crinkle Cookies, Soft & Chewy, 77
Sticky Ginger Apple Loaf, 41

muffins
Chocolate Fudge Swirl Banana, 137
Milk Chocolate Swirl Pumpkin Spice, 28
Blueberry Buttermilk, 129
Chocolate Chip Peanut Butter Banana Oat, 131

N

Neapolitan Layer Cake, 99

New York Style Bagels, 120

nut(s) (see almond, cashew, hazelnut, peanut, pecan, pistachio, or walnut)

O

oats
Cream Cheese Caramelitas, 161
Double Dark Chocolate Oat & Almond Bars, 127
Raspberry Maple Crumble Cheesecake Bars, 34
Salted Peanut Caramel Crumb Bars, 153
Sweet & Salty Chocolate Peanut Butter Granola, 130
Honey Olive Oil Muesli Bars, 126
Vanilla Chai Coconut Granola, 131
White Chocolate & Cranberry Peanut Butter Oatmeal Cookies, 152

olive oil
Cake, Apricot Almond, l 31
Cake, Summer Stone Fruit Almond, 31
Decadent Double Chocolate Loaf Cake, 171
Fennel Orange & Almond Biscotti,
Healthy Whole Wheat Banana Bread, 135
Muesli Bars, Honey, 126
Pumpkin Seed & Black Pepper Crispbreads, 147
Vanilla Chai Coconut Granola, 131

Orange Sables (Butter Cookies), 177

Overnight No Knead Cinnamon Rolls, 123

P

PB & Jelly Sandwich Cookies,

peanut(s)
Caramel Crumb Bars, Salted, 153

peanut butter
Banana Oat Muffins, Chocolate Chip, 131
Chocolate Sandwich Cookies 115
Chocolate Swirl Banana Bread, Oat 133
Chocolate Truffle Cream Cheese Cookie Bars, 51
Cookies, Soft-Baked, Chocolate Chunk, 102
Double Dark Chocolate Oat & Almond Bars, 127
Granola, Sweet & Salty Chocolate 130
Mousse Cake, Chocolate, 109
Oatmeal Cookie, White Chocolate & Cranberry, 152
PB & Jelly Sandwich Cookies, 115
Swirl Brownies, Flourless, 107

Peanut Butter & Chocolate Sandwich Cookies, 115

Peanut Butter & Oat Chocolate Swirl Banana Bread, 133

Peanut Butter Chocolate Truffle Cream Cheese Cookie Bars, 51

pecan(s)
Banana Bread, Whole Wheat Maple, 29
Brown Butter Pecan Cookies, 175
Butter Balls & Batons, Chocolate Chip, 74
Millionaire's Shortbread, Maple,181
Maple Sesame Snickerdoodles, 164
Pie, Maple Brown Butter Bourbon, 57
Seed Loaf, Date Apricot, 25
Shortbread, Rosemary, Press-In, 146
Ultimate Cheeseboard Crisps, 143

Peppermint Crème Chocolate Sandwich Cookies, 75

Pfeffernusse German Spice Cookies, 79

pistachio(s)
Biscotti, Cherry & Chocolate, 67
Butter Cookies, Sour Cherry,
Vanilla Chai Coconut Granola, 131

Pistachio Cherry & Chocolate Biscotti, 67

pumpkin
Chocolate Cheesecake Bars, 59
Spice Muffins, Milk Chocolate Swirl, 28

Pumpkin Chocolate Cheesecake Bars, 59

Pumpkin Seed & Black Pepper Crispbreads, 147

R

raspberry
Maple Crumble Cheesecake Bars, 34
Mocha Berry Cheesecake, 22
Sachertorte, 187
Swirl Cheesecake Brownies, 184
Turnovers, 35

Raspberry Maple Crumble Cheesecake Bars, 34

Raspberry Sachertorte, 187

Raspberry Swirl Cheesecake Brownies, 184

Raspberry Turnovers, 35

rhubarb
Honey Rhubarb Melt Cake, 37

Rich Salted Caramel Sauce, 196

Rosemary Pecan Press in Shortbread, 146

Royal Icing, 63

S

Salted Chocolate Cream Pie, 117

Salted Cinnamon Butterscotch Walnut Bars, 172

Salted Peanut Caramel Crumb Bars, 153

Sea Salt S'mores Cookies, 107

Secret Sauce Chocolate Chip Cookies, 84

sesame seed paste (see tahini)

Shiny Top Fudge Brownies, 110

Silk Cream Cheese Custard Tart with Creamy Caramel, 149

Silky Salted Dark Chocolate Truffles, 177

Soft & Gooey Cream Cheese Caramel Cashew Cookie Bars, 103

Soft & Chewy Molasses Spice Crinkle Cookies, 77

Soft Spicy Gingerbread Cake, 63

Sour Cherry Pistachio Butter Cookies, 155

sour cream
Apple Cinnamon Sour Cream Snack Cake, 125
Best Vanilla Birthday Cake, 85
Chocolate Celebration Cake, 97
Chocolate Fudge Frosting, 91
Coffee Cake, Blueberry, 131
Cream Cheese-Filled Carrot Cakes, 49
Creamy Lemon Squares, 157
Dark Chocolate Mousse Cake, 195
Decadent Double Chocolate Loaf Cake, 171
Double Dark Chocolate Cake, 91
Ginger Cardamom Crumb Cake, 128
Honey Chocolate Cake, 192
Honey Rhubarb Melt Cake, 37
Mocha Berry Cheesecake, 22
Neapolitan Layer Cake, 99
Peanut Butter & Oat Chocolate Swirl Banana Bread, 133
Silk Cream Cheese Custard Tart with Creamy Caramel, 149
Triple Chocolate Cheesecake, 47
Tuxedo Cheesecake Bars, 189
Ultra Moist Chocolate Fudge Cake, 93

Sour Cream & Honey Chocolate Cake, 192

Sticky Apple Ginger Loaf, 41

Sticky Salted Caramel Date Cakes, 178

strawberry
- Apple Pie, 53
- Maple Almond Tart, 39
- Shortcake Swiss Roll, 45

Strawberry Apple Pie, 53

Strawberry Maple Almond Tart, 39

Strawberry Shortcake Swiss Roll, 45

Summer Stone Fruit Almond & Olive Oil Cake, 31

Sweet & Salty Magic Bars, 94

T

tahini
- 3-ingredient Choc Tahini Fudge, 197
- Maple Sesame Snickerdoodles, 164

tempering
- of chocolate, 205

Thick & Chewy Flourless Chocolate Chunk Peanut Butter Cookies, 102

Tiramisu Brownies, 168

Toasted Coconut & Dark Chocolate Chunk Blondies, 176

Toasted Coconut Truffle Tartlets, 174

Triple Chocolate Cheesecake, 47

Triple Chocolate Fudge Cupcakes, 106

truffle(s)
- Coconut Lime Margarita, 199

Icy Chocolate Squares, 204
Silky Dark Chocolate, 177
Squares, Peanut Butter Chocolate, 51

Tuxedo Cheesecake Bars, 189

U

Ultimate Cheeseboard Crisps, 143

Ultra Moist Chocolate Fudge Cake, 93

V

Vanilla Sugar Cookies, 66

Vanilla Walnut Crescent Cookies, 78

Vanilla Chai Coconut Granola, 131

Vanilla Custard Sponge Cake, 163

vegan
- 3-Ingredient Choc Tahini Fudge, 197
- Dark Chocolate Coconut Cream Tart, 198
- Double Dark Chocolate Oat & Almond Bars, 127
- Vanilla Chai Coconut Granola, 131

Vegan Dark Chocolate Coconut Cream Tart, 198

W

walnut(s)
- Banana Bread, Honey, 136
- Bars, Salted Cinnamon Butterscotch, 172
- Cream Cheese-Filled Carrot Cakes, 49
- Crescent Cookies, Vanilla, 78

Healthy Whole Wheat Banana Bread, 135

Whipped Chocolate Ganache, 89

white chocolate
- 3-Ingredient Choc Tahini Fudge, 197
- Brown Butter Pecan Cookies, 175
- Peppermint Crème Chocolate Sandwich Cookies, 75
- Triple Chocolate Fudge Cupcakes, 106
- Tuxedo Cheesecake Bars, 189

White Chocolate & Cranberry Peanut Butter Oatmeal Cookies, 152

whipping cream (see: cream, heavy 35%)

whole wheat
- Banana Bread, Healthy, 135
- Banana Bread, Maple Pecan, 29
- BEST Classic Banana Bread, 132
- Chocolate Peppermint-Dipped Graham Crackers, 81
- Homemade Graham Crackers, 111
- Pumpkin Seed & Black Pepper Crispbreads, 147
- Sea Salt S'mores Cookies, 107

Y

yogurt
- Avocado Mojito Cheesecake Bars, 142
- Healthy Whole Wheat Banana Bread, 135
- Overnight No Knead Cinnamon Rolls, 123
- Triple Chocolate Fudge Cupcakes, 106
- Ultimate Cheeseboard Crispbreads, 143

Made in the USA
Monee, IL
18 September 2024